WHITAKER'S BRITAIN

BLOOMSBURY

LONDON · NEW DELHI · NEW YORK · SYDNEY

First published in Great Britain 2013

Copyright © 2013 Bloomsbury Publishing Plc

Bloomsbury Publishing Plc, 50 Bedford Square, London WC1B 3DP
www.bloomsbury.com

Bloomsbury Publishing, London, New Delhi, New York and Sydney

ISBN 978-1-4729-0305-1

COVER ILLUSTRATION
The frontispiece which has appeared in each edition of *Whitaker's Almanack* since 1868.

Editorial Staff
Project Editor: Ruth Northey
Editors: Scott Hamilton; Nathan Joyce; Oli Lurie; Katy McAdam
Illustration Design: Oli Lurie

Typeset by RefineCatch Ltd, Bungay, Suffolk NR35 1EF
Printed and bound by CPI Group (UK) Ltd, Croydon CR0 4YY

CONTENTS

The British Empire

British Holiday and Health Resorts

Reviews of the Year

FOREWORD

My great grandfather Joseph Whitaker published the first *Whitaker's Almanack* in 1868. Family tradition has it that he compiled that first slender effort from notebooks kept to help answer readers' queries when he had been editor of *The Gentleman's Magazine*.

Family tradition also has it that the Almanack was something of an act of desperation: he had a large brood of children to support, fifteen by the end. Fortunately it was an immediate success.

Optimist that he was I doubt that he would have foreseen how many editions would follow. Nor that the current one would be over 1,000 pages long.

He died in 1895. In the 118 years that have followed, his Almanack has chronicled the events of four reigns (five, if you include Edward VIII); two World Wars, and a frightening number of smaller conflicts; the great slump of the 1930s, and the still present recession from the 1990s; the plays, and films almost from the time cinema was invented; Derby winners, tidal predictions for the years, a section from the Royal Observatory, and much, much more.

The section on countries overseas has grown and grown, but not so much as that given over to government. The European Union has provided its own pressures on space. Not something Joseph could have predicted.

The present editor – only the eleventh in nearly a century and a half – has had much from which to make her selection.

I believe Joseph Whitaker would have been proud of the longevity of his creation, and approve of his successor's choices for *Whitaker's Britain*.

David Whitaker

DAVID WHITAKER

PREFACE

In producing *Whitaker's Britain* we have tried to bring you a selection of some of the gems from our extensive archive, which dates back to 1868 when Joseph Whitaker first published his collection of facts, figures and commentary as an almanack. It proved an almost impossible task trying to choose from such a vast array of information. Everything we read was fascinating, from British holiday and health resort recommendations from 1906 to the macabre murder of 'sweet' Fanny Adams and the record of an early meeting of the British Aeronautical Society from 1869, entitled 'Sailing in the Air'. Hopefully you will find the snippets we have extracted as interesting, informative, moving and intriguing as we did. With its combination of subjects as diverse as politics, finance, royalty and astronomy, the Whitaker's archive provides a unique window into a fascinating world from the height of the British Empire through the twentieth century to the present day. Old editions are extraordinary cultural and social artefacts, offering an historical insight into the major events from the last century-and-a-half as they were recorded at the time.

Whitaker's Britain includes detailed digests of historical events, extensive information on the British Empire and the Royal Family, plus annual summaries, written at the time, on subjects as wide ranging as 'Broadcasting', 'Science and Invention' and 'The Weather'. There is also an eight-page colour insert of brand new infographics, using re-formatted data from the original editions to give a comparative history across the decades, and a selection of truly remarkable advertisements, taken directly from the old editions, and reproduced in their original form.

By its very nature *Whitaker's Britain* can only include a selection of material from the 145-edition archive, but we hope that what we have chosen goes some way to providing a compelling insight into the fascinating information documented in *Whitaker's*.

Where possible we have tried to reproduce the text in its original form, along with all its idiosyncrasies of style and archaic phrasing. In some cases style was altered so that extracts taken from different editions read more smoothly and consistently, but a concerted effort was made to keep this to a minimum. With events which the reader may not be familiar with, further explanation has been provided in boxed notes throughout and names have been qualified where we deemed this to be helpful.

Please feel free to contact us with any feedback – our readers' thoughts and comments have always proved invaluable, especially on a new project such as this, and remember, the 145th edition of *Whitaker's Almanack* will be published, as usual, in November.

The Whitaker's Team
50 Bedford Square
London WC1B 3DP

Email: whitakersalmanackteam@bloomsbury.com
www.whitakersalmanack.com

INTRODUCTION

JOSEPH WHITAKER AND HIS ALMANACK

It is unlikely that Joseph Whitaker imagined, when he published his collection of the notes he had made as a journalist in order to support his growing family, that his almanack would continue to be published for 145 consecutive years.

Joseph Whitaker was born in 1820 the son of a silversmith, and began his career in books at an early age as an apprentice at Parker's, a scholarly bookshop in Oxford. He moved to London when the company sent him there to open a branch on the Strand, and it was in the capital that Whitaker became involved in publishing, founding the *Penny Post*, a monthly church magazine, in 1849.

During the 1850s, he was an editor at *The Gentleman's Magazine* in charge of the correspondence pages. This required him to answer a selection of readers' questions that were notoriously broad in their scope, and Whitaker consequently accumulated a substantial collection of invaluable newspaper cuttings, government statistics and questions and answers from a variety of sources.

In addition to his work at *The Gentleman's Magazine*, he founded and edited *The Bookseller*, the magazine for the book trade that continues to this day, also finding time to marry twice and father 13 children. It was his growing number of financial dependants that prompted his decision to publish his collection of facts as an almanack.

An 'almanack' (or 'almanac') is defined as 'an annual publication that includes a calendar for the year as well as astronomical information and details of anniversaries and events'. The astronomical information in *Whitaker's Almanack* was initially provided by a member of the staff of the Astronomer Royal, Sir George Airy, and the section still forms part of the book, 145 years later.

Such was the immediacy of the Almanack's 'establishment' status that just ten years later it was considered worthy of a space in the time capsule buried beneath Cleopatra's Needle on London's Embankment, alongside a set of contemporary coins and a copy of *The Times* newspaper.

Joseph Whitaker edited his Almanack up to his death in 1895, and was succeeded by his son Cuthbert, later Lt.-Col. Sir Cuthbert Whitaker.

Calendar Information; Royal Family: past and present; Peerage & Precedence; MPs; General Election and by-election results; Government & Public Bodies; Regional & Local Government; European Parliament; Law Courts & Offices; Tribunals; Ombudsmen; Police; Prisons; The Armed Forces; Education; Health; Social Welfare; Utilities; Transport; Religion; Communications; Environment & Heritage; Banking & Finance; Taxation; Law; The Media; Listings of: clubs, charities, societies and trade, professional and sports bodies; economic and demographic information and statistics for the UK and every country of the world; 'Reviews of the Year' in Archaeology, Architecture, Art, Business and Finance, Conservation, Dance, Film, Literature, Music, Opera, Science, Sport, Theatre and Weather; plus last, but not least, the all important Astronomical & Tidal data that makes Whitaker's an almanack.

In his preface to the 1884 edition, and with the number of pages totalling 456 (up from just under 400 pages in the first edition in 1868), Joseph Whitaker stated that: 'Year by year, the scope of the Almanack has widened, and its pages have increased in number; the limit has now been reached.' Little did he know that, 145 years later, the 2013 edition would reach an extent of 1,200 pages!

The fundamental components of *Whitaker's*, such as the peerage listing and directories of government departments and educational establishments, have persisted throughout each edition, being expanded and reduced where necessary and where changes in these areas dictate. Every editor from Joseph onwards (which, to date, only numbers ten) has tried to evolve, modernise and broaden the contents of the book wherever possible.

External factors have also influenced the book's size and scope. For example, the relatively minor effects of the First World War on the Almanack were a lower quality of paper and some slight delays in production. During the Second World War, however, a bombing raid on the City of London on 29 December 1940 hit the Whitaker's premises in Warwick Lane, obliterating almost all of the records and the reference library, and prompting Winston Churchill to write to Sir Cuthbert (Joseph's son, and then editor) to seek reassurance that publication would not be interrupted.

The war also dictated several changes to the content, including the replacement of the usual tidal predictions with tables of black-out and lighting-up times, and throughout the war years publication dates inevitably fluctuated.

On the death of Sir Cuthbert Whitaker in 1950 after 55 years as editor, F. H. C. (Tom) Tatham took over the editorship (although Sir Cuthbert's son Haddon was chairman and Editor-in-Chief) and continued the Whitakers' tradition of long service to the book, staying in the post until 1981. There were several innovations during Tatham's 31 years at the helm, including the Almanack's first colour illustration (a portrait of the Queen as the frontispiece to celebrate her coronation in 1953), the first use of photographs (of the coronation, in the 1954 edition), the introduction of dust jackets in 1960 and sketched maps in 1968.

The next two editors were Richard Blake (1981–6) and Hilary Marsden (1986–99). The latter oversaw the complete redesign of the 1993 edition for the Almanack's 125th birthday; this, the first redesign in its history, aimed to make the book more legible and navigable, by increasing both the size of the font and the page.

In more recent years *Whitaker's* has undergone another redesign, keeping the two-column format, but again introducing a more modern and compact font and different levels of heading for increased clarity. In addition, the means in which information is now portrayed is considerably more varied than the tabular and textual options available for early editions. Timelines, charts, graphs, maps and illustrations now feature alongside the text and tables throughout. But, whatever format, contemporary editions of the book still contain the extraordinary breadth of content that *Whitaker's Almanack* has always been associated with.

THE WORLD WARS

THE FIRST WORLD WAR

The Outbreak of the First World War
As recorded in the 1915 edition
Diary of the European War

The European conflagration broke out towards the end of **July [1914]**, and by the beginning of August practically the whole of the Continent was under arms, if not actually engaged in warfare. Up to the last moment hopes were entertained that the dispute between Austria–Hungary and Serbia might be localised, or even settled without recourse to hostilities, but the Dual Monarchy's hand was forced by Germany's declaration of war upon Russia. It speedily became clear, indeed, that the German plans of campaign and the completeness of the vast military organisation had been the deliberate work of years. The first step leading to the outbreak was the presentation, on **July 23**, of Austria–Hungary's ultimatum to Serbia. The latter's reply within the stipulated 48 hours was considered unsatisfactory.

On **July 27** Sir E. Grey [Foreign Secretary, 1905–16] announced his proposals for a conference of Germany, France, Italy and Great Britain, and their acceptance by France and Italy; but on the following day Austria–Hungary declared war on Serbia and commenced operations, and on **July 30** there was a partial mobilisation of the Russian Army, followed on the next day by a general mobilisation. War was declared upon Russia by Germany on **Aug. 1**, and on the **2nd** French territory was entered at Ciréy by German troops, while Russian forces crossed the German frontier. On **Aug. 3** the British Fleet was mobilised, and Germany sent an ultimatum to Belgium, which led to the British ultimatum to Germany on **Aug. 4**, on which day, at 11 p.m., war was declared between Great Britain and Germany. On **Aug. 10** France declared war upon Austria–Hungary, and Great Britain made a similar declaration two days later.

The following is a digest of events taken from the 1915 edition detailing the first three months of the First World War:

Aug. 5. [1914] The German mine-layer *Königin Luise* was sunk by the cruiser *Amphion;* but while reconnoitring on the following day the cruiser struck a mine and foundered, with the loss of 131 lives. **6.** Tremendous German assault on the Liège forts repulsed with enormous loss. German Dreadnought cruiser *Goeben* and light cruiser *Breslau* put to sea from Messina, where they had taken shelter. **9.** Liège was invested. French troops entered Alsace and occupied Mulhaüsen. German colony of Togoland, West Africa, seized by British and French forces. A British cruiser squadron attacked by German submarines without success. The cruiser

Birmingham sank German submarine U 15. **10.** Liège city occupied by Germans, most of the forts holding out. The *Goeben* and *Breslau* escaped to the Dardanelles, where they were taken over by Turkey. **13.** Germans repulsed by Belgians at Diest-Haelen. **14.** Transportation of French troops into Belgium announced to be complete. Serious attention directed to German inhumanity and atrocities in Belgium. Raid by British on Dar-es-Salaam, German East Africa; ships in harbour dismantled or sunk. **15.** Field-Marshal Sir John French [Commander, British Expeditionary Force, 1914–15] arrived in Paris. Japanese ultimatum to Germany to deliver up leased territory of Kiao-Chau. Visé (Belgium) burned and destroyed by Germans. **16.** Information published that British Expeditionary Force had been safely landed in France. The French contained their advance in Alsace-Lorraine. The French Fleet in the Adriatic sunk an Austrian cruiser. **19.** The Belgian Government removed from Brussels to Antwerp. The news was confirmed that the Serbians had routed the Austrians at Shabatz. The Belgian forces retired from Louvain, which was occupied by Germans. **20.** The Germans arrived at Brussels, the Belgian retirement being dictated by strategical situation. The Russians took the offensive along the whole line, and occupied Gumbinnen, in West Prussia. **21.** A war contribution of £8,000,000 was imposed by Germany upon the city of Brussels. It was announced that Britain proposed to lend Belgium £10,000,000. Battle of Charleroi began, and ended following day by withdrawal of French. **23.** Japan declared war on Germany. Russian victory over Germans in East Prussia, and occupation of Insterburg announced. Germans destroyed three forts at Namur. The cruiser *Bristol* engaged German cruiser *Karlsruhe* south of Bermuda, but the latter escaped owing to superior speed. A great battle began in the Charleroi-Mons region between Germans and the Allied troops, the British holding their ground. In the Namur region the Allies fell back to the French frontier, and Namur was captured by the Germans. The French were checked in Alsace and fell back upon Nancy and Belfort, the Germans entering France and occupying Luneville. **24.** The destroyer *Kennet* was fired at by the Tsingtau forts and lost a few men. The Liège forts were finally destroyed by the German siege artillery. **25.** Mr. Asquith [Prime Minister, 1908–16] announced that the British casualties to date were approximately over 2,000. A Zeppelin passed over Antwerp and dropped bombs, killing 12 civilians and causing considerable damage. The Germans destroyed Louvain. **26.** The Russians in East Prussia surrounded and defeated the Germans, and further south repulsed the Austrians. **27.** British Marines were landed at Ostend. The German cruiser *Magdeburg* was blown up in the Gulf of Finland. The armed German liner *Kaiser Wilhelm der Grosse* was sunk on the West African coast by the cruiser *Highflyer*. The Germans recaptured Malines and bombarded the Cathedral. **28.** Destroyers and cruisers of the Grand Fleet in the Heligoland Bight intercepted and attacked German destroyers and cruisers, sinking four vessels, while another disappeared on fire and many destroyers were damaged; British vessels were scarcely damaged, the casualties numbering 69 killed and wounded. An Austrian destroyer was sunk off

Corfu by a British destroyer. In the House of Commons, Mr. Asquith announced a great feat of arms by the British troops against a superior German force in the fighting near Cambrai and Le Cateau. **29.** Particulars reached London of the sack of Louvain, the chief buildings being burned. Accounts of German barbarism and outrage in Belgium multiplied. **31.** The War Secretary [Earl Kitchener], describing the retirement from Mons, said the British troops offered a superb and most stubborn resistance against tremendous odds, and extricated themselves in good order, though with serious losses, the Germans making desperate but unsuccessful efforts to drive the British into Maubeuge. A bomb was dropped in Paris from a German aeroplane, but no damage done. Apia, in German Samoa, surrendered to a New Zealand force.

Sept. 1. The Anglo-French troops had to give way in France, but nowhere were they broken through. The British casualties were officially given as 163 killed and 4,974 wounded and missing. **2.** The German advance on Paris was steadily continued, the enemy's cavalry reaching the forest of Compiègne. The Allies retired in good order, inflicting heavy losses. Details arrived of a heavy Austrian defeat at the hands of the Russians near Lemberg. **3.** The French Government transferred the seat of the Central Administration to Bordeaux. A further British casualty list brought the number of killed to 233, and wounded and missing to 10,345. The torpedo vessel *Speedy* struck a mine in the North Sea and foundered. **4.** Belgians opened the dykes near Antwerp, the Germans losing heavily. Seven German destroyers and torpedo-boats arrived at Kiel in a damaged condition, and it was believed that one squadron had mistaken another for enemy ships. Lemberg, the capital of Galicia, was captured by the Russians. Nearly half the Austro-Hungarian army had been rendered useless for offensive purposes by Russia and Serbia. **5.** The light cruiser *Pathfinder* struck a mine and was blown up, most of the crew being lost. Great Britain, France and Russia agreed not to treat for peace separately. The Germans were defeated in, and abandoned, the attempt to envelop the Allies' left flank, and the Allies checked the German advance. **9.** Sir John French's first despatch was published, and, alluding to the retirement from Mons, spoke in terms of deep appreciation of General Sir Horace Smith-Dorrien in saving the left wing of the British Force on **Aug. 26.** The Germans fell back about 26 miles, and the British crossed the Marne. **10.** A German defeat and retirement was admitted in Berlin, with a loss of 50 guns and thousands of prisoners. The British losses amounted to 346 killed and 18,383 wounded and missing. The "war contributions" demanded by Germany from various towns in Belgium and France amounted to over 28 millions sterling. **11.** Further information proved that the Allies' victories at the Marne and at Meaux had saved Paris. At Petrograd it was announced that the chief Austrian army, although reinforced by Germans, was fleeing in disorder. **13.** General Joffre described the result of the five days' battle as "an incontestable victory." The Russians gained a victory in which 30,000 Austrian and German prisoners were taken and several hundred guns.

14. The British troops crossed the Aisne in spite of strong opposition. The army of the Crown Prince [Crown Prince Wilhelm] was reported to have been driven back. **15.** Sir John French paid a notable tribute to the work of the Royal Flying Corps, which had gained "something in the direction of the mastery of the air." The Germans succeeded in checking their retreat and occupied strong positions to the north of the Aisne. **16.** A new battle developed over a front of 90 miles from Noyon to the Meuse, near Verdun, the main German army aiding the rearguard. The German cruiser *Hela* was sunk by submarine E 9 off Heligoland. **18.** After six days' furious fighting on the Aisne there was little change in the position, though the Germans lost heavily. **20.** Great indignation was caused by the destruction by German bombardment of Rheims Cathedral. The British cruiser *Pegasus* was surprised at Zanzibar and disabled by the German cruiser *Königsberg*. The German cruiser *Emden* captured six British merchantmen in East Indian waters, and shelled the oil tanks at Madras. The British auxiliary cruiser *Carmania* sank the German armed merchant cruiser *Cap Trafalgar*. **21.** The Austrians were beaten by the Serbians on the Drina, and fled in a state of panic. The number of German merchantmen captured was 92, and 95 ships were detained in British ports, against 82 British ships in all. **22.** German submarines torpedoed the cruisers *Aboukir, Hogue,* and *Cressy,* the loss of life amounting to about 1,400 officers and men, 900 being saved. It was thought that the *Cressy* sank one submarine. Jaroslav, east of Lemberg, was captured by the Russians. **23.** The Allies' left wing advanced despite fierce fighting. Flight-Lieutenant Collet flew to Düsseldorf and dropped three bombs upon the Zeppelin shed, returning safely. The Russian cruiser *Bayan* sank three German war vessels in the Baltic. **24.** The Allies occupied Péronne. The Germans in Northern France were reported to have been strongly reinforced. A British force was landed to co-operate with Japanese in movements in Kiao-Chau. **25.** The seat of Government in Kaiser Wilhelm's Land, German New Guinea, was occupied by Australians, who annihilated Germans at Herbertshohe. **27.** Lüderitzbucht, German South-West Africa, was occupied by South African troops. The Allies' left wing was described as having made "marked progress" on a very extended front in North France. **29.** Germans bombarded Antwerp's first line of defence. Serbians re-captured Semlin. German cruiser *Emden* sank four more British steamships. German advance from East Prussian frontier on river Niemen was checked, and the main Russian armies in Galicia pushed on towards Cracow. **28.** The British and Japanese forces attacked the advanced positions at Tsingtau, and, driving back the Germans, occupied the high ground overlooking the main line of defence. German casualties during August were stated to number 117,000.

Oct. 2. In the final speech of his campaign Mr. Asquith, at Cardiff, disclosed the fact that two years before the war Germany asked Great Britain to pledge itself to absolute neutrality in the event of Germany being engaged in a war. The left wing of the Germans, operating near the Niemen, was thrown back. **3.** The Russians captured Augustovo, the enemy retreating in disorder. **4.** The Allies' left wing in Northern France resumed the offensive, after repulsing German attacks. The Admiralty announced that the Government had authorised a mine-laying policy in a defined area in the North Sea. M. Poincaré [President of France, 1913–20] left Bordeaux to visit the Allies' troops in the field. After seeing the British forces the President and King George exchanged cordial messages. **5.** The National Relief Fund reached £3,000,000. **6.** The Allies' left wing in France was declared to be extending more and more, and north of Soissons an advance was recorded. A British submarine, E 9, sank a German torpedo-boat destroyer off the Ems River and returned safely. The Japanese landed a force at Jaluit, in the Marshall Islands, without resistance. The Belgian Government was transferred to Ostend, owing to the fierce bombardment of Antwerp. **7.** It was announced that the barracks at Tsingtau had been destroyed by the Japanese. The Colonial Office intimated that attempts by the enemy to raid the East Africa Protectorate and cut the Uganda Railway had been repulsed with slight British losses. **9.** Simultaneously with the official statement that the Indian troops had arrived at Marseilles, the text was issued of messages sent by the King-Emperor [term used to describe the British King as ruler of India] to the Force. The Belgian troops, with a British marine brigade and two naval brigades sent to their assistance, having withdrawn from Antwerp, the Germans occupied the city. One British naval brigade, numbering 2,000 was cut off and entered Dutch territory, where they laid down their arms. **10.** British airmen returned safely after a successful attack on the Düsseldorf airship shed, a Zeppelin being destroyed. **11.** On the Allies' left wing the German cavalry were forced to retire, and all along the front positions were held. Two German aeroplanes flew over Paris and, besides killing three and injuring fourteen persons with bombs, damaged the cathedral of Notre Dame. **12.** The Germans occupied Ghent without opposition. The rebellion of Lieut.-Col. Maritz in the north-west of the Cape Province, assisted by Germans, was announced. Martial law was at once proclaimed throughout the Union, and a punitive force was despatched. The announcement was made of the loss of the Russian cruiser *Pallada*, with all hands, after an attack by a German submarine in the Baltic. The Russians claimed to have sunk two German submarines. **13.** The Belgian Government left Ostend for Havre, and the civil population hurried away to France and England. Franco-British troops occupied Ypres, inside the Belgian frontier. Lille was captured by the Germans, but elsewhere in France "perceptible progress" was reported by the Allies. It was reported from Constantinople that the *Goeben* was leading an attack on the Russian Fleet in the Black Sea. **14.** The press Bureau announced that British troops had been engaged with the enemy towards the Allies' left, the Germans being pressed back slightly. The Canadian troops arrived at Plymouth amid great enthusiasm. A Zeppelin was brought down by a Cossack patrol near Warsaw. **15.** The *Theseus* and the *Hawke* were attacked by submarines in the North Sea, and the latter was sunk, there being about 70 survivors. The bombardment of Cattaro was resumed by the

Allied Fleet. **17.** The new light cruiser *Undaunted,* with four destroyers, engaged off the Dutch coast four German destroyers, all of which were sunk. The damage to our vessels was slight, and only one officer and four men were wounded. **18.** The Press Bureau stated that during the previous few days the Allies had driven the enemy back more than thirty miles in the northern area. **19.** Two vivid despatches from Sir John French were published dealing with the retreat and the victory on the Marne. With them was issued a long list of officers and men "mentioned in despatches." The Allies advanced as far as Roulers, in Belgium, German attacks upon Nieuport and Dixmude being repulsed. **20.** The German Army which had advanced upon Warsaw was forced into a precipitate retreat, vigorously pursued by the Russians. **21.** The sinking of five further British steamers by the *Emden* was announced. The Government ordered the removal from the Suez Canal of all enemy vessels. In the operations on the Belgian coast the Allies were assisted by the three British monitors firing on the enemy's right flank and doing great execution among the trenches. **23.** British vessels continued to bombard the German right, the enemy suffering severely. A few shells were fired at Ostend. **24.** German forces succeeded in crossing the Yser between Nieuport and Dixmude. The destroyer *Badger* rammed and sank a German submarine. All hope was abandoned for the British submarine E 3. **26.** The Germans in Poland were driven back to Lowicz, Skierniewice and Rava, the Russian advance being continued. General Christian de Wet and General Beyers joined the South African rebels, and Heilbron was seized. **27.** The German attacks in Belgium slackened, and the Allies made progress near Ypres. General Botha drove Beyers' men headlong, capturing 80. Many of Maritz's rebels were also taken prisoners. **28.** The Russian Headquarters announced that they had broken the resistance of the last units of the enemy remaining on the north of the Pilitza. On the front beyond the Vistula all Austro-German army corps were in retreat. Russian cavalry had entered Radom. The German cruiser *Emden* entered Penang disguised, and sank a Russian cruiser and French destroyer. It was stated that German-Turkish warships had bombarded Russian ports in the Black Sea. **29.** The British vessels continued their splendid work off the Belgian coast, receiving only trifling structural damage from German guns. Beyers' commandoes were scattered by the Union Force, Beyers himself escaping. **30.** Ground was steadily gained in Belgium, the enemy falling back across the Yser. **31.** The Turkish Fleet bombarded Sebastopol, doing considerable damage. The Foreign Office issued a statement setting out Turkey's infractions of treaties and international law, and giving evidence of Turkey's intention to invade Egypt. The old British cruiser *Hermes* was sunk by a torpedo fired by a German submarine in the Straits of Dover. The British Ambassador left Constantinople. The London Scottish made a brilliant charge and drove the enemy from a village in Flanders.

Great War Casualties, 1914–1919

As recorded in the 1940 edition

British Empire		
Total Number Mobilized, 8,904,000		
	Deaths	**Wounded**
Gt. Britain and Ireland	812,317	1,849,494
Canada	62,817	166,105
Australia	60,456	154,722
New Zealand	18,212	45,946
South Africa	9,032	17,843
Newfoundland	1,609	3,628
Colonies	52,044	78,535
India	73,432	84,715
Total, British Empire	**1,089,919**	**2,400,988**

Allied and Associated Countries			
	Mobilized	**Deaths**	**Wounded**
France	8,410,000	1,393,388	1,490,000
Belgium	267,000	38,172	44,686
Italy	5,615,000	460,000	947,000
Portugal	100,000	7,222	13,751
Roumania	750,000	335,706	No record
Serbia	707,000	127,535	133,148
U.S.A.	4,355,000	115,660	205,690

Enemy Countries			
Germany	11,000,000	2,050,466	4,202,028
Austria and Hungary	7,800,000	1,200,000	3,620,000
Bulgaria	1,200,000	101,224	152,400
Turkey	2,850,006	300,000	570,000

The End of the First World War

As recorded in the 1919 edition
Diary of the War

The following is a digest of events taken from the 1919 edition detailing the last three months of the First World War:

Sept. 1. [1918] Enemy in retreat on almost his whole front from S. of Ypres to Soisons, except between La Bassée and Lens. Allies progressed and captured Péronne and Sailly-Saillisel: Bouchavesnes and Rancourt taken by the British: recapture of Bullecort and Heudecour: capture of Neuve Eglise on the Lys front. 57,318 prisoners, including 1,263 officers and 657 guns; 5,750 machine guns, 1,000 trench mortars taken by British in France during August. Maj.-Gen. G. F. Ellison appointed Q.M.G. [Quartermaster-General] to Forces in Great Britain. **2.** Great German system of defences, the Drocourt-Quéant line, covering Douai and Cambrai broken through on a front of six miles by Canadians: capture of Dury, Cagnicourt, Williers, Le Transloy and St. Pierre Vaast Wood. French, under Gen. Mangin, advanced and took Neuilly and Terny Sorny. **3.** English, Scottish and Naval force, under Gen. Fergusson, penetrated Hindenburg defences of Quéant and Prouville: Drecourt taken: advance on Inchy and Moeuvres: Baralle, Rumancourt and Lécluse captured. The Somme crossed by French at Epenancourt. Germans evacuated Lens. **4.** British still advancing E. on a wide front between the Scarpe towards Cambrai: enemy fighting rearguard actions: Moeuvres and Ecourt taken by British: Ruyaulcourt taken by New Zealand troops: N., capture of Ploegsteert and Hill 63. Supplement on agreements to Brest-Litovsk Treaty signed by German and Bolshevist Governments. **5.** French under Gen. Humbert advancing N. E. from Noyon to St. Quentin. The Aisne between Condé and Vieil-Arcy reached by French. Khabarovsk, Bolshevist base against Vladivostok, taken by Japanese. **6.** French between Somme Canal and the Oise captured the whole of the Autrécourt *massif,* Ham, and railway junction of Chauny. Germans in rapid retreat from the line of the Somme, from Péronne S. to the Hindenburg line, from which they opened their offensive **Mar. 21. 7.** Hurried retreat of Germans continued on a wide front towards St. Quentin, La Fère and Laon before the armies of Gens. Débeney, Humbert and Mangin. Publication by Admiralty of commanders' names of 150 U-boats disposed of by Navy. **8.** 150,000 prisoners taken since the Allied counter-offensive of **Jul. 18. 9.** Crozat Canal crossed by French: strong counter-attacks by Germans near Laffaux, between Soissons and Laon, repulsed. **10.** Special Order of the Day issued by Sir Douglas Haig [Commander, British Expeditionary Force, 1915-18] on the completion of a month's most successful fighting: 75,000 prisoners and 750 guns captured in four weeks. **11.** Attilly, Vermand and Vendelles, between Cambrai, taken by British. Arrival in Archangel of U.S. troops to assist Allies in restoring order in N. Russia. **12.** Gen. Pershing, with 1st U.S. Army, co-operating with French Army, supported by Tanks, attacked Germans on both flanks of St. Mihiel salient: on the

S. on a front of 11 miles they carried Thiancourt, captured Pannes and Nousard and gained Bois de Gargantua: W. Combres carried. British S. W. of Cambrai captured Havrincourt, Trescault, Gouzeaucourt Wood and Moeuvres. Union Castle liner *Galway Castle*, with over 1,000 on board, including many women and children, torpedoed without warning: 154 passengers and crew missing. Important speech by Mr. Lloyd George [Prime Minister, 1916–22] at Manchester – "the worst is over, but the end not yet": casualties one-fifth of those in the advance over same ground in 1916. **13.** Registration in the U.S. of 13,000,000 citizens between 18 and 21 and 32 and 35 for military service. Reign of terror in Petrograd reported: many anti-Bolshevists put to death. **14.** Turks attacked Baku: evacuated by British. Germany stated to have made an offer of "peace" to Belgium: reversion to neutrality; maintenance of old commercial treaties; "Flemish question" to be dealt with; no indemnities, no reparation. **15.** German retreat between the Meuse and Loselle continued; enemy after evacuating the St. Mihiel salient retiring towards the Conflans-Metz-Longwy railway on a 33-mile front, closely pursued by Americans and French. Note addressed by Austro-Hungarian Government to all belligerent and neutral Powers, communicated in special form to the Holy See, proposing a conference between representatives of the States at war to discuss in a "non-binding" manner, but secretly, the general conditions of peace. **16.** President Wilson's [U.S. President 1913–21] reply to the Austrian Note. Offensive by French and Serbians in the Balkans: first Bulgarian position on the Dobrolpolje front carried. Air raid on Paris: six killed, 15 injured, two enemy machines brought down. Mr. Balfour [Foreign Secretary, 1916–19] in speech described the Austrian "peace" conference proposal as a cynical attempt to divide the Allies. Recognition by Japan of the Czech-Slovaks as an Allied and belligerent army. **17.** Austrian "peace" proposal contemptuously rejected by French Government. **18.** Outer defences of the Hindenburg line stormed by British 3rd and 4th armies: Lempire captured. French on a six-mile front and depth of 1½ miles advanced and took Saxy Wood and Fontaine-les-Cleres. Bulgarians in retreat before Serbian cavalry. Blagoveshtchensk and Alexeievsk occupied by Japanese. **19.** Moeuvres recaptured. Appointment of Mr. John Davis, U.S. Solicitor-General as U.S. Ambassador to London announced. **20.** Nazareth occupied. Benay, S. of St. Quentin, taken by French. Dr. Page, U.S. ex-Ambassador presented with the freedom of Plymouth, enclosed in a silver model of the *Mayflower*. **21.** Further advance of Gen. Allenby in Palestine. Franco-Serbian armies reach the Vardar. **22.** 7th and 8th Turkish armies *hors de combat*. **23.** Withdrawal of 4th Turkish Army towards Amman; Colonial and Jewish troops in pursuit reached Es Salt: Capture of Acre and Haifa: Maan occupied by King Hussein's Arabs. Prilep entered by French cavalry: Bulgarians fleeing in disorder N. from Monastir to Veles harassed by Allied troops. **24.** Francilly-Selenay captured by French. Resignation of Japanese Cabinet announced. Congratulations from the citizens of London to Gen. Allenby on his splendid victories in Palestine. **25.** "Italy's Day" celebrated in London. Armistice proposed by Bulgaria. Ishtip and Veles captured by Serbians: British enter Bulgaria opposite Kosturino: 10,000 prisoners, 200 guns taken. Selency captured by British. Tiberias on the Sea of Galilee, and Amman on the Hedjaz railway occupied by Gen. Allenby: 45,000 prisoners, 265 guns to date. **26.** French and U.S. armies attacked enemy in the Argonne on a front of 40 miles and captured Montfaucon, Varennes and numerous villages. Strumnitza entered by British. **27.** Hindenburg line in front of Cambrai broken by British, who took Beaucamp, Graincourt and other important enemy positions: Bourion Wood carried by Canadians: Franco-Americans progressed in the Champagne: 23,000 prisoners captured. **28.** British and Belgians under King Albert, attacking from Dixmude to Ploegsteert on a front of 23 miles, captured Houthulst Forest and numerous prisoners: British warships and many aeroplanes co-operated on Zeebrugge and vicinity. Further French advance in Champagne and on the Aisne: withdrawal of Germans to the Ailette. Armistice with view to peace negotiations asked for by Bulgaria. **29.** Anglo-Belgian armies progressed and occupied Dixmunde, Passchaendale, Gheluvelt and Messines: outskirts of Cambrai reached by British, who broke the Hindenburg line between Cambrai and St. Quentin: 22,000 prisoners to date. New Japanese Cabinet formed with Mr. Kei Hara as Premier. **30.** Surrender of Bulgaria: Allied terms accepted. "Feed the Guns Campaign" to raise second War Loan of £1,000,000,000 opened by the Chancellor of Exchequer.

Oct. 1. Resignation of Count Hertling, German Imperial Chancellor and all German secretaries, announced. Damascus entered by British: 7,000 prisoners. Fall of St. Quentin. Advance of Gen. Gourand towards Challerange in the valley of the Aire: Aure and Marfaux taken: further progress and capture of Binarville, Condé, Autry and Vaux. British flag hoisted at Ebeltoft Harbour, Spitzbergen. **2.** Rumilly–Beaurevoir–Fonsome, enemy line of defence between Cambrai and St. Quentin, broken through by Australians; swift retreat of Germans between the Vesle and the Aisne as far as Rheims; enemy withdrawal from Armentières, La Bassée and Lille; British cross the Lys between Wervicq and Comines. Italian and British warships attacked Durazzo, sank an Austrian torpedo-boat destroyer, and completely destroyed the base. **3.** Prince Max of Baden appointed successor to Count Hertling. British Infantry, with Tanks, attacked on an 8 mile front and advanced some 3 miles north of St. Quentin. Gen. Moiner appointed Military Gov. of Paris. **4.** German Note by Prince Max sent to Pres. Wilson proposing an armistice to open peace negotiations on the basis of Pres. Wilson's 14 points of **Jan. 8**; Germany now to have a "People's Government"; offer to join the League of Nations. Advance of British on a 20 mile front east of Armentières and Cambrai; French and U.S. troops advanced between Rheims and Verdun; in Champagne they captured Challerange. Abdication of King Ferdinand of Bulgaria in favour of his son Boris. Japanese steamer *Hiramo Maru,* torpedoed off the Irish coast: 28 saved out of a total 320. **5.** Gen. Gourand's left wing and centre and the 5th Army on their left, north of Some-Py, east of Rheims, flung back the enemy on a 25 mile front, freeing Rheims and capturing

Brumont and Nogent l'Abasse; capture by Gen. Berthelot's army of the old French line of the Aisne-Marne Canal; German retreat on a front of 30 miles to the line of the Suippe, surrendering without a fight Morouvillers Ridge. British, east of the breach in the Hindenburg line, advanced and captured Montbrehain, Beaurevoir, and high ground to the north: 1,000 prisoners taken; Germans forced to retire from the Scheldt Canal. Germans in their retreat towards Lille set Douai in flames, and were systematically laying waste the country. Capture of Vrange by Franco-Serbian troops. **6.** Solemn warning to Germany issued by French Government "that the authors and directors of German crimes on French territory, such as the treatment of refugees, and the destruction of towns, will be held responsible, morally, judicially and financially…The account with them is opened and will have to be settled." Fresnoy, north of the Scarpe, taken by British: by its capture, enemy now definitely on a 100 mile front from Dixmude down to the Oise, behind the line from which he started for the "Kaiser's Battle" of **March 21**. Sir Douglas Haig awarded the American Cross of Honour. H.M. armoured mercantile cruiser *Otranto* carrying U.S. troops lost by collision: 431 drowned, including 351 soldiers; 367 rescued. **7.** Berry-au-Bac taken by French, and north-east of St. Quentin, Remancourt, Oppy and Biache St. Vaast captured by British. Rapid advance from Damascus of Gen. Allenby, who reported that he, with the King of the Hedjaz, had since **Sept. 18** taken 79,000 prisoners. Sidon occupied by British, and Beirut by French. German Armistice and Peace Note, with its Austrian appendix, received in Washington. Evidence confirming the non-democratic sympathies of Prince Max brought to light by a letter to a relative **Jan. 18**, in which he mocked at "parliamentarisation," and demanded that Germany should "take the enemy by the throat," and exact as much as possible from the Allies. **8.** Full text of Pres. Wilson's reply to the German Peace Note published: President firmly refuses an armistice until all the territories occupied by Germans have been evacuated by them, before the discussion of peace terms. British, French and Americans delivered a strong attack on a 21 mile front from Cambrai to St. Quentin towards Le Cateau and Guise. **9.** Attack resumed on the whole front of the 3rd and 4th Armies; 23 German division defeated between Cambrai and St. Quentin; Cambrai taken by Canadians of the 1st Army. Grand, Ham and Lançon in the valley of the Aisne captured by French. **10.** Fall of Le Cateau to British, who pushing north-east reached Solesmes-Le Cateau road; great progress made between Lens and the Scarpe towards Douai. Line of the Oise, east of St. Quentin, reached by French. Irish mail boat *Leinster* from Kingstown torpedoed: 650 passengers, 70 crew; 527 lost, 193 saved. **11.** Germans forced by British thrust beyond Le Cateau to retreat on the whole front between Soissons-Laon road and Grand Pré, they evacuated the Chemin des Dames, left the Suippe, and the main pass through the Argonne; enemy in Champagne forced to retreat on a front of 37 miles, pursued by French cavalry and infantry; the Suippe crossed and enemy first positions captured by French. British east of Cambrai won the high ground at St. Aubert; north of the Scarpe they advanced through the north stretch of the

Drocourt-Quéant line. Big raid by Allied troops on Austrian positions north of Monte Grappa. King sent a message of congratulation to Sir Douglas Haig. **12.** U.S. troops overseas numbered over 1,900,000. Nish occupied by Allies and the direct line Berlin-Constantinople broken. **13.** Laon and La Fère occupied by French; retreat of Germans on a front of 100 miles from the Oise east of St. Quentin to the Argonne; St. Gobain Forest evacuated; whole of the bend of the Aisne facing Rethel, west bank of the Sensée Canal captured by British near Douai. Tripolis occupied. Capture of 90,000 prisoners and over 2,000 guns by Allies in the Balkans since **Sept. 15. 14.** Belgian, British and French forces, acting under King Albert, resumed the offensive on a front of 28 miles from Dixmude on the north to Wervicq in the south, the British fleet co-operating off the Belgian coast; Merion, Roulers and Iseghem taken. Sissone, in the Hunding line, captured by French. Durazzo occupied by Italians. **15.** Pres. Wilson's reply to Germany. The Allies and U.S. must judge about "the process of evacuation and conditions of an armistice," Germany warned to expect no armistice while German outrages on sea and land continue. The ruling power in Germany, too, is an arbitrary power. Haute Deule Canal, south-west of Lille, crossed by British. **16.** Wervicq, Comines, Hallim and Welveghem captured by 2nd British Army, under Gen. Plumer, fighting east of Ypres in the Valley of the Lys; northern half of Courbrai and river bank to Bavichove secured. Ingelmunster and Lichtervelde taken by French, who also outflanked Thourout. In three days Gen. Plumer advanced 8 miles, took 4,000 prisoners and 150 guns. **17.** Germans in retreat on the whole of the Flanders front, and south as far as Douai; Ostend evacuated; Vice-Adm. Sir Roger Keyes landed from the Fleet, and Belgian troops entered; visit of King and Queen of Belgians. British troops of 5th Army. Gen. Birdwood occupied Lille, and breaking German resistance on the Haute Deule Canal entered Douai. British and French carried the line of the Selle and part of Le Cateau. **18.** Allied troops operating east of Ostend captured Blankenberghe. British crossed the Sensée north of Coutrai. British-Americans continuing their offensive from Le Cateau to Bohain, co-operating with French, took Ribeauville and Wassigny. Operations against the Turks on the Tigris by three columns under Gen. Marshall. Bolshevist force, between 2,000 and 3,000, defeated in North Russia by British troops on the Dvina; Allied troops in Murman region reported advancing on Saroka, south-west of White Sea. **19.** Reply of Pres. Wilson to the Austrian Note published; mere autonomy for Czech-Slovaks and Jugo-Slavs no longer an adequate basis for peace. Zeebrugge and Bruges occupied by Belgians; Denain taken by 1st British Army. Hunding line on a front of 3 miles broken through by French operating between the Oise and the Serre. **20.** Belgian coast cleared of Germans, retreating east towards Antwerp and still retiring from Dutch frontier to south of Valenciennes: British 2nd Army close to the Scheldt. Enemy on the Selle attacked by English, Scottish and Welsh troops from Denain to Le Cateau, and passage of river forced; 3,000 prisoners. Franco-Serbian troops close to Danube near Roumanian border. **21.** Reply by German Government to Pres. Wilson dealing with the evacuation of North France and Belgium, and the charges of illegal and inhumane actions against the German sea and land forces, and the status of the German Government. Germans find temporary refuge behind a line of rivers and canals from the Dutch frontier to St. Amand, north of Valenciennes, the Lys Canal, the Lys and the Scheldt and its canals **22.** French and Belgians attacked along the line of the Lys Canal towards Ghent; Canal crossed and 1,100 prisoners taken. French advance on the Serre front. West suburb of Valenciennes entered by 1st British Army. Lord Northcliffe [owner of *The Times* and *The Daily Mail*, and Director of Propaganda], in a speech to a large gathering of U.S. officers, uttered a warning that the great German peace offensive, now in progress, might prove more dangerous than the offensive in the field earlier in the year: "no haggling with Germany about peace terms." Despatch from Sir Douglas Haig published, dealing with the reasons for the retirement of the 5th Army. **23.** Great attack opened by 3rd and 4th British armies east and north-east of Le Cateau on a 20 mile front to a depth of 4 miles; between Valenciennes and Tournay, 1st British Army pushing through Raismer Forest captured Bruay, Bicharies and Espain. The Souche crossed by French, overcoming stubborn resistance of the enemy. Mr. Balfour, speaking in London, said "that in no circumstances was it consistent with the safety, security and unity of the British Empire that the German colonies should be returned to Germany." **24.** 3rd and 4th British armies extended their advance beyond the Oise-Sambre Canal and the Scheldt, a distance of 17 miles: 7,000 prisoners, 100 guns taken: Landrecies approached and the Forest of Mormal. Offensive opened on a wide front by Italians, French and British against Austrians on the Trentino front and Middle Piave: bitter fighting on Monte Grappa region: Monte Solarolo taken by Italians, and Sisemol by French: 84 officers, 2,791 men prisoners. Reply of Pres. Wilson to Germany, demanding "extraordinary safeguards, because the present war is not under the German peoples' control." **25.** British 1st Army north of Valenciennes advanced through Raismes Forest into the Condé loop of the Scheldt. 3rd Army south won eight miles of the Valenciennes-Avesnes Railway: 9,000 prisoners, 150 guns taken in two days' fighting. Between the Oise, Serre, Souche and Aisne rivers, French attacked on a front of 25 miles. Piave crossed by Anglo-Italian 10th Army, under Lord Cavan. **26.** Aleppo taken, completing the conquest of Syria, and cutting the Baghdad Railway. South of Valenciennes, Artnes, Famars, and Englefontaine captured by British. Resignation of Gen. Ludendorff. **27.** Austrian reply to Pres. Wilson, accepting his Note of **Oct. 18** (refusing to accept mere autonomy for the Czecho-Slovaks) and stating readiness to negotiate peace, and an immediate armistice on all the Austro-Hungarian fronts. Germans retreated between the Oise and the Serre towards Hirson. Port of Alessio taken by Italians. Mr. Lloyd George and Mr. Balfour with their naval and military advisers, and Col. House, U.S., in Paris for Conference of Allies. **28.** Conference, at Versailles, of Allied Chiefs. Prof. Lammasch appointed Austrian Premier in succession to the Hussarck Cabinet resigned. Piave, in Montello region, crossed by Italians. Kalat Shergat, on the Tigris, taken by Gen. Marshall.

Count Andrassy, new Austro-Hungarian Foreign Minister, applied to Mr. Lansing [U.S. Secretary of State, 1915–20] asking him to use his influence with Pres. Wilson, to effect an immediate armistice. **29.** Further progress of great Italian advance begun **Oct. 24** extending from the Brenta to the sea: enemy's successive lines of resistance on the mountain front being overcome: the Allied line carried across the Piave well north of Valdobbiadene and of Conegliano as far as Vittorio: Lower Piave crossed at St. Donà di Piave and Zenson: Austrian Trentino line threatened: 33,000 prisoners and hundreds of guns taken since **26th Oct**. Turks heavily engaged by Gen. Marshall five miles north of Kalat Shergat, 50 miles south of Mosul, and routed: 7,000 prisoners. Conclusion of Tigris campaign. Desperate fighting by French for ancient castle of Guise. Important debate in the House of Commons on the treatment of British prisoners at the hands of the Germans. **30.** Czecho-Slovak state proclaimed at Prague: independence of Croatia and all the Southern Slav territories proclaimed in Agram Diet. Surrender of Turkish army on the Tigris. Turkey out of the war: unconditional surrender: armistice signed to take effect from noon next day. Great activity of British air squadrons on the Western front: 82 German machines down: 18 British missing. Mr. Bonar Law [Chancellor of the Exchequer, 1916–18] joined Mr. Lloyd George at Versailles. **31.** British captures Aug., Sept., Oct., in series of successful battles fought in France: 172,659 prisoners, including 3,957 officers, 2,378 guns, 17,000 machine-guns, 2,750 trench mortars. Austrian Army occupying the Trentino separated and isolated from occupying the Venetian Plains: enemy's only line of communications down to the Piave Gorge from Bellona and along the Val Sugana, 50,000 prisoners to date. Austrians chased back across the Livenza towards the Tagliamento, in the mountainous Asiago, and the whole of strong positions between the Brenta and Piave regained. Austrian Dreadnought *Viribus Unitas*, flagship of the Austrian fleet, sunk by Italians at Pola. End of Dual Monarchy: revolutionary outbreaks at Vienna and Budapest: demonstrations against the Hapsburgs: Hungarian National Government, at Budapest, took over the Government and proclaimed a Republic. Bosnian National Council, at Sarajevo, proclaimed the amalgamation of Bosnia and Herzegovina with the kingdom of Serbia. Austrian commander-in-chief on Italian front applied to Gen. Diaz for an armistice. King and War Cabinet sent a warm message of thanks to Gen. Allenby: the G.C.B. conferred. Nancy bombed by Germans: severe casualties and damage.

Nov. 1. Versailles Conference opened: naval delegates present. English and Canadians forced the passage of the Rhonelle, captured villages of Maresches and Aulnoy, and, attacking on a 6-mile front, reached S. outskirts of Valenciennes. British, French, and U.S. troops E. of the Lys forced their way to the Scheldt as far as Gavere, 10 miles S. of Ghent: combined push of U.S. and French from the Aisne to the Meuse. Continued retreat of Austrian armies on the whole front of the Venetian Alps and Plain. Imperial decree issued handing over the Austrian Fleet to S. Slav

Council at Agram and Pola: Danube flotilla transferred to Hungarian Government. Count Tisza [Hungarian Prime Minister, 1913–17] shot at Vienna. **2.** British at Valenciennes: capture by French of Semuy and S. bank of the Canal des Ardennes from Semuy to Neuville. Mass meeting of Trade Unionists, to consider Labour's part in the Peace, held at Albert Hall. **3.** Surrender of Austria, accepting all conditions: armistice signed by Gen. Diaz, Italian Comm.-in-Chief, to take effect at noon, **Nov. 4.** Mutiny of sailors of German Fleet at Kiel. Advance of French and Americans 8 miles on a front of 30 miles: Neuville, Les Aileux, Noival, Buzancy, Bois de Tailly, and woods N. W. of Dun, on the Meuse, taken: the Argonne completely cleared of Germans. Italian military and naval forces landed at Trieste: Italian troops in Trent and Udine. Belgians advanced S. of Dutch frontier and took Baasvelde and Steydinge. Prof. Lammasch handed over to the Austrian State Council the government "to far as it relates to German localities." Hungarian National Council, with Count Karolyi at its head, in power at Budapest. **4.** French reached the line of the Ardennes Canal: La Chesne captured: Americans on the right near Beaumont and Stenay: 17 German divisions defeated, 5,000 prisoners, 100 guns taken: Great offensive by the 1st, 3rd and 4th British Armies, with Army of Gen. Débeney on the right, on a front of 30 miles, E. of Valenciennes to Guise: Landrecies taken: British half-way through the Forest of Mormal: over 10,000 prisoners, 200 guns captured. The defences of the Sambre-Oise Canal broken through by 1st and 32nd British Divisions operating on the right N. British several miles E. of Le Quesnoy after fierce fighting. German retreat towards the Meuse, flowed by Allies. Scutari entered by Italians. Spread of revolution to Hamburg and other parts of Germany. **5.** Rapid retreat of Germans on wide sections of the Western Front. Forest of Mormal occupied by British: Le Quesnoy captured with its garrison of 1,000 men. French advance between the Oise and Aisne towards Hirson. French over the Ardennes Canal: Beaumont taken by Americans. Germans still retreating between the Aisne and the Meuse. In the House of Commons Mr. Lloyd George announced that the Versailles Conference had reached complete agreement as to the terms of armistice with Germany, which the Premier read to the House: Gen. Foch placed in supreme direction of all the forces operating against Germany on all fronts "in this last and decisive phase of the war." Allied reply to Germany through President Wilson: "Germany must apply for the conditions of armistice to Gen. Foch in the usual military form." **6.** Sedan reached by U.S. troops: main lateral line of German communications cut. French captured Vervins and Rethel. Great German retreat continued and became general from the Scheldt N. of Valenciennes to the Meuse. 1st, 3rd and 4th British Armies continued their pursuit towards Mons, Maubeuge and Avesnes. German delegates left for Western Front to receive Allied terms of armistice from Gen. Foch and Adm. Sir R. Wemyss. **7.** Formal entrance into Valenciennes by 1st British Army: Bavai taken N.: Avesnes entered S.: Haumont, in the Sambre Valley, reached. Kiel and Hamburg reported to be in the hands of Committees of Workmen and Soldiers: their demands granted by the German

Government: part of the German Fleet "flying the Red flag." Maj. W. C. Barker, D.S.O., a Canadian, fought 60 enemy aeroplanes, brought down 10, and returned to the British Front severely wounded. Approximate number of German prisoners captured on the Western Front, Jan. 1–Nov. 5: by British, 200,000; French, 140,000; U.S., 50,000; Belgians, 15,000. **8.** Resignation of Prince Max of Baden, Imperial Chancellor. Spread of revolutionary movement over Germany. Bavaria proclaimed a Republic. Further progress of British: W. part of Tournai occupied: the Scheldt crossed to the S.: Condé captured: advance towards Mons on both sides of the Mons-Condé Canal: Maubeuge taken: 18,000 prisoners, several hundred guns taken since **Nov. 1** by British. French continued their progress towards Mézières and Charville: 3,500 prisoners captured. **9.** German envoys received by General Foch. "Abdication" of the Kaiser announced. Revolution in Berlin: flight of the King of Bavaria: Bavaria, Würtemburg, Saxony, the Mecklenburgs, Brunswick, Hesse, and other countries reported to be suppressing their Governments.

Armistice Declared

Nov. 9. [1918] Mr. Lloyd George, at the Lord Mayor's banquet, announced the abdication of the Kaiser, and said "Germany's doom was sealed." Flight of the Kaiser to Holland. **10.** French captured Hirson, surrounded Mézières and crossed the Meuse: few German troops remaining on French soil. U.S. troops pushed forward towards Montmédy and the Briery basin. Death of Herr Ballin, Director of the Hamburg-Amerika Line. **11.** Mons entered at dawn by Canadians. Armistice signed by German plenipotentiaries. **11 a.m.** firing ceased on all fronts. Allies' terms including the giving up of 6 battle-cruisers, 10 battleships, 8 light cruisers, 50 destroyers and all submarines, specified number of military guns etc immediate evacuation of all invaded countries, release of British prisoners, and the occupation by Allies of the left bank of the Rhine. Messages of congratulation and appreciation sent by the King to the Navy, Army, and Air Force. Scenes of great rejoicing in London and the provinces.

OFFICIAL END OF THE WAR

The *Official Termination of the War,* when Treaties of Peace had been ratified by the respective Governments, was Aug. 31, 1921. The Ottoman Empire was excluded from the Order in Council, and War with Turkey was declared at an end on August 6, 1924.

THE SECOND WORLD WAR

The Approach to War: Six Months of Hitlerism

A selection of events as recorded in the 1940 edition

Mar. 10. [**1939**] The President of Czecho-Slovakia dismissed Dr. Tiso, the Slovak Premier, and three other Ministers to prevent attempt at separation [*see* 'Munich Agreement' below]. Dr. Tiso appealed to Herr Hitler, who summoned midnight conference. **12.** German storm-troopers appeared in Bratislava, and shops were wrecked. **13.** Bomb explosions occurred at Bratislava. Dr. Tiso saw Herr Hitler in Berlin. Troop movements occurred in Germany. **14.** Slovakia declared her independence and Prague Government resigned. Dr. Hacha, Czecho-Slovakian President, hurried to Berlin and had conference with Herr Hitler, Herr von Ribbentrop [German Foreign Minister, 1938–45] and Field-Marshal Goering. Hungary presented ultimatum to Prague Government, demanding withdrawal of Czech troops from Ruthenian territory. Hungarian troops entered Carpatho-Ukraine, and, later, German troops invaded Czech territory and occupied several towns. **15.** German troops poured into Prague, being frequently greeted with hostile demonstrations from weeping crowds. In the evening Herr Hitler drove into the city and hoisted swastika above former President's official home. German generals were appointed military governors of Bohemia and Moravia. Trade talks which British Ministers had intended to begin in Berlin were cancelled. In Commons, Mr. Chamberlain said that owing to internal disruption, Britain could no longer hold itself morally bound to guarantee the Czecho-Slovak frontiers. He would not regard method by which changes had been brought about as in accord with spirit of Munich Agreement. **16.** Hitler, before leaving Prague, proclaimed Bohemia and Moravia as a German protectorate, garrisoned by German troops, and Slovakia as another German protectorate, but with different system of government. Thousands of Czechs arrested in Prague. Hungary and Poland inaugurated their new frontier in Carpatho-Ukraine. **17.** British and French Ambassadors in Berlin were recalled to report. Mr. Chamberlain at Birmingham strongly denounced Germany's action and reproached Führer for breaking his solemn assurance that he had no further territorial aims. United States Acting Secretary of State, Mr. Welles, condemned Germany's "wanton lawlessness." German troops in Prague moved eastwards. **19.** Hitler returned to Berlin and was given mass welcome. Britain, France and Russia sent strong protests to Germany, refusing to recognise annexation. **20.** Replying to British and French suggestions for co-operation to stop aggression, Russia proposed immediate calling of conference of peace-loving Powers. United States sent note refusing to recognise the annexation. **21.** Germany gave Lithuania three days within which to hand over the Memel Territory. Fascist Grand Council in Rome declared its adhesion to the Rome-Berlin axis in the face of threatened front of the democracies.

MUNICH AGREEMENT

An agreement between Italy, France, Germany and the UK, ratified in the early hours of 30 September 1938, but dated 29 September, which permitted Nazi Germany to annex the 'Sudetenland'. The Sudetenland was an area within Czechoslovakia, along the border with Germany, and mainly inhabited by German speakers. The settlement was negotiated at a conference in Munich without the presence of any representatives from Czechoslovakia.

British Prime Minister Neville Chamberlain returned from the Munich Conference on 30 September 1938, and on landing at Heston Aerodrome, announced to the awaiting crowds, "The settlement of the Czechoslovakian problem, which has now been achieved is, in my view, only the prelude to a larger settlement in which all Europe may find peace…We regard the agreement signed last night and the Anglo-German Naval Agreement as symbolic of the desire of our two peoples never to go to war with one another again.

Later that day Mr Chamberlain stood outside 10 Downing Street and concluded, "My good friends, for the second time in our history, a British Prime Minister has returned from Germany bringing peace with honour. I believe it is peace for our time. We thank you from the bottom of our hearts. Go home and get a nice quiet sleep."

22. Memel formally surrendered to Germany. **26.** In speech on 20th anniversary of Fascism, Signor Mussolini said he considered a long period of peace necessary for safeguarding of development of European civilization. **29.** M. Daladier [French Prime Minister, 1938–40], in a broadcast speech, declared France would not cede an acre to Italy, but would examine any proposals. Because of German military preparations, Poland's mobilization was speeded up, and President conferred with Opposition leaders. **31.** Mr. Chamberlain in Commons said that Britain and France had given assurances that if Polish independence were threatened and Poland considered it vital to resist, Britain and France would lend all support in their power.

Apr. 3. Mr. Chamberlain explained that Britain and France would immediately go to assistance of Poland if she were threatened. All Parties supported Government's policy. Colonel Beck, Polish Foreign Minister, arrived in London. **4.** Anglo-Polish talks opened, Colonel Beck stating Poland desired to make the guarantee against aggression reciprocal. **5.** Berlin announced that General Franco had joined the anti-Comintern Pact. **6.** Mr. Chamberlain, in Commons, said Colonel Beck's conversations had shown that the two governments were in complete agreement upon general principles and were ready to enter into agreement of permanent and reciprocal character. **7.** Italian troops invaded Albania, landing at four points, and advanced towards Tirana, the capital. King Zog, his wife and two-day-old heir fled to Greece. Albanian army resisted where possible but were greatly outnumbered by invaders. **9.** Roumania and Turkey decided to stand together in seeking Balkan Entente policy. Provisional Albanian Government formed in Tirana. Italian troops advanced further. **10.** British Cabinet sent strong protest to Rome. Occupation of Albania considered complete, troops being flown to many points. **12.** Albanian Constitutional Assembly at Tirana abrogated existing constitution, set up a new government and offered the Crown of Albania to King Victor Emmanuel. **13.** Prime Minister in Commons and M. Daladier in Paris announced that Britain and France had decided to extend all support in their power to Greece and Roumania if their independence were threatened. Mr. Chamberlain declined to denounce Anglo-Italian Agreement, as it would add to international tension. He stated that Italy had assured Greece no attack on Corfu was contemplated. Fascist Grand Council approved Italian King's acceptance of Crown of Albania. **14.** President Roosevelt sent personal appeals for peace to Herr Hitler and Signor Mussolini, inviting them to give a 10-year, or, if possible, a 25-year assurance that they would not attack or invade 30 named countries [the Arabias, Belgium, Bulgaria, Denmark, Egypt, Estonia, Finland, France, Great Britain and Ireland, Greece, Hungary, Iran, Iraq, Latvia, Liechtenstein, Lithuania, Luxemburg, The Netherlands, Norway, Palestine, Poland, Portugal, Rumania, Russia, Spain, Sweden, Switzerland, Syria, Turkey and Yugoslavia]. **16.** British Government cordially approved the message. **21.** Germany asked several small States whether they considered themselves threatened by the Axis Powers. **23.** Several States replied to Germany in diplomatic terms. **26.** Mr. Chamberlain announced Government's decision that young men between 20 and 21 should undergo compulsory military training for six months. **28.** Herr Hitler, in Reichstag, denounced Anglo-German Naval Agreement of 1935 and Polish-German Non-Aggression Pact of 1934, but expressed willingness to negotiate with Britain on naval problem. He rejected President Roosevelt's appeal for conference, and offered guarantee to the 30 States, provided it was asked for with appropriate proposals. **29.** Lord Halifax [Foreign Secretary, 1938–40] discussed with M. Maisky, Soviet Ambassador, proposals for Anglo-Soviet agreement.

May 5. Colonel Beck, in Polish Parliament, refused to hand over Danzig to Germany as a free city or to grant route to Germany through the Corridor. **7.** It was announced that Italy and Germany had decided to fix their relations in final form in political and military pact, involving, it was understood, combined commands in war and pooling of arms. **8.** The Pope proposed a conference to settle Polish-German dispute. British proposals for pact presented to M. Molotov [Russian Foreign Minister, 1939–49]. **10.** Mr. Chamberlain stated it was not Britain's intention to commit the Soviet to intervention unsupported by Great Britain and France. **11.** Prime Minister warned Germany that if attempt was made to change Danzig situation by force and Polish independence were thereby threatened, it would start a conflagration in which Britain would be involved. **12.** Mr. Chamberlain announced that Britain and Turkey had agreed to conclude long-term pact of mutual aid in Mediterranean area, including the Dardanelles and Black Sea. **17.** Norway, Sweden and Finland declined Germany's offer of non-aggression pact and Denmark announced readiness to negotiate, but on conditions. **20.** Polish Customs House near Danzig attacked and wrecked by crowd and shots were fired. **22.** German-Italian political and military pact signed in Berlin. **24.** Mr. Chamberlain said he hoped as result of new proposals of Britain and France full agreement would be reached at an early state with Russia. Polish-British military talks began at Warsaw. **31.** M. Molotov said Anglo-French-Soviet Pact must be exclusively of defensive character and be concrete agreement for assistance if one of signatories were attacked. Non-aggression Pact between Germany and Denmark signed in Berlin.

June 3. "Registration Day" for young men of 20 brought almost unanimous response, over 219,000 attending. **5.** Japan informed Germany and Italy that while friendly to the Axis Powers she was unwilling to undertake European commitments. **7.** Government decided to send special Foreign Office representative to Moscow to accelerate negotiations. Non-aggression pacts between Germany and Latvia and Estonia signed at Berlin. **14.** Mr. William Strang, of Foreign Office, arrived in Moscow. Poland called more men to the colours. Germany protested against treatment of their minority in Poland. **15.** Mr. Strang and other delegates had interview with M. Molotov. **18.** Dr. Goebbels, speaking in Danzig, pledged German support for the Free City Germans in their wish to return to the Reich. **23.** Danzig decided to form a Nazi Corps. Franco-Turkish declaration of mutual assistance signed in Paris, and agreement signed in Ankara by which France ceded the Hatay to Turkey. Franco-British Far East defence talks began in Singapore. **25.** Unanimous agreement reached on all matters of policy at Singapore discussions. **26.** Admiralty announced that Fleet would carry out exercises in August. **28.** In Note to Germany, Britain denied encirclement, said it could only be hostile to Germany if latter committed act of aggression, and offered discussions on trade if mutual confidence could be established. **29.** In speech broadcast to the world Lord Halifax declared plainly that Britain would use whole of her strength to resist aggression by Germany.

July 1. French Foreign Minister [Georges Bonnet] told German Ambassador that France would not accept any alteration in Danzig. **9.** Soviet Government announced that renewal of talks had not produced any definite result. **10.** Mr. Chamberlain in Commons, said that a threat to Danzig would at once raise grave issues affecting Polish national existence and independence and Britain would carry out her undertaking to assist Poland if her independence were threatened. Orders served on foreigners in Italian Tyrol to leave within 48 hours, as result of agreement between Germany and Italy that German inhabitants should emigrate to the Reich.

13. Sir John Simon [Chancellor of the Exchequer, 1937–40] stated Britain's expenditure on defence for the year now totalled £730,000,000. **17.** Moscow talks resumed. **18.** General Sir Edmund Ironside began staff talks with Polish war chiefs in Warsaw. **24.** Mr. Chamberlain, in Commons, denied reports of proposal for loan to Germany. **29.** Home Fleet left ports for two-month exercises in North Sea. **31.** Mr. Chamberlain stated that Naval, Military and Air Force Mission would be sent to Russia immediately because Soviet Premier thought political difficulties could thus be removed.

Aug. 1. Britain agreed to guarantee Polish purchases for £8,000,000. **2.** Poland decided to reject demand of Danzig Senate for reduction of Polish Customs officers in the Free City. **4.** In Note to Danzig, Poland declared that threat to open Customs frontier with East Prussia might lead to open conflict. **7.** Stated that 7,000 German-speaking peasants had been driven from their homes in South Tyrol by Italian Government. Danzig Senate said no discrimination would be introduced against Polish officials. **10.** Herr Förster, Nazi leader in Danzig, after visiting Hitler, declared in speech that the hour of liberation and reunion with the Reich would come. **11.** British and French mission arrived at Moscow for staff talks. Hitler and Count Ciano [Italian foreign minister, 1936–43] discussed policy of Axis powers. **12.** The Moscow conferences began. **15.** Hungary rejected Germany's demand for military pact. **16.** President of Danzig Senate conferred with Polish Commissioner. **18.** Germany signed military treaty with Slovakia and assumed military protection of Slovak territory between Poland and Hungary. **20.** Germany began concentrating troops near Polish frontier. Pope sent high prelate to Warsaw to urge Poland to negotiate with Germany. Agreement announced in Berlin which granted trade credit to the Soviet to buy German goods and called on Germany to buy Soviet goods. Announced that obstructions were to be placed immediately in the Firth of Clyde. **21.** World sensation caused by official announcement in Berlin that Germany and Soviet Union had agreed to conclude a non-aggression pact with each other. British subjects advised to leave Poland by British Consul in Warsaw. **22.** British Cabinet decided to recall Parliament to pass Emergency Powers (Defence) Bill. Certain personnel for Defence Services and Civil Defence called up. Government declared use of force involving European war was not justified by difficulties between Germany and Poland. Japan indignant at news of Soviet-German Pact. **23.** Von Ribbentrop and M. Molotov signed Russo-German Pact in Moscow. Each country undertook for ten years to refrain from acts of force or aggressive acts against each other and not to support a third Power which took warlike actions against one of them or join any group of Powers directed against them. Herr Hitler, after receiving from British Ambassador letter from Mr. Chamberlain announcing Government's view, declared that this view could not cause Germany to renounce pursuance of her national vital interests. Final concentration of German troops completed. King of the Belgians broadcast appeal for peace on behalf of the rulers of Belgium, Denmark, Finland, Luxemburg, Holland, Sweden and Norway. France called up further class of reserves. **24.** Hitler conferred with military leaders. Berlin declared Poland's preparations had assumed offensive character. Herr Förster appointed Führer of Danzig. Britons and French recommended to leave Germany. Poland called up 500,000 reserves. President Roosevelt urged King of Italy to put forward peace proposals. Parliament met specially. Mr. Chamberlain and Lord Halifax declared Britain and France would fulfil their obligations to Poland. Emergency Powers Bill passed through all its stages and became law. Hitler twice saw Sir Nevile Henderson [British Ambassador to Germany, 1937–40]. He told other Ambassadors that his patience was almost exhausted by Poland. German ships ordered to remain in or return to German ports. British and French Missions left Moscow. Anglo-Polish Treaty signed in London. Poland protested against appointment of Herr Förster. Mr. Roosevelt sent appeals to Hitler and Polish President. **26.** Sir Nevile Henderson flew to London and attended meeting of Cabinet. **27.** Hitler, replying to message from French Premier, demanded not only Danzig, but the return of the Polish Corridor. Admiralty assumed control of British merchant fleet. Polish-German frontier closed. **28.** German troops occupied Silesia. Sir Nevile Henderson flew back to Berlin and gave Hitler British Government's reply. France closed her frontier with Germany. Admiralty closed Mediterranean and Baltic to British shipping. Britain and France promised to respect Belgian neutrality. **29.** Hitler's reply to Britain handed to Ambassador and telegraphed to London. Mr. Chamberlain told Commons entire Fleet was ready and all defences were manned. **30.** Hitler ordered Polish delegates to come to Berlin to negotiate settlement. British reply to Hitler's last message offered to assist negotiations, and urged both parties to take no military action during negotiations. Poland called up final reserves. French Army took over control of railways. Paris school-children evacuated. Hitler set-up permanent Council of Ministers for Defence of the State. **31.** Germany announced her proposals for settlement with Poland, but declared she considered them rejected because no delegate had come to Berlin. They had been given to Polish Ambassador only two hours before and Poland had consequently never seen them. Frontier fighting in which Poles and Germans were killed reported. British Government ordered full mobilization of the Fleet and calling up of further naval, military and Air Force reserves. Soviet Army increased by 500,000 men.

The Outbreak of the Second World War

As recorded in the 1940 edition
The War Against Aggression: The First Phase

Sept. 1. [1939] At dawn German troops began invasion of Poland on all fronts –
without either ultimatum or declaration. German planes raided many Polish cities
and towns, including Warsaw and claimed to have gained upper hand. Few hours
after military action began, Polish Ambassador called on Lord Halifax and formally
invoked Anglo-Polish Treaty asking for Britain's assistance against aggression.
Polish President called the whole nation to arms. British and French Ambassadors
in Berlin presented document to German Government warning Germany that
unless aggressive action were suspended and all German forces withdrawn from
Polish Territory, Britain and France would go to the aid of Poland. Hitler told Signor
Mussolini that he would not need military aid from Italy but thanked him for
diplomatic and political aid he had given. In declaration to Reichstag, Hitler said
that his proposals were rejected and denied that there had been undue pressure.
Herr Förster decreed Danzig part of the Reich. Mr. Chamberlain in Commons
outlined Britain's efforts for peace and was supported by all parties. House voted
sum not exceeding £500,000,000 for Defence of Realm and prosecution of war.
Labour Party in manifesto gave Government's decision full support. State took
control of railways. France announced general mobilisation and proclaimed martial
law. Italian Council of Ministers announced that Italy would take no initiative in
military operations. Britain and France sent favourable replies to President
Roosevelt's appeal not to bomb civilians and unfortified cities. Evacuation of
children, mothers, blind and disabled from danger zones in Britain began, over
1,000,000 being moved without mishap. **2.** German troops advanced further and
made further raids on open towns. **3.** Britain became at war with Germany at
11.15 a.m. Mr. Chamberlain announced the news in broadcast to the nation.
Germany, he said, had given no undertaking to withdraw troops from Poland by
stipulated time and consequently we were at war. France entered the struggle at
5 p.m., the time she had fixed. General Viscount Gort appointed Commander-in-
Chief of British Field Forces, General Sir Edmund Ironside Chief of Imperial
General Staff and General Sir Walter Kirke Commander-in-Chief of the Home
Forces. War Cabinet formed and held first meeting. It consisted of Mr. Chamberlain,
Sir John Simon, Lord Halifax, Lord Chatfield, Mr. Churchill (new First Lord of the
Admiralty), Mr. Hore-Belisha, Sir Kingsley Wood, Sir Samual Hoare (now Lord
Privy Seal) and Lord Hankey (Minister without portfolio). Mr. Eden was appointed
Dominions Secretary; Lord Stanhope, Lord President; Sir Thomas Inskip, Lord
Chancellor and Sir John Anderson, Home Secretary and Minister of Home Security.
Labour and Liberal Parties were invited to accept offices but declined although
giving wide co-operation. The King broadcast to the nation, asking the people to
stand calm and firm and united.

The End of the Second World War

As recorded in the 1946 edition
Chronicle of the War 1945

THE END DRAWS NEAR: FIGHTING IN THE BERLIN SUBURBS

April 21. [1945] Russians fighting in suburbs of Berlin, three miles from heart of city. In the west British bridgehead over the Elbe expanded. Tanks shelled enemy cruiser defending Hamburg and U-boat leaving dry dock. Eighth and Fifth Army freed Bologna and advanced beyond city. **22.** Many suburbs of Berlin captured by the Russians; city invested on 3 sides. In the south French occupied Stuttgart and reached Swiss border, sealing off enemy forces in Black Forest. Germans retreating across the Po Valley bombed with devastating results. **23.** Russian troops broke into Berlin from the south as advance from the Oder made progress. American Third Army suddenly switched attack upon Bavaria and took Germans by surprise, advancing rapidly towards mountain redoubt of Nazis. Both Fifth and Eighth Armies reached River Po. **24.** Soviet troops from east and south made contact in Berlin, more suburbs of which were captured. American drive into Bavaria continued, enemy making stand at Regensburg. French occupied Ulm and crossed the Danube. British fought their way into suburbs of Hamburg and Bremen. In Italy Allies crossed River Po, and captured Ferrara, Modena and Spezia. **25.** Armies of Marshal Zhukov and Koniev joined north-west of Potsdam, thus surrounding Berlin. Lancasters dropped 12,000 lb. bombs on Berchtesgaden hitting Hitler's chalet and barracks in grounds and Hitler's mountain refuge. Resistance in Italy slackened as the two Armies advanced. Oilfields of Burma cleared of Japanese with capture of Yenanyaung. **26.** Firm contact established between Americans and Soviet troops at Torgau, north-east of Leipzig, cutting Germany in two. Russian troops poured into Berlin, radio centre being taken. Port of Stetting occupied, Bremen surrendered. New crossings of Danube made by General Patton's Americans. Göring relieved of command of Luftwaffe owing to illness. Allies in Italy entered Verona and crossed River Adige. 14th Army in Burma took Toungoo. **27.** Mr. Churchill, President Truman and Marshal Stalin issued messages reaffirming their determination to complete destruction of the Reich. Russians captured Potsdam, Spandau and Tempelhof aerodrome. Third Army entered Regensburg and crossed frontier in Austria. Fifth Army occupied Genoa after partisans had seized part of the city. Arrest of Mussolini reported. **28.** Himmler offered unconditional surrender to Britain and United States but not to the U.S.S.R. Offer was refused as only unconditional surrender to the three major Powers would be entertained. Fifth Army captured Brescia and Bergamo. Mussolini and his mistress and 12 members of his Cabinet were executed by Italian partisans in village and their bodies taken to Milan. **29.** British crossed Elbe near Lauenburg, south-east of Hamburg, and gained substantial bridgehead. American Seventh Army entered Munich; Third advanced from the Danube to east of the city; and French troops came into line on Austrian border. Russians captured Berlin district of Moabit. Fifth Army occupied Milan and London Division of Eighth Army entered Venice. Formation of provisional government in Austria announced. **30.** Soviet troops isolated Baltic port of Swinemünde and Czechoslovakia stormed Moravska Ostrava. In Berlin they captured Reichstag building and hoisted Red Flag. Last Japanese defensive position before Rangoon broken by 14th Army.

DEATH OF HITLER

May 1. [1945] In wireless announcement Grand Admiral Dönitz said Hitler had died in Berlin after appointing him as his successor. New Führer said struggle would continue. Russians took Brandenburg and Stralsund and cleared more districts of Berlin, their tanks being in the Tiergarten. New Zealand troops of Eighth Army crossed River Isonzo, and made contact with Marshal Tito's army; other forces entered Udine and Fifth Army advanced along Gulf of Genoa.

SURRENDER IN ITALY

May 2. [1945] Hostilities ceased in Italy, nearly a million Germans surrendering unconditionally to Field Marshal Sir Harold Alexander as result of document signed at Caserta three days earlier, large part of Austria being included in capitulation area. Field Marshal Alexander in Order of the Day told his troops they had won victory which had ended in complete and utter rout of German armed forces in Mediterranean. Russian High Command announced capture of Berlin and surrender of garrison. Soviet troops captured Rostock on the Baltic, and 20 miles away British Airborne division took Wismar, other forces taking Lubeck. Australian troops invaded Borneo. British Forces landed south of Rangoon. **3.** Enemy collapsed in northern Germany and prisoners flocked in, British Second Army taking at least 500,000 in two days. Hamburg and Oldenburg surrendered and British troops crossed Danish frontier. In Burma British entered Rangoon after rapid advance. **4.** Field Marshal Montgomery reported that all enemy forces in Holland, north-west Germany, and Denmark had surrendered. In the south the "redoubt" was split into fragments. Salzburg and Innsbrück falling. Seventh Army went through Brenner Pass to join with Fifth Army in Italy. **5.** An Army Group in Southern Germany surrendered to Sixth Army Group under General Devers, some 300,000 troops being involved. Patriots in Czechoslovakia rose and Czech flags flew again in Prague. In north-west Germany more than 400,000 Germans laid down their arms and hostilities ceased in accordance with surrender arranged with Field Marshal Montgomery. Soviet troops took Swinemünde and Peenemunde. **6.** Third Army advanced north-east into Czechoslovakia, taking Pilsen. Blaskowitz, leader of German 25th Army, with about 120,000 troops in western Netherlands, unconditionally surrendered to Canadian Commander, General Foulkes. Release from prison camps announced of Daladier, Reynaud, Generals Gamelin and Weygand, Kurt Schuschnigg, Leon Blum, and Lord Lascelles.

Édouard Daladier, Paul Reynaud and Leon Blum were all major political figures (and former Prime Ministers) in the Cabinet of the Third Republic who were arrested for not cooperating with the Vichy Government and handed over to the Germans. Generals Maurice Gamelin and Maxime Weygand were both Commander-in-Chiefs of the French Forces: Gamelin refused to collaborate with the Vichy regime and was arrested, Weygand collaborated at first but was later arrested. Kurt Schuschnigg was the former Austrian Chancellor and Lord Lascelles (later 7th Earl of Harewood), a British hereditary peer and first cousin of Queen Elizabeth II. Lord Lascelles was taken prisoner of war in Italy in June 1944 while serving as Captain in the Grenadier Guards. Hitler signed Lascelles' death warrant in March 1945, but his execution was not carried out by the camp commander.

ALL GERMANY SURRENDERS UNCONDITIONALLY

May 7. [1945] New German Foreign Minister broadcast to German people announcing the unconditional surrender of all German fighting troops. Surrender was signed at **2.41 a.m.** in school-room at Rheims serving as General Eisenhower's Headquarters, by General Jodl, German Chief of Staff, in presence of General Bedell Smith, Allied Chief of Staff and other Allied officers. German emissaries were afterwards presented to General Eisenhower and Air Chief Marshal Tedder, whom they assured that they were ready to carry out the terms. German forces in Norway capitulated. Admiral Dönitz ordered U-boats to cease hostilities and return to port. British armoured cars arrived in Copenhagen to join airborne troops flown in. Field Marshal Montgomery met Marshal Rokossovsky at Wismar. Eighth Army crossed Italian frontier into Austria north of Udine. Garrison at Breslau ceased resistance and surrendered. Fighting still going on in Prague, where populace revolted against Germans. Victory in Europe [VE] celebrated in all Allied capitals.

VE DAY

May 8. [1945] Mr. Churchill broadcast end of hostilities one minute after midnight, although "Cease Fire" had been sounded already all along the front. Agreement signed at Rheims was ratified and confirmed at Berlin, being signed by Air Chief Marshal Tedder, Marshal Zhukov, and General de Lattré de Tassigny for the Allies and by Keitel for the German forces. Huge crowds rejoiced in London, where King and Queen and the Princesses appeared on the balcony of Buckingham Palace several times, once with Mr. Churchill, and were enthusiastically cheered. Prime Minister spoke to great assembly in Whitehall, with his Cabinet standing by his side. Oslo liberated. Russians occupied Dresden. **9.** German garrison on Channel Islands surrendered to small force of British troops amid deep emotion of the people. Rejoicings continued on second VE Day. Last German warships, including cruisers *Prinz Eugen* and *Nürnberg,* surrendered to British Fleet at Copenhagen.

POTSDAM DECLARATION

The Potsdam Declaration or the 'Proclamation Defining Terms for Japanese Surrender' was a document issued on 26 July 1945 by President Truman, Prime Minister Winston Churchill and Chairman of the Nationalist Government of China, Chiang Kai-shek (the Soviet Union was not yet at war with Japan), which called for the surrender of the Empire of Japan and outlined the terms of any such surrender. The declaration was issued towards the end of the Potsdam Conference held in Potsdam, Berlin in occupied Germany from 17 July to 2 August 1945. The ultimatum stated that if Japan did not surrender, it would face "prompt and utter destruction", although it made no specific reference to the use of atomic weapons.

WARTIME CONFERENCES

The Potsdam Conference was the third of three wartime conferences among 'the Big Three' – Britain, United States and the Soviet Union, represented respectively by Winston Churchill (who was replaced mid-point by the newly elected British Prime Minister Clement Attlee), Harry Truman (who had replaced the late President Roosevelt) and Joseph Stalin. As well as outlining the terms of the Japanese surrender, the goals of the conference included the establishment of post-war order, the prosecution of Nazi war criminals and countering the effects of the war.

The other two major wartime conferences were the Yalta Conference, held in the Soviet Union 4–11 February 1945, for the purpose of deciding Europe's post-war reorganisation, and the Tehran Conference, held 28 November to 1 December 1943, in the Soviet Embassy in Tehran, Iran to decide upon a strategy for the war.

THE ATOMIC BOMB

July 26. [1945] In proclamation [*see* above] issued by President Truman, Mr. Churchill and General Chiang Kai-shek Japanese people were given choice of surrender or prompt and utter destruction. Another fire-bomb raid on cities on Japanese mainland. **28.** Japanese battleship beached and another damaged and explosion caused on aircraft carrier by raid by carrier-borne planes. By leaflets 11 Japanese cities were warned to avoid destruction. **29.** Tokyo area again raided by 1,000 aircraft and warships bombarded south coast of Honshu. **30.** Allied vessels entered Suruga Gulf in southern Honshu and bombarded Shimizu. **31.** Attack on Japanese mainland continued; in previous 21 days 1,023 surface ships and 1,257 aeroplanes destroyed or damaged. 12 more Japanese cities warned that they would be destroyed by fire-bombs.

Aug. 1. 800 Super-Fortresses dropped record load of 6,000 tons of bombs on 5 industrial towns. Wake Island shelled and bombed. **3.** All Japanese harbours mined by Allied aircraft and there was complete shipping blockade of the homeland. **4.** More Japanese cities warned of coming destruction. **5.** The first atomic bomb dropped by United States aircraft on Hiroshima, important Japanese base on Honshu. President Truman, from cruiser *Augusta* in Mid-Atlantic, announced that British and American scientists had "harnessed the basic power of the universe" and that the bomb had explosive power equal to 20,000 tons of T.N.T. and more than 2,000 times the blast power of largest bomb previously used. Impenetrable cloud of dust and smoke covered target area. **7.** Tokyo and Yokohama areas bombed, and 800 tons dropped on Toyokawa naval arsenal. **8.** Soviet Foreign Minister announced that the Allies had requested Russia to join in war against Japan and that Russia had agreed. Japanese Ambassador in Moscow was told Soviet Government considered this policy the only means of bringing peace nearer. Mr. Attlee welcomed "great decision." Official photographs of Hiroshima showed that 4 square miles of the city were completely destroyed by one atomic bomb. Ordinary bomb attacks on mainland continued. **9.** Russia at war with Japan, Soviet troops crossed Manchurian frontier at many points and several places captured. Second and more powerful atomic bomb dropped on Nagasaki with devastating results. **10.** Japanese Government made offer of unconditional surrender on declaration of Potsdam with the understanding that prerogatives of the Emperor were not prejudiced. The Four Allied Powers concerned consulted through regular diplomatic channels. Russians drove 100 miles into Manchuria. **11.** Allies told Japan that from the moment of surrender authority of Emperor and Japanese Government should be subject to Allied Supreme Commander, Emperor being required to ensure signature of surrender terms and to command all forces to cease active operations. Japanese Government must transport prisoners of war and civilian internees to places of safety. **12.** Japanese Cabinet considered Allied reply. Tokyo area bombed. Pacific Fleet warned to be vigilant. **13.** Operations continued with more raids on Tokyo area and farther advance by Russians into Manchuria.

JAPAN SURRENDER
Aug. 14. [1945] Broadcasting at midnight, Mr. Atlee announced that Japan had surrendered and that the Emperor had agreed to authorize and ensure signature of necessary terms for carrying out provisions of Potsdam declaration and to order cessation of active operations. President Truman made similar announcement and said General MacArthur had been appointed Supreme Allied Commander to receive the surrender. News came after yet further air attacks on many targets in Japan and Russian advance in Manchuria, but offensive action was then suspended. **15.** General MacArthur ordered Japanese to cease hostilities and to send to Manila a representative fully empowered by the Emperor to receive instructions. **16.** Emperor ordered all Japanese forces to cease fire. Suzuki Cabinet resigned and was

succeeded by one under Prince Higashi-Kuni, Emperor's cousin. Fighting continued in Manchuria; Russian Commander sent ultimatum to Japanese to surrender. **17.** On several sectors of the Manchurian front Japanese forces surrendered to Russians. **19.** Japanese envoys arrived at Manila and began conference with Allied High Command representatives to provide information asked for. **20.** Manila talks ended and Japanese envoys returned to Tokyo. Soviet troops occupied Harbin and Mukden. **23.** Stalin announced whole of Manchuria had been occupied, Japanese Army surrendering. **25.** Occupation of Japan postponed because of series of typhoons. **26.** Japanese envoys arrived at Rangoon and handed over detailed information to British Officers. **27.** First Allied troops landed by air at Japanese airfield near Tokyo. Advance flotilla of Allied Fleet moved into Tokyo Bay in readiness for occupation. Announced that Governors of Hong Kong, North Borneo and Straits Settlements had been released from Japanese camps in Manchuria. **28.** Occupation of Japan began, advance airborne force being landed. **29.** Main landings began in Japan, both by air and from sea, huge Allied fleet being massed in Tokyo Bay. **30.** Occupation forces spread out over Yokosuka, Yokohama and Tokyo plain. General MacArthur landed and set up his headquarters at Yokohama. Strong British naval force entered harbour of Hong Kong which was occupied and British administration set up.

Sept. 2. Japanese envoys signed instrument of unconditional surrender on board United States battleship *Missouri* in Tokyo Bay. General MacArthur and representatives of all the Allies added their signatures.

THE ROYAL FAMILY

THE DEATH OF QUEEN VICTORIA

As recorded in the 1902 edition
Remarkable Occurrences, 1900–1901

> Her Most Gracious Majesty ALEXANDRINA *VICTORIA*, Queen of the United
> Kingdom of Great Britain and Ireland, Defender of the Faith, Empress of India,
> in the 64th year of her Reign, aged 81 – January 22, at Osborne.

Jan. 18. [1901] Great public consternation at the news in the *Court Circular* that the Queen was not in her usual health, that she "was to abstain for the present from transacting business," and that her health demanded a certain degree of quiet and retirement. **19.** Universal sympathy was excited by the definitive announcement that the Queen was "suffering from great physical prostration accompanied by symptoms that cause anxiety." **20.** A bulletin was issued from Osborne at midnight stating that "The Queen's condition has late this evening become more serious, with increased weakness and diminished power of taking nourishment." – The German Emperor arrived in London, driving to Buckingham Palace, where he remained during the night. **21.** Owing to the serious nature of the last official statement from Osborne, the gravest apprehensions were aroused throughout the empire. The bulletins issued from time to time and posted at the Mansion House in London and at all the Town Halls in the Kingdom were anxiously read by sorrowful yet hoping crowds, the greatest love and veneration for the aged Sovereign being expressed by all classes of the community. – The German Emperor, accompanied by the Prince of Wales, the Duke and Duchess of York, and the Duke of Connaught, travelled from London to Osborne. – At **11.30 p.m.** a bulletin slightly more hopeful in tone was issued from Osborne House, though the advanced age of the illustrious sufferer precluded any genuine hope for her recovery. **22.** Bulletins were issued hourly during the day conveying the sorrowful news that the Queen was "slowly sinking," and in the evening the Lord Mayor received a telegram announcing the death at **6.30 p.m.** of the beloved monarch who had passed away "surrounded by her children and her grandchildren." **23.** Universal signs of mourning for the death of Queen Victoria were exhibited in every part of the British Empire, in America, and the whole world. – His Majesty the King arrived in London and drove to St. James's Palace, where, at a Privy Council attended by all the most important personages in the realm, he announced his intention to be known by the title "King Edward VIIth." His Majesty further expressed his determination to be guided in the execution of his kingly duties by the noble example of his illustrious mother. **24.** The King was proclaimed "our only lawful and rightful Liege Lord Edward the Seventh, by the grace of God, King of the United Kingdom, Great Britain and Ireland, Defender of the Faith, Emperor of India," with all traditional ceremony at St James's Palace, Temple Bar, and the Royal Exchange. **26.** The German Crown Prince arrived at

Osborne. – Memorial services for the late Queen were held in every place of worship throughout the British Empire. **30.** The King of Portugal, the King of Greece, the King of the Belgians, the Grand Duke of Baden, and the Duke of Sparta arrived in England in order to attend the funeral of Queen Victoria.

THE FUNERAL OF QUEEN VICTORIA

Feb. 1. [1901] The body of Queen Victoria was removed from Osborne House, carried by Highlanders and Bluejackets, to the Royal yacht *Alberta* and conveyed across the Solent, from east Cowes to Portsmouth Harbour, between an imposing line of British and foreign war vessels, each warship saluting as the *Alberta* slowly steamed along. Portsmouth was reached at **4.30 p.m.**, and the yacht was moored in the harbour during the night, guarded by the Fleet. **2.** At **8.30 a.m.** the remains of Queen Victoria were placed in a train for conveyance to London (Victoria Station), which was reached by **10.50.** Placed upon a gun-carriage adapted as a funeral car, the coffin was drawn by the eight cream-coloured horses which had been used in the Jubilee procession of 1897. The route taken by the funeral cortège on the journey from Victoria to Paddington was by way of Buckingham Palace Road, The Mall, St James's Street, Piccadilly, Hyde Park (from Apsley Gate to the Marble Arch), Edgware Road, and London Street. The streets, which were lined by troops, were filled by millions of the late Queen's subjects eager to pay their last tribute of respect to their beloved Sovereign. Behind the coffin, as chief mourners, were the King, the German Emperor, and the Duke of Connaught. These were closely followed by the Kings of Portugal and Greece, and by the King of the Belgians, the German Crown Prince, Prince Henry of Prussia, and some forty other royal personages. The procession included representatives from every European state, as well as an imposing array of soldiers, sailors and Colonial and Indian troops. Paddington was reached by **12.30,** and the Royal train conveying the coffin of the late Queen and the illustrious mourners reached Windsor at ten minutes after two. From Windsor Station a procession was formed to the Albert Memorial Chapel, where the Queen's body remained until **Feb. 4,** when it was transferred to the Mausoleum at Frogmore and laid by the side of the tomb of her husband.

THE DEATH OF KING GEORGE V AND
THE ACCESSION OF KING EDWARD VIII

As recorded in the 1937 edition
Events of the Year (1935–1936): The British Isles

Jan. 17. [1936] It was announced from Sandringham that King George was suffering from bronchial catarrh and that signs of cardiac weakness were regarded with some disquiet. Prince of Wales went by special train to Wolferton and motored to Sandringham. Oxygen apparatus was sent from London. **18.** Although the King had some hours of restful sleep, the cardiac weakness and embarrassment of the circulation increased and gave cause for anxiety. **19.** His Majesty, it was announced, maintained strength and passed a quiet day. Prince of Wales and Duke of York motored to London, and Duke of Kent and Archbishop of Canterbury went to Sandringham. Crowds gathered outside Buckingham Palace to read bulletins, and prayers were said in churches of all denominations throughout the Empire. **20.** In the country house that he loved so dearly, King George the Fifth, in his 71st year and 26th year of his reign, passed away peacefully at five minutes before midnight in presence of the Queen, Prince of Wales, Duke of York, Princess Royal and Duke and Duchess of Kent. Earlier in the day Prince of Wales had flown to Sandringham, and Privy Council was held to appoint Counsellors of State to act for the dying Sovereign, who, however, was too weak to sign the document. Nation was prepared by bulletin in late afternoon and at **9.25 p.m.** it was stated: "The King's life is moving peacefully towards its close," a sorrowing Empire heard the news on the wireless. The end was announced soon after midnight in the poignant words: "Death came peacefully to the King."

THE FUNERAL OF KING GEORGE V

Jan. 21. [1936] Coffin containing body of King George was borne on hand-bier to Sandringham Parish Church, followed on foot by Queen Mary, Princess Royal, Duke and Duchess of Kent and Lord Harewood. Tributes arrived from rulers and peoples of the world. **22.** Thousands of people filed past the coffin of King George guarded by four foresters. Queen Mary, Princess Royal and Duke of Kent visited the church, and later King Edward and Duke of Gloucester prayed beside coffin. **23.** King Edward and his three brothers walked behind body of their royal father as it was borne on gun-carriage from parish church to Sandringham station, Queen Mary, Princess Royal and her three daughters-in-law driving. At many points along train route people watched reverently. Dense crowds lined streets in London as their beloved Sovereign's body passed on gun-carriage, the coffin being draped with Royal Standard on which lay the Crown. Behind walked his four sons. The coffin was taken to Westminster Hall, where in presence of Queen Mary and all the Royal Family with Peers and M.P.'s a short impressive service was held. Both Houses adopted resolutions of condolence and loyalty. **24.** Vast pilgrimage of mourners began to file past King George's body, lying in State in Westminster Hall, guarded

2

┌─ TAKE UP PELMANISM ─┐
For Successful Living

PELMANISM is beneficial in all the affairs of life. That is its outstanding recommendation to those who wish to make the best of themselves in their occupations, in their social and cultural relations and in their recreations.

Every line written in the Pelman Course is directly applicable to some aspect of human life and conduct. The intention of every word in the Course is to make clear to men and women the means by which they can develop their powers to the fullest extent so that they can live more happily, and be more successful—so that, on the one hand, they will make and use occasions for profit and advantage and, on the other hand, be at ease in any company. Both conditions are necessary to complete self-respect and a full life.

Personal and Individual

Pelmanists are not left to make the applications themselves. An experienced and sympathetic instructional staff shows them, in exact detail, how to apply the principles of Pelmanism to their own circumstances and aspirations. Thus every Pelman Course is an individual Course.

Half an hour a day of spare time for a few weeks is enough. Everything is simply set out and described and no drudgery is entailed. The books are printed in a handy "pocket size," so that you can study them in odd moments during the day. Even the busiest man or woman can spare a few minutes daily for Pelmanism, especially when minutes so spent bring in such rich rewards.

What Pelmanism Does

Pelmanism enables you to overcome defects and failings. Amongst those most often met with are the following :

Inertia	Pessimism
Timidity	Forgetfulness
Indecision	Indefiniteness
Depression	Procrastination
Weakness of Will	Mind-Wandering

But Pelmanism does more than eliminate failings. It awakens dormant faculties. It develops powers you never thought you possessed. It strengthens mental attributes which are valuable in every career and every aspect of living. It develops :—

—Optimism	—Initiative
—Judgment	—Reliability
—Self-Control	—Will-Power
—Concentration	—Resourcefulness
—Self-Confidence	—Presence of Mind

Reduced fees for serving and ex-Service members of Her Majesty's Forces.
(Apply for Services Enrolment Form.)

Pelmanism is a true philosophy of living for ordinary sensible people who wish to make the best of themselves at all times and under all circumstances. The Pelman Institute has won and held its unique position through all wars and worries, trials and tribulations, during the last half-century.

The general effect of the training is to induce an attitude of mind and a personal efficiency favourable to the happy management of life.

Send for the Free Book

The Pelman Course is simple and interesting and takes up very little time ; you can enrol on the most convenient terms. The Course is fully described in *The Science of Success*, which will be sent you, gratis and post free, on application to :—

PELMAN INSTITUTE
200 Norfolk Mansions
Wigmore Street, London, W.1
Established over 50 years   Callers welcomed

PELMAN (OVERSEAS) INSTITUTES : DELHI, 10 *Alipore Road. MELBOURNE,* 396 *Flinders Lane. DURBAN, Natal Bank Chambers (P.O. Box* 1489*). PARIS,* 176 *Boulevard Haussmann. AMSTERDAM, Prinsengracht* 1021.

150

PEARS' SOAP,

AS RECOMMENDED BY

PROF.ᴿ **ERASMUS WILSON,**

I have found matchless for the Hands and Complexion.

Adelina Patti.

"CLEANLINESS IS NEXT TO GODLINESS."
Specially drawn for Messrs. A. & F. PEARS
By H. STACY MARKS, R.A.

continuously by Life Guards, Gentlemen-at-Arms and Yeomen of the Guard. **27.** Nearly a million people had paid homage to a noble Sovereign by the time the doors of Westminster Hall had to be closed. Queen Mary and most members of Royal Family and foreign mourners passed through the hall on last evening, and at midnight King Edward, Duke of York, Duke of Gloucester and Duke of Kent, in full uniform, kept vigil beside body of their father, standing motionless with the other guardians for over quarter of an hour, while public continued to file past the catafalque. **28.** Multitudes of sorrowing people, in London and at Windsor, paid final tribute to King George as his body was taken from Westminster Hall to its last resting-place in St. George's Chapel, Windsor. Whole route to Paddington was thronged with silent crowds as the funeral procession moved slowly along. The gun-carriage bearing the coffin, draped in the Royal Standard, was drawn by sailors, and behind walked King Edward and his three brothers. Then followed Kings of Norway, Denmark and Rumania, the French President, King of the Belgians, King of Bulgaria and representatives of every country in the world. Queen Mary, accompanied by Queen of Norway, Princess Royal and Duchess of York, were in a glass coach. The Services were represented by many detachments. At Windsor, scene in the chapel was beautiful and impressive. As coffin sank into vault, King Edward cast handful of earth upon it, and then, with his mother, returned to London. Two minutes' silence was observed throughout the Empire during the service. **29.** Great crowds inspected thousands of wreaths covering lawns outside St. George's Chapel.

KING EDWARD VIII STARTS HIS REIGN

Jan. 20. [1936] The first public message of King Edward VIII was telegram to Lord Mayor of London announcing death of his father. **21.** King Edward flew from Sandringham to London, and held Privy Council at St. James's Palace and signed Proclamation of Accession. Privy Councillors took the oath to the new monarch, who made a declaration referring to the irreparable loss suffered by the British Commonwealth of Nations by the death of King George. "I am determined to follow in my father's footsteps", said King Edward, "and to work as he did throughout his life for the happiness and welfare of all classes of my subjects." He sent messages to the three Services expressing thanks for their devoted services to his father. Court ordered to wear mourning for nine months, changing to half mourning on July 21, and to go out of mourning on Oct. 21. **22.** King Edward the Eighth was proclaimed King in London and many provincial cities amid loyal demonstrations. Mr. Baldwin was received by the King. **27.** King Edward entertained at dinner at Buckingham Palace Kings of Norway, Denmark, the Belgians, Rumania and Bulgaria, and French President. **29.** Queen Mary sent message to the Empire expressing gratitude for sympathy with which she had been surrounded, and commending to the people "my dear son." **30.** King Edward assumed rank of Admiral of the Fleet, Field-Marshal and Marshal of the Royal Air Force.

Feb. 4. King received deputation of Party leaders, who brought address of loyalty from Houses of Lords and Commons. **18.** King decorated officers and men who took part in King George's funeral ceremony.

March 1. King Edward from Broadcasting House addressed the Empire, speaking of his father's constant devotion to duty and concern for welfare of his subjects, and sending his greetings and assurance that his constant effort would be to continue to promote the well-being of his fellow-men.

April 2. King received loyal addresses from various public bodies and promised to remember his motto as Prince of Wales, "I serve."

THE ABDICATION OF KING EDWARD VIII

As recorded in the 1938 edition
Events of the Year (1936–1937): The British Isles

Nov. 3. [1936] King Edward motored from Buckingham Palace to Westminster to open the new Session, and in presence of his three brothers in House of Lords made declaration of his Protestant faith and read Royal Speech. **11.** King Edward laid wreath at foot of the Cenotaph and led the Great Silence which was observed throughout the Empire. Duke of York and Duke of Kent were present, and Queen Mary, Duchess of York and Duchess of Gloucester witnessed the tribute from a window. In evening the King attended the ex-Servicemen's Festival of Remembrance at Albert Hall, and, in pouring rain, planted wooden cross in the Field of Remembrance outside Westminster Abbey. **12.** King Edward spent a day with Home Fleet off Portland, and attended lower deck concert on aircraft carrier *Courageous.* **13.** He went aboard new minelayer submarine *Narwhal* and other vessels, and returned to Fort Belvedere. **14.** Queen Mary visited new People's Palace and other places in East London. **18.** King Edward toured the Rhondda Valley and discussed with the unemployed their problems.

Dec. 1. Duchess of York received Freedom of Edinburgh. **2.** King Edward went to Fort Belvedere. **3.** The nation was informed of the grave constitutional crisis. The King saw the Duke of York, Queen Mary and Mr. Baldwin, who conferred with Dominion representatives. **4.** Mrs. Ernest Simpson left England for France. **7.** Duke of York visited his brother. In a statement read by Lord Brownlow at Cannes, Mrs. Simpson declared she had invariably wished to avoid any action which would hurt or damage the King or the Throne, and expressed her willingness to withdraw from a situation rendered both unhappy and untenable. **King Edward's Decision. 10.** In a House crowded to its utmost capacity, Mr Baldwin announced that King Edward VIII had decided to abdicate, and that he would be succeeded by the Duke of York as King George VI. Amid tense silence the Speaker read a message from the King renouncing the throne and referring to "my final and irrevocable decision." **11.** King Edward ceased to be King; and King George VI began his reign. "Prince Edward," as he was announced, broadcast to whole world a message declaring his allegiance to the new sovereign. After dining at Windsor with the Royal Family, he motored to Portsmouth and boarded destroyer *Fury,* which left for France. Queen Mary issued message to the people expressing gratitude for sympathy shown to her and commending the new King and his Consort. **12.** Prince Edward, created Duke of Windsor, landed at Boulogne and boarded Vienna express. **13.** On arrival at Vienna, he drove to the Schloss Enzesfeld, home of Baron Eugene de Rothschild.

THE ACCESSION OF KING GEORGE VI

As recorded in the 1938 edition
Events of the Year (1936–1937): The British Isles

Dec. 11. [1936] On the Abdication Bill receiving the Royal Assent, Duke of York ascended the throne as George VI. He attended family farewell dinner party to his brother at Royal Lodge, Windsor, and returned to London, as did Queen Mary, Princess Royal, Duke of Gloucester, Duke of Kent, Princess Alice and Earl of Athlone. **12.** King George held his Accession Council and made his declaration of adherence to the strict principles of constitutional government. He announced conferment of Dukedom of Windsor on the former King. Announced that Queen Elizabeth was suffering from mild attack of influenza. Both Houses of Parliament met, and Peers and M.P.'s were sworn in. King sent messages to the three Services. **14.** On the King's birthday, he conferred the Garter on the Queen. Family luncheon party held at his Piccadilly home. In message to Parliament King George said he was resolved to do his duty, and he would endeavour to promote the happiness of the people. Both Houses agreed to present an Address of Loyalty. **15.** Lord Wigram appointed Permanent Lord-in-Waiting. King received address from Commons, and in his reply spoke of his loss in his brother's decision.

THE DEATH OF KING GEORGE VI AND THE ACCESSION OF QUEEN ELIZABETH II

As recorded in the 1953 edition
Home Affairs: The Royal House

SUDDEN DEATH OF THE KING

Feb. 6. [1952] The world was shocked to learn that King George VI, who had retired to rest in his usual health, passed peacefully away in his sleep at Sandringham. It was afterwards learned that cause of death was coronary thrombosis. The Queen and Princess Margaret were at Sandringham, and sad news was broken to the new Queen by Duke of Edinburgh in Kenya. Accession Council signed proclamation of Queen Elizabeth II. Messages of condolence were received from every part of the Commonwealth and in almost every country in the world warm tributes were paid. **7.** Queen Elizabeth the Queen Mother and Princess Margaret attended private service at Sandringham village church. In Broadcast to the nation, Prime Minister said that during his last months the King walked with death as if death were an acquaintance whom he did not fear. In the end death came as a friend. **8.** Coffin containing the King's body was taken from Sandringham House to Church of St. Mary Magdalene on the estate and placed before altar, estate workers keeping watch throughout the night. **10.** Services were held in churches all over the country in memory of King George. **11.** After short service the coffin was carried by Grenadier Guards to gun carriage on which it was conveyed to Wolferton, followed by Queen Elizabeth, the Queen Mother and members of Royal Family, and from there taken to London by train. At King's Cross the coffin, now surmounted by the Imperial State Crown was reverently placed by guardsmen upon gun-carriage, which was drawn by the King's Troop, Royal Horse Artillery, through streets packed with mourners, to Westminster Hall, the Duke of Edinburgh and the Duke of Gloucester walking behind. The Queen, the Queen Mother and Princess Margaret drove by different route and with Queen Mary and other members of Royal Family awaited arrival of the cortège at Westminster Hall, where Peers and M.P.'s had assembled. Royal mourners followed coffin to catafalque in centre of hall, and after Archbishop of York had conducted service, members of two Houses of Parliament filed past the coffin on which a day and night vigil was kept. Tributes to King George were paid in Lords and Commons and both Houses agreed to send loyal motions and condolences to the three Queens. **12.** Lying-in-state began and all day people filed past the catafalque. **13.** Duke of Windsor arrived in London and with Queen Mary attended the lying-in-state. **14.** The Queen and Duke of Edinburgh with Princess Margaret and later the Queen Mother visited Westminster Hall. Lying-in-state was continued all night and it was estimated that over 300,000 people had filed past catafalque. **15.** With impressive yet simple pageantry, remains of King George were taken from his capital, through streets lined with great crowds paying a final homage, and laid to rest in St. George's Chapel, Windsor. The mile-long cortège included representatives of all the Services. The gun-carriage bearing the coffin covered with the Royal Standard, on which were placed the Crown, the Orb and the Sceptre, and drawn reverently at a slow march by naval ratings, was followed by a coach in which were the Queen, the Queen Mother, Princess Margaret and Princess Royal. Behind, walking, were the Duke of Edinburgh, the Duke of Gloucester, the Duke of Windsor and the Duke of Kent, followed by the Heads of State, among them the Kings of Denmark, Sweden, the Hellenes and Iraq and the Presidents of France, Turkey and Yugoslavia. In the carriage were the King of Norway and the Queen of the Netherlands. At Paddington the coffin and the mourners entered royal trains and proceeded to Windsor, where shorter procession was formed, gun-carriage being again drawn by bluejackets. When the cortège reached St. George's Chapel, a two-minutes silence was observed throughout the country. During service the Queen laid upon the coffin the King's Colour of the King's Company, Grenadier Guards, and sprinkled on it earth from a gilded bowl as it sank slowly into the vault, both Her Majesty and the Queen Mother bowing their last farewell. Commemoration services were held in many cities throughout the world. **16.** Queen Elizabeth the Queen Mother expressed her gratitude to all who had sent flowers in memory of King George. In ten days 200,000 people visited Windsor to see floral tributes on lawns surrounding the chapel. **17.** The Queen Mother issued message of thanks to all who had given her sympathy and commending to the people "our dear daughter," who would need protection and love "in the great and lonely station to which she has been called." Memorial services were held in many parts of the Commonwealth.

QUEEN ELIZABETH II FLIES HOME

Feb. 6. [1952] The new sovereign, Queen Elizabeth II, was resting in her hunting lodge in Kenya when the Duke of Edinburgh broke to her the news of the death of King George. Her Majesty and the Duke drove to airfield at Nanyuki from where they flew to Entebbe, Uganda. There they took off for El Adem, Libya, after being delayed by sudden electrical storm. **7.** Queen Elizabeth and her husband arrived at London Airport after flying from El Adem. Duke of Gloucester welcomed Her Majesty, and when she alighted she was greeted by Mr. Churchill, Mr. Attlee, and leading Privy Councillors. The Queen drove to Clarence House where Queen Mary awaited her. **8.** At her first Privy Council Her Majesty made her Accession Declaration, in which she expressed her resolve to follow her father's shining example of service and devotion. The accession was proclaimed with picturesque ceremonial throughout Britain and the Commonwealth. The Queen accompanied by Duke of Edinburgh went to Sandringham. **9.** Court mourning for the King ordered for 10 weeks, until May 31. **10.** The Queen, the Queen Mother and other members of Royal family attended brief service in estate church of St. Mary Magdalene. **11.** They accompanied coffin of the King to London and at Westminster Hall followed it as it was placed on catafalque for lying-in-state. **12.** The Queen received Mr. Churchill at Clarence House, her first audience as Queen. **13.** Mr.

Churchill, heading deputation of all parties in House of Commons, presented address to Her Majesty at Buckingham Palace. Duke of Windsor saw the Queen and Queen Mother. **14.** The Queen received in audience High Commissioners and other representatives of the Commonwealth and was visited by many of the foreign Royalties in London for the funeral, including Kings of Sweden, Denmark and the Hellenes and Queen of the Netherlands, as well as the French, Turkish and Yugoslav Presidents. French President also visited Queen Elizabeth the Queen Mother (her new style) and Queen Mary. **16.** The Queen and Duke of Edinburgh joined the Queen Mother and Princess Margaret at Royal Lodge, Windsor. **17.** They attended memorial service in the private chapel there. **19.** Deputations from both Houses of Parliament were received by the Queen Mother and Queen Mary to whom they handed messages of condolence on death of the King. The Queen received Dr. Adenauer, German Chancellor, and British, United States and French Foreign Ministers. **22.** The Queen held Council at which Duke of Edinburgh was present. **27.** Her Majesty held first investiture of her reign at Buckingham Palace, first to be decorated being Private William Speakman, awarded V.C. for gallantry in Korea. **28.** Duke of Windsor left England for New York. **29.** The Queen approved Orders in Council providing for wording of prayers for the Royal Family.

THE QUEEN'S CORONATION

As recorded in the 1954 edition.
Home Affairs: The Royal House

QUEEN ELIZABETH IS CROWNED

June 2. [1953] With traditional ceremony and a religious symbolism that stirred millions of people throughout the world, Queen Elizabeth II was crowned in Westminster Abbey, receiving the acclaim of hundreds of thousands of her subjects as, with the Duke of Edinburgh, she made her royal progress through the capital before and after the impressive service. Great throngs lined the decorated streets but even larger multitudes, in their homes and in places of assembly, saw by means of television or heard by wireless, all but the most sacred and personal portions of the ceremony. In the Abbey the Queen, with superb grace and dignity, made the ancient promises to govern well, and confirmed those promises with solemn oath, and after the anointing beneath canopy of cloth of gold and the presentation of the regalia the Archbishop of Canterbury placed the Crown upon her head to the cry from all over the Abbey of "God Save the Queen" and the sound of fanfares. Her Majesty then ascended the throne and the peers, led by Her Majesty's own consort, swore the oath of homage, after which the whole congregation acclaimed their sovereign. The Coronation was completed and shortly afterwards the Queen, the central figure of a colourful procession, left the Abbey to meet again her people, waiting patiently in showers of rain, to show their affection. All the members of the Royal Family were present, including for a time, which covered the actual crowning, the young Duke of Cornwall, in the care of the Queen Mother and Princess Margaret. The Prime Ministers of the Commonwealth, with Sir Winston Churchill at their head, were also there, as were representatives of all the nations. A great cheering met the Queen when, with her husband and wearing her crown, she set out in the golden coach on the longer return journey to the Palace, and the enthusiasm continued throughout the slow progress home. Afterwards the vast concourse near the Mall flocked to the front of the forecourt and presently Her Majesty, her husband and children and all the members of the Royal Family came to the balcony to watch the brilliantly executed fly-past of the Royal Air Force in honour of their sovereign. Other balcony appearances followed and in the evening Her Majesty broadcast to the Commonwealth and Europe and declared that her abiding memory of the day would be not only the solemnity and beauty of the ceremony but the inspiration of the loyalty and affection of her people. At dusk she pressed switch which turned on illuminations and searchlights and was signal for lighting of bonfires and celebrations all over the United Kingdom.

NOTABLE ROYAL BIRTHS

The following is a record of the births of all future monarchs or heirs to the throne, from the first edition of *Whitaker's Almanack* published in 1868, to the Duke of Cambridge's birth in 1982. The births are written exactly as they were recorded at the time; some are just brief mentions, especially in cases when the future monarch was not necessarily directly in line to the throne at the time of birth, although, in the case of Queen Elizabeth II, parallels were drawn between her situation at birth and that of Queen Victoria.

BIRTH OF KING EDWARD VIII
As recorded in the 1895 edition: Remarkable Occurrences 1894

June 23. [1894] Birth of a son (Prince Edward) to the Duke and Duchess of York [later King George V and Queen Mary], at White Lodge, Richmond. **26.** The Queen [Queen Victoria] visited White Lodge, Richmond, to see her great-grandson in the direct line.

BIRTH OF KING GEORGE VI
As recorded in the 1897 edition: Remarkable Occurrences 1895

December 14. [1895] Birth of a second son to the Duke and Duchess of York.

BIRTH OF QUEEN ELIZABETH II
As recorded in the 1927 edition: Questions of the Day – Succession to the Throne

The birth in April [**April 21. 1926**] of Princess Elizabeth Alexandra Mary, the daughter of the Duke and Duchess of York [later King George VI and Queen Elizabeth], had an interesting bearing upon the succession to the throne. As the daughter of the King's second son, the Princess is in the direct line, and, ranking after the Prince of Wales and her own father, is third in succession. She takes precedence over the King's two younger sons, Prince Henry and Prince George, and over Princess Mary and her two sons, who fill the next three places in the order of succession. According to the Act of Settlement, an elder brother's daughter is preferred in the succession to a younger brother, and it was owing to this provision that Queen Victoria ascended the throne ninety years ago instead of the Duke of Cambridge, who was next surviving brother to King William IV, but was junior to the young Queen's father, the Duke of Kent. In the event of the Prince of Wales marrying and having children, Princess Elizabeth of York would go out of the line of succession, and the birth of a brother would place her one position lower. At the moment the little Princess is the fourth lady in the realm in the order of precedence, being preceded only by the Queen, Princess Mary, and her mother, the Duchess of York.

BIRTH OF THE PRINCE OF WALES

As recorded in the 1950 edition: Events of the Year 1948–1949, Home Affairs

Nov. 14. [1948] *Birth of Prince Charles:* Princess Elizabeth safely delivered of a Prince at Buckingham Palace. Official announcement added that Her Royal Highness and her son were both doing well. Crowd waiting outside Palace received news with enthusiasm. **15.** Cabinet and City of London sent congratulations on birth of the Prince. Royal Salute of 41 guns was fired in Hyde Park, salutes were fired at Edinburgh and other places, and peals of bells were rung. President Truman sent cable of congratulations, and throughout the British Commonwealth and Empire news was received with jubilation. **16.** Bulletin stated that the Princess was making satisfactory progress and that infant Prince continued to do well. Both Houses of Parliament carried loyal address of congratulation to King and Queen, Princess Elizabeth and Duke of Edinburgh unanimously. **18.** Palace bulletin announced that the infant Prince was a healthy baby. **19.** Final bulletin said Princess and her son were maintaining steady and satisfactory progress.

BIRTH OF THE DUKE OF CAMBRIDGE

As recorded in the 1983 edition: Events of the Year 1981–1982, Royal House

June 21. [1982] The Princess of Wales gave birth to a 7 lb 1½ oz. boy, who became second in line to the throne, in St Mary's Hospital, Paddington at **9.03 p.m. 28.** Buckingham Palace announced that the baby son of the Prince and Princess of Wales was to be named William Arthur Philip Louis and would be known as Prince William of Wales.

THE KING AND COURT

The extract below is from the 'Events of the Year' or 'Annual Summaries' section of the 1927 edition.

The period covered is from 1 November 1925 to 31 October 1926 and includes the announcement of the Queen's birth and the death of Queen Alexandra among other day-to-day events of the Royal House.

(1925) Nov. 3. Prince of Wales had fall while hunting with the Whaddon Chase, but was not hurt. **11.** The King, Prince of Wales, Duke of York, the Cabinet and four ex-Premiers headed crowd at the Centotaph on Armistice Day during the Silence. **19.** Queen Alexandra taken suddenly ill with severe heart attack at Sandringham. **20.** Her Majesty passed away peacefully at 5.25 p.m. in presence of King and Queen and members of Royal Family. World-wide tributes paid to the Queen Mother. Three months' Court mourning ordered. **22.** Impressive memorial service for Royal Family held at Sandringham Church. **25.** Body lay in state in Sandringham Church. **26.** Coffin removed to Chapel Royal, followed by King and Royal Family. **27.** First part of funeral service read in Westminster Abbey, following which thousands filed past Queen Mother's coffin. **28.** Final part of funeral ceremonies took place in private in Albert Memorial Chapel, Windsor. In message to his people the King expressed his gratitude for flood of sympathy shown all over the world.

Dec. 1. To mark his work at Locarno, King conferred the Garter upon Mr. Austen Chamberlain, Mrs. Chamberlain being made a D.B.E.

> Sir Austen Chamberlain, half-brother of Neville Chamberlain, was a politician and Secretary of State for Foreign Affairs (1924–29), who won the Nobel Peace Prize in 1926 for his part in negotiating what is now known as the Locarno Pact of 1925. Following the First World War, Sir Austen, together with French foreign minister and co-laureate, Aristide Briand, German foreign minister, Gustav Stresemann, and representatives from Belgium and Italy, signed an agreement to settle all future differences between the nations by arbitration and never resort to war.

15. King and Queen approved suggestion that memorial to Queen Alexandra should take form of fund for extending the work of Queen Victoria Jubilee Institute for Nurses. **17.** Princess Mary launched HMS *Rodney* at Birkenhead. **19.** Prince of Wales attended birthday celebrations of Toc H and lit lamps of maintenance of 32 new branches. **25.** Royal Family spent Christmas at York Cottage, Sandringham.

(1926) Jan. 1. New Year Honours included barony for the Master of the Rolls [Sir Ernest Pollock/Baron Hanworth, Master of the Rolls 1926–35] and Companionship of Honour for Prebendary Carlile [founder of the Church Army]. **27.** While Prince of Wales was hunting with Belvoir Hounds his horse fell dead under him; he was thrown but only bruised. **28.** Prince fractured his collar bone while out with the Fernie Hounds, being thrown at high rail.

Feb. 15. Prince of Wales attended British Industries Fair banquet at Mansion House and appealed to manufacturers to keep on the alert for trade opportunities overseas. **18.** King and Queen visited British Industries Fair at the White City.

Mar. 1. Prince of Wales inspected Welsh Guards. **11.** King visited Chatham, inspected Royal Engineers and examined their war memorial. **15.** Owing to mild attack of influenza Duke of York cancelled several engagements. **16.** King inspected Brigade of Guards at Caterham. **28.** Prince of Wales underwent slight operation on the ear. **29.** Princess Victoria suffering from influenzal pneumonia and her condition caused some anxiety for a time.

Apr. 1. Queen of Norway arrived in England. **16.** Prince of Wales arrived at Biarritz for short rest. **20.** Marquessate conferred upon Lord Reading. **21.** Duchess of York gave birth to a daughter. **28.** Queen visited Guildford and presented colours to the 5th Queen's Royal Regiment.

May 3. King held Privy Council connected with strike [The 1926 general strike lasted nine days, from 4 May 1926 to 13 May 1926; the strike was called by the general council of the Trades Union Congress in defence of miners' wages and hours]. **22.** Duke of York admitted to freedom of Fishmongers' Company. **23.** Prince of Wales and Earl Haig attended British Legion ceremony at the Cenotaph and led march past King and Queen. **27.** Their Majesties attended performance at the Alhambria in aid of Variety Artistes' Benevolent Fund. King received delegates of 40 Parliaments attending International Parliamentary Commercial Conference in London. **29.** Princess Elizabeth, daughter of Duke and Duchess of York, christened in Buckingham Palace Chapel. **31.** Queen opened new College for Nurses in London.

June 2. King and Queen saw the Derby and His Majesty gave customary dinner at the Palace. **9.** Prince of Wales unveiled Kitchener memorial on Horse Guards' Parade. Their Majesties held first Court of the season. **21.** King, who was accompanied by the Queen, commemorated jubilee of Wimbledon Lawn Tennis meeting by presenting medals to ex-champions. **25.** Prince of Wales visited number of institutions at Reading. **26.** King opened extension of Tate Gallery.

July 3. King's birthday honours deferred owing to the strike [*see* May 3], included one new peer, three Privy Councillors and six baronets. **6.** Their Majesties were present at Royal Show at Reading. **9.** Prince of Wales presided at demonstration to mark tenth anniversary of National Savings Movement. **22.** Prince of Wales visited Isle of Wight. 15,000 guests attended Royal garden party at Buckingham Palace.

23. Prince of Wales became first freeman of City of Portsmouth. **30.** King and Queen arrived at Cowes on Royal yacht.

Aug. 3. Duke and Duchess of York admitted to the Order of Bards at Eisteddfod at Swansea. **4.** As President of British Association, Prince of Wales opened its meeting at Oxford with address eulogising science. **6.** Prince attended camp of Welsh scouts at Llandrindod Wells. **11.** King arrived at Bolton Abbey for grouse shooting. **24.** His Majesty arrived at Balmoral. **29.** Queen paid visit to Princess Mary at Goldsborough Hall. **31.** Prince of Wales left London for holiday in Biarritz.

Sept. 1. Queen arrived at Balmoral. **9.** Their Majesties were present at the Braemar Highland Gathering. **15.** Prince of Wales returned to England.

Oct. 8. On arriving back in London from Scotland, King and Queen were greeted at Euston by nine veteran drivers who had driven Royal trains 18,000 miles. **9.** Duke of York admitted as honorary freeman of Edinburgh. **12.** Prince of Wales unveiled memorial tablet in Westminster Abbey to British Empire's million dead who fell in Great War. **20.** As Earl of Chester, Prince opened new school of agriculture at Chester.

REMARKABLE
OCCURRENCES

REMARKABLE OCCURRENCES

A selection of 'Remarkable Occurrences', later re-named 'Events of the Year', as recorded in editions of *Whitaker's Almanack* dating from the first edition in 1869.

The first section 'A Year through the Ages' is a calendar year of events, but with each month's events taken from a different decade, starting with the first edition in 1869.

The second part consists of themed selections on accidents and disasters, aviation, crime, exploration and shipping; all topics which have had their own sections within the Remarkable Occurrences chapter of *Whitaker's Almanack*.

A Year through the Ages

Each month below details 'occurrences' or 'events' one decade on from the previous month.

JANUARY (1868)
From the 1869 edition

4. Slight shock of, earthquake felt in the Vale of Parret, and other parts of Somerset. **4–11.** General swearing-in of special constables throughout England, in consequence of the Fenian outrage at Clerkenwell. – Great eruption of Mount Vesuvius, with earthquakes, descent of lava, etc. **6.** Arrival of the Duke of Edinburgh at Hobart Town. **7.** Visit of the Prince of Wales to the patients (at St. Bartholomew's hospital) who were injured by the explosion (caused by Fenians) at Clerkenwell prison in December. **8.** Sudden and mysterious disappearance of the Rev. B. Speke, causing great sensation throughout the country. He was discovered alive and well in Cornwall shortly afterwards. **9.** Committal of Burke, Casey, and Shaw, to Warwick gaol for Fenianism, from the Bow Street police-office, London. **11.** Wreck of the screw steamer, "Chicago," on a reef of rocks near Cork harbour; all lives saved. **16.** Landing of the remains of the Emperor Maximilian of Mexico, at Trieste. **17,18.** Severe gales on all coasts of the United Kingdom, with many wrecks and great loss of life. **18.** Explosion of gunpowder at Newcastle-on-Tyne, with death of two men and injury to others – Attempted murder by Clancy, a Fenian, of two policemen, in Bedford Square. **18–25.** Heavy gales throughout the Kingdom, with much loss of life and property at sea and on land. Loss of nineteen fishing vessels, and fifty-two lives near the Burry river on the Welsh coast.

FEBRUARY (1878)
From the 1879 edition

5. Midhat Pacha [political reformist and leader of the Ottoman constitutional movement of 1876] is expelled from Turkey. – Railway riots in Quebec before the Parliament House by about 6,000 persons. **7.** Death of Pope Pius IX, at Rome. – A rumour of the entry of the Russians into Constantinople caused great excitement, and a special Cabinet Meeting was held in London. **8.** Opening of the Canadian Parliament by Lord Dufferin. **9.** Funeral of the celebrated caricaturist, George Cruikshank, at Kensal Green Cemetery. – Banquet given by the Royal Geographical Society to Mr. H.M. Stanley, the African explorer. – The terms of the Military Armistice between Russia and Turkey were made known. **13.** Russians take possession of Erzeroum. – The British Fleet anchored near to the Prince's Islands, in the Sea of Marmora. **14.** Entombment of Pope Pius IX took place at Rome in the Basilica. – The notorious Madame Rachel charged with fresh frauds in "beautifying" ladies. **15.** Opening of the Spanish Cortes by the King, with the Queen and his sisters. **16.** Announcement was made that negotiations had been completed between all the Powers for a Congress on the Eastern Question [the diplomatic and political issues relating to the dissolution of the Ottoman Empire]. The British Fleet withdrew to a position about 40 miles south of Constantinople. Part of the Channel Squadron sailed from Vigo for Gibraltar. – Mr. Blands's Silver Bill passed by the United States Senate. **20.** Election of the new Pope, Cardinal Pecci, as Leo XIII, by the Cardinals at the Vatican. **21.** The terms of the Treaty of Peace (San Stefano) between Russia and Turkey, in part published. The Russians threatened an ultimatum if the signatures were delayed by Turkey. **22.** Master of the Rolls shot at by a clergyman named Dodwell. **24.** Tumultuous meeting in Hyde Park on the Eastern Question. Mr. Gladstones' house in Harley Street was assailed. – Failure of Messrs. Willis, Percival & Co., London Bankers, for about £700,000.

MARCH (1888)
From the 1889 edition

1. M. Wilson, son-in-law of ex-President Grévy, sentenced to two years' imprisonment and other penalties for trafficking in decorations. – The Panama Canal shareholders resolved to issue bonds for 340,000,000 francs to complete the canal. **2.** The Upper House of Convocation discuss a memorial on "the desecration of the Sabbath by the upper classes". **3.** Dinner to the Marquis of Ripon and Mr. John Morley by the Oxford University Home Rule League. **5.** Four brothers drowned by the breaking of ice at Ledsham, near Chester. – The Porte telegraphed to Prince Ferdinand that his presence in Bulgaria is illegal. **6.** Waterloo Cup won by Burnaby; Purse by Miss Glendyne; Plate by Winfarthing. **7.** The Prince of Wales held a levée on behalf of the Queen. **9.** Collision between the *City of Corinth* and the *Tasmania* off Dungeness, and wreck of the *Lanoma* in Portland Bay, with loss of 25 hands. – Prize fight, £100 a side near Amiens, between John L. Sullivan, American, and Charles Mitchell, English: after 39 rounds, a draw was agreed upon. **10.** The Prince and Princess of Wales celebrated their silver wedding. **12.** Lying-in-state of the German Emperor. – Fearful snowstorm in America, putting a stop to all business and traffic in New York. **15.** General Boulander's dismissal from the French army announced. – Bank rate reduced from 2½ to 2 per cent. – Marriage of Prince Oscar of Sweden to Miss Ebba Munck at Bournemouth. **16.** Funeral of William I of

Germany. – Heavy snowstorms in Scotland and the north of England. **17.** Annual football match between England and Scotland won by England. **20.** The Baguet Theatre, Oporto, destroyed by fire, and about 100 lives lost. **21.** The Queen left Windsor for Italy. – The Prince of Wales held a levée on behalf of the Queen. **22.** A British expeditionary force captured the Thibetan post of Lingtn. **23.** The Grand National won by Playfair. **24.** The Queen arrived at Florence. – University boat-race won by Cambridge. – The Princess of Wales held a Drawing Room on behalf of the Queen. **27.** The *Nile,* the heaviest armoured ship yet built, launched at Pembroke Dockyard. **30.** Resignation of the ministry of M. Tirard, after an adverse vote in the French Chamber: succeeded by M. Floquet. – The Emperor Frederick and the Empress enthusiastically received in Berlin.

APRIL (1898)
From the 1899 edition

1. Special performance at the Royal Theatre in Madrid to raise a fund for increasing the Navy. **2.** The judgment in the Zola trial quashed on appeal. **4.** Great industrial disturbance caused by stoppage in the South Wales coal mines; nearly 100,000 men thrown out of work. **5.** The government of Natal offered the British naval authorities 12,000 tons of steam coal per annum at Durban. – Mr. Balfour stated in the House of Commons the Great Britain had obtained from China a lease of Wei-Hai-Wei, in order to restore the balance of power which had been disturbed by Russia's acquisition of Port Arthur. **8.** The Sirdar with his Anglo-Egyptian force, attacked the Khalifa's Emir Mahmoud, who was encamped on the banks of the Atbara River, within a zareeba, and utterly defeated the opposing forces, capturing their leader. **13.** The British South Africa Company issued a report on the progress and prospects of Rhodesia as evidenced by the experience of the past two years. **16.** The United States Senate continued a debate upon the report of their Foreign Relations Committee, and decided to reorganise the independence of the Republic of Cuba. **20.** President McKinley sent an ultimatum to the Madrid Government regarding the situation in Cuba, but before it reached its destination Senor Polo de Bernabe, the Minister at Washington, was instructed to ask for his passport. – Telegraphic communication established between Cape Town and Lantyre. **21.** The Madrid Government notified General Woodford, the United States Minister, that as they had withdrawn their own minister from Washington, diplomatic relations had been broken off. On learning this the United States Government dispatched a squadron from Key West for Havana. – The Rt. Honble. Cecil Rhodes was re-elected a director of the British South Africa Company. **24.** The Regular Army of the United States was increased to 61,000 men, and arrangements made for the enrolment of 125,000 volunteers. **25.** The Senate of the United States (to avoid the difficulties that had arisen owing to the fact that neither their own Government nor that of Spain had declared war) announced that a state of being at war with Spain had existed since April 21st. – Mr. Day became Secretary of State in succession to Mr. Sherman, who resigned in consequence of the work entailed by the outbreak of the war. **27.** The United States squadron, forced to leave Hong Kong owing to the declaration of the 25th, sailed for Manila, the capital of the Philippines. **29.** The House of Representatives at Washington passed a Bill for raising a War Revenus.

MAY (1908)
A selection from the 1909 edition

1. Serious tram accident between Bournemouth and Christchurch; 7 killed and 10 injured. – The Kaiser and the principal German Sovereigns assembled at Vienna, and congratulated the Emperor Francis Joseph on the attainment of the 60th year of his reign. Congratulatory messages were sent from the whole of Europe. **4.** The King and Queen arrived in London after a visit to the Continent. **6.** At the annual meeting of the National Art-Collections Fund Mr. Duveen had offered to provide a new wing to the Tate Gallery to house the Turner Collection. **9.** After a most strenuous contest Mr. Winston Churchill (L.) was elected Member for Dundee. **11.** The Prime Minister of Nepal was received by the King. **13.** A heavy thunderstorm raged over Lincolnshire; one of the pinnacles of the famous Boston "Stump" displaced by lightning. **14.** The Prince of Wales formally opened the Franco-British Exhibition, in the most deplorable weather. **15.** The Unionist candidate returned for Mid-Shropshire with an increased majority – The Court of Criminal Appeal sat for the first time. **16.** The Bishop of London presided at a large demonstration at the Albert Hall in favour of the Licensing Bill – A demonstration of the Hop and Allied Trades was held in Trafalgar Square, urging that steps should be taken to protect the English hop trade. **19.** A daring robbery took place at the Central Railway Station, Manchester, a package containing goods and securities to the value of £15,000 being removed from a guard's van by a woman who was subsequently arrested in Liverpool. – The Earl of Lytton presided at a representative meeting to support the movement to establish a national theatre as a memorial to Shakespeare. – First appearance for the season of Madame Melba in *La Bohème* at Covent Garden. **20.** In connection with the recent Poor Law Scandals in Mile End, seven of the Guardians were arrested. **21.** An express train ran into the rear of a pilgrim train at Contich, near Antwerp; 38 were killed and over 100 injured. **26.** The King and the President of the French Republic visited the Franco-British Exhibition. In the evening a State Ball was given at Buckingham Palace. – The decision of the Winchester City Council to remove some railings round a Russian gun captured in the Crimean War and placed in a public position, led to such serious riots that the troops were called out. **28.** The Prince and Princess of Wales opened the new Public Library in Mare Street, Hackney. **30.** The International Balloon Race, starting from the Hurlingham Club, with 31 entries, resulted in four places out of the first five being gained by British competitors.

JUNE (1918)

A selection from the 1919 edition

1. Great fire at Constantinople, covering a distance of over 2½ miles: more than 2,000 houses destroyed, about 20,000 people homeless. **3.** New decorations for airmen instituted by His Majesty. – Explosion at Beausenq, France, munitions works: about 100 killed, 50 injured. **5.** The King in residence at the Royal Pavilion, Aldershot. **6.** Highly encouraging survey of the food position given by Mr. Clynes in the House of Commons. **7.** Speech by Mr. Lloyd George, in which he eulogized the unsurpassed sacrifices of the British peoples and their Allies. **8.** American SS *Pinar del Rio* sunk by U-boat off Maryland. **9.** Boating accident, with loss of 17 lives, in Ulverton Channel, off Peel Island, Barrow-in-Furness. **10.** 400 people killed by an explosion of a munitions depôt at Jassy. **12.** Statue of John de Witt unveiled in the Hague with State ceremonial. **13.** In the House of Commons Mr. Bonar Law [Chancellor of the Exchequer 1916–19] was closely questioned as to the present position of German banks in this country. – Bill for the damming of the Zuyder Zee finally passed by the Dutch States-General **14.** Bernard A. Kupferburg sentenced at the Old Bailey to 3 years' penal servitude for aiding and abetting Samuel Reardon (sentenced to 18 months' hard labour) wrongfully to apply Government marks to war material with intent to deceive. **15.** Decision of the War Cabinet announced to set up a Committee of Ministers of Home Affairs. – British Colony at Shanghai during "Tank Week" subscribed £429,655. **17.** 34,879 pensions and 3,013 gratuities awarded in Canada during the war. **19.** Debates in both Houses of Parliament on Cabinet control. **20.** Maj.-Gen. the Maharajah of Patiala received in audience by His Majesty, who invested him with the G.B.E. – Mr. Griffith, Sinn Fein, elected M.P. for East Cavan by majority of 1,214 votes over Mr. O'Hanlon, official Nationalist. – Maj.-Gen. Sir E. Northey, K.C.M.G., C.B., appointed Governor and Commander-in-Chief of the East African Protectorate, and H.M. High Commissioner for Zanzibar. **21.** Government announced the abandonment, for the present, of Home Rule and conscription for Ireland. **22.** Redistribution of Departments at the Ministry of Munitions. – Disastrous railway collision near Hammond, Indiana: 59 killed, 115 injured. **23.** Proposal for a permanent Anglo-American Union for the preservation of the liberties of the world put forward by Lord Reading. **24.** Duke of Connaught opened the Washington Inn for U.S. officers in St James's Square. – First Canadian aerial mail started: special bag carried from Montreal to Toronto. – Capt. Amunsden left Christiania on a N. Polar expedition in the *Maud*. **29.** Peerage conferred on Col. Sir A.H. Lee, K.C.B., M.P. (the donor of the Chequers Estate to the Nation), in recognition of his public services as Director-General of Food Production, 1917–18.

JULY (1928)
A selection from the 1929 edition

2. Royal Assent given to bill enfranchising women on the same terms as men. – British cruiser *Dauntless* ran on shoal outside Halifax, Nova Scotia, but afterwards refloated, entire crew being saved. **5.** Car dashed into hawser by which tractor was hauling timber near Oxford and three occupants were killed. **6.** International Liberal Conference opened in London. – At Gloucester Assizes, Mrs. Beatrice Annie Pace was found not guilty on charge of murdering her husband by administering arsenic, and she was discharged amid remarkable demonstrations of enthusiasm. **7.** Liner *Carmarthenshire* caught fire in the Thames outward bound for China and was beached, passengers being landed. Chilean Army transport foundered off coast of Chile with 80 passengers and crew of 215. **9.** Electric train collided with light engine outside London Bridge station, one man being killed and several persons injured. **11.** British liner *Demerara* rammed by cargo boat and badly damaged off Portuguese Coast – French Cabinet expressed approval with the anti-war pact. **12.** Germany accepted Mr. Kellogg's anti-war pact. **13.** Both majority and minority reports of the tribunal set up to investigate police interrogation of a woman at Scotland Yard urged change in the system. – Labour candidate won the ex-Speaker's seat at Halifax in a triangular fight. – Three young men were sentenced to death at Sussex Assizes for murder of a Brighton man. They appealed unsuccessfully, but were reprieved on eve of day fixed for execution, their sentences being commuted to penal servitude for life. **16.** King received at Buckingham Palace delegates to International Conference on Cancer. **17.** King inspected new Australian cruisers at Portsmouth, and the reconditioned *Victory*. **18.** Britain's reply accepting the anti-war pact proposed by United States presented. Australia, New Zealand, South Africa, and India all accepted. **19.** Prince of Wales carried out number of engagements at Grimsby, flying there and back. **20.** Boat mail train ran off rails 30 miles from Madras, owing apparently to rails having been tampered with. **23.** Queen consulted oculist regarding eye strain – Industrial Transference Board published report declaring that 200,000 miners might not again find employment in coalfields. **25.** King received Sultan of Muscat and Oman. – Indian States Committee, in London, heard case for group of India's ruling Princes for more satisfactory political relationships between their States and Indian Government. **26.** Their Majesties gave garden party at Buckingham Palace. **29.** Light engine and excursion train collided at Ardwick, Manchester, a guard being killed and 22 passengers injured – The Olympic Games were inaugurated at Amsterdam.

AUGUST (1938)
A selection from the 1939 edition

2. The King left the royal yacht and spent a day at his boys' camp at Southwold. **3.** Lord Runiciman arrived in Prague. **4.** Their Majesties and the Princesses disembarked at Aberdeen and motored to Balmoral. – Lord Runiciman met President Benes [of Czechoslovakia] and the Premier and saw representatives of the Sudeten-German Party. 5–7. Britain's air exercises to test coast defences began. As they ended two bombers crashed, 6 men being killed. 6. Mr. Malcolm MacDonald arrived in Palestine by air and discussed situation with High Commissioner and Commander of British troops before walking unrecognised through Jerusalem. 7. Lowerstoft trawler *Aleazar* sank in Irish Sea after collision in thick fog with a cross-Channel steamer, 7 lives being lost. 8. Duke and Duchess of Gloucester visited Empire Exhibition at Glasgow. 9. Prime Minister returned to London to receive treatment for nasal catarrh. – Spanish troops began offensive near Lerida and crossed River Segree. 11. German monoplane flew 3,942 miles non-stop from Berlin to New York in 25 hours. 12. Duke and Duchess of Gloucester flew from Hendon to Marseilles and embarked on liner for Alexandria. 14. The German monoplane arrived back in Berlin after flight of 19 hrs. 59 mins. 15. Spanish Government and General Franco agreed to appointment of British Commission to assist in exchange of prisoners. 17. Sudetan-Germans, at conference with Czech Ministers, rejected Government's proposals for equality for all citizens, elections on principle of proportionality, and civil servants and schools according to race percentage. 20. The Duke and Duchess of Gloucester arrived at Nakuru, Kenya, to begin their holiday. 25. Japanese troops captured Juichang, China. 26. Grave tension in Jaffa after several serious incidents. In 3 weeks, 174 people were killed or died of wounds and 183 wounded. 27. After carrying out full-load trials at Hatfield, one of the monoplanes built for Transatlantic service broke its back. – 27. Sir John Simon, speaking at Lanark, repeated Mr. Chamberlain's former declaration that it would be a mistake to assume that in event of trouble in Czechoslovakia Britain would necessarily remain outside. 30. Berlin Ambassador attended special meeting of British Cabinet which expressed entire agreement with action taken and policy to be pursued [in Czechoslovakia]. Herr Hitler sent for Herr Henlein to discuss position. Dr. Benes explained new proposals for cantonal autonomy to Sudetan-Germans.

SEPTEMBER (1948)
A selection from the 1949 edition

1. Chinese leader found murdered by insurgents near Penang. 2. Vickers Viscount, four-engined jet-propelled air liner, gave satisfactory demonstration flight. 3. Dr. Benes, former President of Czechoslovakia died. 4. Queen Wilhelmina abdicated and became Princesss of the Netherlands, and huge crowds at Amsterdam acclaimed the new Queen Juliana. 5. Princess Margaret flew to Amsterdam to represent King and Queen at inauguration of Queen Juliana. – New air liner Hermes IV flew for first time and performed perfectly. 6. Avro Tudor VIII, first all jet-propelled four-engined civil transport aircraft, made its initial test flight. – Berlin Assembly met in British sector. 7. Indian Premier announced Government had asked Nizam of

Hyderabad to disband volunteer force immediately and facilitate return of Indian troops to Secunderabad to restore law and order in the State. **8.** Mr. Atlee announced to be suffering from an early duodenal ulcer which would require dietetic treatment for some weeks. – All political meetings in British sector adjoining Soviet sector in Berlin were banned. **9.** King and Queen attended Braemar Gathering. Princess Margaret returned from Netherlands and flew to Balmoral. – Great crowd attended anti-Communist demonstrations at junction of British and Soviet sectors in Berlin: red flag on top of Brandenburg Gate was torn down and shots were fired into British sector, one person being killed. **10.** British residents in Hyderabad were evacuated by air. **13.** Indian troops invaded Hydarabad on Nizam's refusal to disband volunteer force and severe fighting took place. State of emergency declared throughout India to deal with possible internal disturbances. **17.** Count Bernadotte and United Nations official were shot dead while driving through Jewish area of Jerusalem, assassin being presumed to be member of Stern Gang. **18.** Hyderabad Army formally surrendered and Indian troops entered Secunderabab. **30.** Leader of Stern Gang was arrested in Haifa.

OCTOBER (1958)
A selection from the 1960 edition

1. At Labour Party conference at Scarborough, Mrs. B.A. Castle was elected chairman of party for ensuing year. – British plan for Cyprus officially took effect. Greek Cypriots staged strike throughout island. – Soviet Government sent notes to U.K. and U.S.A. agreeing to talks on suspension of nuclear tests at Geneva on Oct. 31 and proposing that they should be at foreign ministers' level. **3.** British sergeant's wife murdered by terrorists in Famagusta and another seriously wounded. Archbishop Makarios sent message to Greet Cypriots urging them to react "vigorously" against implementation of British plan. **4.** Comet jet passenger service across Atlantic began. **6.** The Pope was stated to be gravely ill after a stroke. **9.** After suffering a second stroke on previous day Pope Pius XII died in early hours of morning. **11.** Rocket aimed at moon was successfully launched from Cape Canaveral, but slight error in aiming angle prevented it from reaching its destination and on following day it was believed to have re-entered earth's atmosphere and burnt out over Pacific. **16.** The Queen and the Duke of Edinburgh left Balmoral after their holiday and travelled to Carlisle, which Her Majesty had been prevented from visiting due to her illness in July. – Russian trawler drifted on rocks in Shetlands and sank with loss of more than 20 men. The skipper and two seamen were rescued by Lerwick lifeboat and later handed back to Soviet authorities. **20.** Twenty members of crew of London tanker *Stanvac Japan* killed in Persian Gulf when explosion blew out whole midships section of vessel. **22.** B.E.A. Viscount aircraft collided with Italian fighter near Anzio and crashed with loss of all 31 persons on board. **23.** Mr. Krushchev said that Soviet Government was granting credit of £33,000,000 to United Arab Republic towards building of Aswan dam.

30. Mr. Boris Pasternak, who had been awarded Nobel Prize for literature, declined to receive it after he had been expelled from Writers' Union and criticised in Soviet press. **28.** The Queen opened new session of Parliament, the ceremony being broadcast and televised for the first time. — Cardinal Angelo Giuseppe Roncalli, Patriarch of Venice, was elected Pope, taking title of John XXIII.

NOVEMBER (1968)
A selection from the 1970 edition

1. The Queen left Heathrow Airport for state visits to Brazil and Chile. **3.** Many people lost their lives when dam burst at Vallemosso in northern Italy during severe flooding. Nearly 200 homes were flooded and roads closed as River Ouse at York rose to its highest level for 20 years. **7.** In Presidential election, Mr. Nixon narrowly defeated Vice-President Mr. Humphrey; final results showed that Mr. Nixon won 31,770,237 (43.4 per cent) of the popular votes to Mr. Humphrey's 31,270,533 (42.7 per cent). – Thousands of armed police, backed by troops, quelled anti-Russian march by 3,000 young people in Prague. **8.** Bruce Reynolds, sought for more than five years by police investigating the Great Train Robbery of 1963, was arrested in Torquay; he was remanded in custody. **10.** Her Majesty watched Lent carnival in grounds of residence of British Ambassador. **18.** New York teachers voted to end their strike which had closed most of the city's schools for five weeks. – About 60,000 students throughout Bohemia and Moravia began three-day strike to demonstrate their opposition to the way in which reform policies by Dubcek regime were being slowly eroded under pressure from Russians and conservative forces within Czechoslovak leadership. **19.** Chancellor of the Exchequer flew to Bonn to attend emergency discussions on international monetary crisis. – The French Prime Minister announced spending economies after continued speculation against franc in favour of German Mark. – West Germany decided not to revalue Deutsche Mark, but to take immediate tax measures in import and export sectors aimed at stabilizing internal prices and warding off foreign pressure to revalue. **22.** On his return from Bonn Mr. Jenkins announced new deflationary measures; details of severe curbs in bank lending to private sector were also given. **24.** Despite international monetary crisis, France decided not to devalue franc. **26.** It was reported that U.S. and South Vietnam troops had entered demilitarized zone and fought battle with Vietcong there for the first time since bombing halt on Nov. 1. **28.** John Lennon, of the Beatles pop group, was fined £160 at Marylebone Magistrates' Court for unauthorized possession of drug cannabis. **30.** A rocket, carrying Europe's first space satellite, was successfully launched from the Woomera Range in Australia.

DECEMBER (1978)
A selection from the 1980 edition

6. The Prime Minister told the Commons that Britain would not join the European Monetary System but that the U.K. would be free to join the exchange rate mechanism at a later date if it wished, or to remain outside it, but Mrs. Thatcher said that it was a sad day for Europe that nine member countries had been unable to agree a major new initiative. **10.** The confidential draft of Labour's election manifesto "Keep Britain Labour" was leaked to the Communist *Morning Star* newspaper. **12.** Bakers' Union leaders decided to recommend a full return to work from Dec. 17 after branches voted by a narrow margin to call off the five-week-old bread strike and accept the 14.4 per cent pay offer from the Bakers' Federation. **13.** Thousands of peak-hour commuters experienced long delays in the Midlands when signalmen operating three power boxes controlling the network came out on unofficial strike in support of signals and telecommunications men who were suspended without pay after their refusal to accept a new pay and grading system. **19–26.** Mrs. Gandhi was taken to Tibar jail, New Delhi, after the Lower House of Parliament, the Lok Sabha, voted to expel her and send her to prison for breach of privilege and contempt of the House, the sentence lasting until the present parliamentary session ended; On Dec. 21 it was reported that 12 people had been killed and more than 30,000 arrested in several states across India as party supporters demonstrated against the jailing of Mrs. Gandhi and her expulsion from Parliament; Mrs. Gandhi was released on Dec. 26 after a week in jail. **21.** The Queen received a loyal address from the Isle of Man to mark the millennium of Tynwald. **25.** The Queen's Christmas broadcast to Britain and the Commonwealth on BBC 1 and Independent TV departed from its traditional format and was one of her longest Christmas messages, lasting 20 minutes.

ACCIDENTS AND DISASTERS

The date in parentheses indicates the edition each of the following extracts was taken from.

5 Oct. 1867 (1869): Explosion of Boxer cartridges at Woolwich Arsenal; twenty-four boys dreadfully burnt, and two instantaneously killed.

8 Nov. 1867 (1869): Explosion in a coal-mine at Rhondda Valley, South Wales, with loss of 170 lives.

6 Dec. 1867 (1869): Destruction by fire of Her Majesty's Theatre, Haymarket, London. **7.** Explosion at gunpowder works near Lake Windermere, with loss of several lives. **13.** Terrible explosion at the House of Detention, Clerkenwell, London, caused by Fenians intending to rescue Burke, confined in that prison. A whole street was laid in ruins, many lives were lost, and the surrounding neighbourhood greatly injured. **17.** Remarkable explosion of nitro-glycerine at Newcastle-on-Tyne, with loss of four lives. **28.** Explosion at the gunpowder mills, Faversham, with loss of eleven lives.

25 July 1868 (1869): Death, by explosion of a new torpedo, of Lieutenant Meade, a son of Lord Clanwilliam, at Portsmouth; and also of one of his assistants named White. **26.** Fires at Colyton and Collumpton, Devonshire, with destruction of 21 houses. **30.** Fearful accident at the Victoria Music Hall, Manchester, by a panic, caused through a false alarm of fire. Thirty persons crushed to death, and many others seriously injured. **31.** Fire at the Jarrow Chemical Works, Gateshead, near Newcastle-on-Tyne, with estimated loss of £100,000.

19 Aug. 1868 (1869): Fire at Northumberland House, Charing Cross, the town residence of the Duke of Northumberland, with heavy loss of art treasures, etc. Amongst these was a Sèvres China vase, formerly belonging to Charles X. of France, and valued at £10,000, which was much injured.

22 Jan. 1873 (1874): The ship *Northfleet* is cut down and sunk by the Spanish steamer *Murillo*, off Dungeness, with loss of upwards of 300 lives.

24 Mar. 1878 (1879): Foundering of the *Eurydice*, a naval training ship, off the Isle of Wight, during a snow squall, with loss of about 330 lives.

3 July 1883 (1884): Capsizing of the steamer *Daphne*, whilst being launched on the Clyde; nearly 150 people drowned.

23 June 1894 (1895): Terrible disaster at the Albion Colliery, Pontypridd; 300 lives lost. [The disaster stemmed from a massive explosion caused by the ignition of coal dust from an explosion of firedamp; following an inquest the manager and chargeman were both fined.]

27 Jan. 1896 (1897): Disastrous colliery explosion in South Wales: over 55 lives lost.

27 Jan. 1903 (1904): A dreadful fire broke out at Colney Hatch Lunatic Asylum, resulting in the death of 52 women inmates.

5 Dec. 1905 (1907): A large portion of the roof of Charing Cross station collapsed suddenly, doing great damage to the avenue theatre; six lives lost.

21 Dec. 1910 (1912): An explosion occurred in the Pretoria Pit, near Bolton, and, notwithstanding the utmost efforts of the mine authorities and rescue parties, the death-roll exceeded 300.

14 Oct. 1913 (1915): An explosion occurred at the Universal Colliery, Senghenydd, near Cardiff, when over 900 men were below, and despite magnificent heroism, by which some 500 were rescued, the death-roll numbered 429.

22 May 1915 (1916): The worst disaster in the history of British railways took place at Quintin's hill, a mile north of Gretna Green, on the Caledonian Line, a heavily laden troop train, going southward with 500 officers and men, running into a local passenger train, the Scotch express from Euston crashing into the wreckage of them both; 157 killed (among them many of the 7th Royal Scots, including 3 officers) and 200 injured.

26 Apr. 1915 (1916): The premature explosion of a grenade at Borden Camp resulted in the death of four soldiers and injuries to 30 others.

11 July 1915 (1916): 70 persons were injured, four seriously, by the overturning of a tramcar between Warwick and Ranelagh Bridges, Paddington. **21.** An explosion occurred at a munitions factory in Yorkshire, 39 persons being killed and 60 injured.

1 July 1918 (1919): Explosion at a national shell-filling factory in the Midlands: 100 killed, 150 injured. [Eight tons of TNT exploded; 134 people were killed and 250 injured; sympathetic telegrams were sent on behalf of the King and Winston Churchill, then Minister of Munitions.]

1 Jan. 1919 (1920): Naval Steam yacht *Iolaire*, with 300 seamen on leave, wrecked outside Stornoway Harbour with loss of 174 lives. **29.** Steamer *Nimrod* of Antarctic expedition fame foundered near Yarmouth, 10 lives lost.

23 Aug. 1921 (1922): While engaged on trial trip preparatory to crossing Atlantic, and after flight of nearly 35 hrs., R38 broke in two and fell in flames into the Humber. Of the 49 officers and crew, including 17 American airmen, only five were saved. [At the time of her first flight, the R38 was the largest airship in the world; the crash resulted in more deaths than the Hindenburg disaster.]

20 Dec. 1928 (1930): Series of gas main explosions tore up number of streets of Bloomsbury over considerable area, great damage being caused to property and several persons injured. Residents in district had to leave their homes in case of further fires and explosions. A Post office workman was blown out of inspection hole and fatally injured.

31 Dec. 1929 (1931): Panic followed cry of "fire" in cinema at Paisley during a "penny matinée" for children, and 70 children under 16 were killed and 36 injured. Actual fire was slight, but spread of fumes created alarm.

13 June 1930 (1931): Sir Henry Segrave killed on Lake Windermere when attempting to break water speed record on his motor boat.

10 Feb. 1930 (1931): French air liner crashed at Marden, Kent, a young married couple being killed and four persons injured.

22 Sept. 1933 (1935): Explosion and fire occurred at Gresford Colliery, near Wrexham, during night shift, 265 out of 400 men in pit being killed. All rescue parties had to be withdrawn and shafts sealed.

12 Dec. 1934 (1936): Floor of church school in Liverpool collapsed during concert, and 300 women and children fell 40 feet, 1 woman being killed and over 100 injured, 18 seriously.

10 Nov. 1937 (1938): During heavy blizzard of whirling snow, express from Edinburgh to Glasgow crashed into rear of stationary train at Castlecary, Stirlingshire, 35 persons being killed and a large number injured. **27.** One man was killed and £100,000 damage done by Boxing Day fire in Oxford Street, W.

31 Mar. 1937 (1938): Part of floor of new building on Blackpool pleasure beach fell while under construction, 4 men being killed and several injured.

10 May 1937 (1938): Explosion, cause of which remained unknown, occurred in Markham Colliery, near Chesterfield, in which 80 miners lost their lives and many were injured.

19 Jun. 1937 (1938): Blackpool Pier pavilion destroyed by fire.

15 Oct. 1940 (1941): Night raid on London was one of the heaviest experienced. Many lives lost when bomb holed roof of a Tube.

A bomb fell on the road above Balham underground station where people were sheltering during an air raid; a bus crashed into the crater made by the explosion and part of the northbound tunnel collapsed filling with earth and water due to a burst water main; 66 people (according to the Commonwealth War Graves Commission) were killed.

30 Nov. 1940 (1942): German Raiders made heavy attack, lasting seven hours, on Southampton, explosives following hail of incendiaries. Considerable damage was caused in centre of city. **Dec 1.** Heavier attack made on Southampton, causing further serious damage. In the two raids killed and injured was about 370.

5 Jan. 1941 (1942): Miss Amy Johnson, pioneer woman aviator, drowned when machine she was piloting crashed into Thames Estuary.

Johnson was the first woman to fly solo from England to Australia, receiving a CBE, the Harmon Trophy and the No. 1 civil pilot's licence in Australia. Until her death, Johnson flew for the Air Transport Auxiliary, as part of the war effort.

---

1 Jan. 1942 (1943): "Silent" explosion shattered workings of Sneyd Colliery near Burslem, 57 men and boys being lost.

13 Apr. 1942 (1943): During joint exercises in Southern England fighter plane fired with live ammunition on troops and tanks, death roll numbering 25.

6 June 1942 (1943): German bomb, undiscovered for 13 months, exploded in cellar of partly wrecked house in Elephant and Castle district of London, and 19 persons, including several children, were killed and over 50 injured, while 300 families were made homeless.

3 Mar. 1943 (1944): Disaster occurred in London tube shelter after night alert had been sounded. Through a woman tripping on stairs, scores of men, women and children fell on top of each other in the darkness, completely blocking the stairway. Others continued to press forward, and by the time the bodies could be extricated 173 persons had died of suffocation and others had to receive hospital treatment. There was no panic and no bomb fell in the district. **April 24.** Eighty-one members of the Forces drowned when 2 barges were overwhelmed by rough seas off Welsh coast.

23 Aug. 1944 (1945): In severe thunderstorm a Liberator crashed in flames on school at Frackleton, near Preston, 38 children and 22 adults being killed, including some of the crew. [The aircraft was a United States Army Air Forces Consolidated B-24 Liberator heavy bomber; three houses were destroyed alongside a snack bar.]

27 Nov. 1944 (1946): Serious explosion occurred at R.A.F. underground depot a few miles from Burton-on-Trent, bombs being hurled over surrounding countryside and causing widespread damage; 70 were killed or missing.

10 Jan. 1945 (1946): Workmen's train and motor-train collided near Belfast, 19 persons being killed and over 40 injured. 20 soldiers killed and 25 injured when mine exploded during lecture in hut at camp in Kent.

30 May 1945 (1946): Worst railway accident for several years occurred near Bourne End, Herts, 43 persons being killed when Perth to London express on L.M.S. line ran off rails and engine and 3 coaches plunged down embankment.

24 Oct. 1945 (1946): Mine drifting in heavy gale off south coast exploded off Folkestone, causing considerable damage.

3 Feb. 1950 (1951): British submarine *Truculent* sank in Thames estuary after being in collision with Swedish motor tanker *Divina* while surfacing. *Divina* and other vessels picked up 15 survivors, but 48 of crew and 16 dockyard workmen were lost, although they were all believed to have left vessel, being swept away by the tide.

8 Oct. 1952 (1954): One of the worst railway disasters in England occurred at Harrow and Wealdstone station, resulting in death of 112 persons and injuries to more than 100. Express from Perth to Euston ran into crowded local train, and almost immediately express from Euston to Manchester crashed into wreckage, engines and coaches being hurled across platforms.

28 June 1960 (1961): Forty-five miners were killed in pit explosion, accompanied by falls of roof, at Six Bells colliery near Abertillery.

6 July 1965 (1966): All 41 servicemen on board R.A.F. Transport Command Aircraft during parachute training flight were killed when plane crashed at little Baldon, Oxfordshire.

4 June 1967 (1968): At Stockport, Cheshire, 72 of the 84 people on board died when Argonaut airliner crashed while returning with holiday makers from Majorca.

18 June 1972 (1973): All 118 persons on B.E.A. Trident died when it crashed in field at Staines shortly after taking off from Heathrow airport for Brussels; this was worst disaster in history of British Aviation.

8 Oct. 1974 (1976): Two hot-air balloonists plunged 1,500 ft. to their death watched by thousands of spectators at Saltley, Birmingham when their balloon fell on to a canal towpath two minutes after take-off.

28 Feb. 1975 (1976): The death toll in London Underground's worst disaster was 42, including the driver, following a crash at Moorgate where the train smashed into a cul-de-sac tunnel. Verdicts of accidental death were returned on all the victims at the end of the four-day inquest on April 18. The 43rd victim died in hospital on June 10.

27 May 1975 (1976): Thirty-two people, mostly elderly women, all from Thornaby, Teeside, were killed after their day-trip coach plunged through a bridge parapet into a ravine at Dibble's Bridge, Hebden, in the Yorkshire Dales; 14 people also being injured.

17 Dec. 1983 (1985): Five people, including a police sergeant and a police woman, were killed and 91 injured when an I.R.A. terrorist bomb exploded outside a rear entrance to Harrods in Hans Crescent, Knightsbridge; on **Dec. 24** a police inspector became the sixth victim when he died from his injuries.

23 May 1984 (1985): Nine people were killed and over 20 injured by an explosion at the underground water treatment plant at Abbeystead, Lancs., as a group of local visitors from the village of St. Michael's on Wyre were being shown around the installation; on **June 4** the death toll rose to 15.

9 Jul. 1984 (1985): Lightning was blamed for causing a fire which destroyed the south transept at York Minster and caused damage estimated at over £1 million.

12 Oct. 1984 (1986): Sir Anthony Berry, M.P. for Enfield Southgate, was one of four people who were killed in an I.R.A. terrorist bomb attack on the Grand Hotel, Brighton, headquarters of the party leaders at the annual Conservative conference; among the injured in the attempt to assassinate the Prime Minister and members of the Cabinet and Government were Mr. Norman Tebbit, Trade and Industry Secretary, and his wife, Mr John Wakeham, Government Chief Whip, whose wife was one of the dead, and Sir Walter Clegg, M.P. for Wyre and his wife; on **Nov. 13** the death toll rose to five when Mrs. Muriel McLean, wife of the Scottish Conservatives' president, died.

11 May 1985 (1986): Fifty-three soccer spectators died and over 200 were injured when fire swept through the main stand at Bradford City's football ground during the match with Lincoln city; the death toll subsequently rose to 55.

22 Aug. 1985 (1986): Fifty-four people died and 83 escaped when a British Airtours Boeing 737 burst into flames as the pilot aborted its take-off for Corfu at Manchester Airport; two firemen were also hurt; on **Aug. 28**, the death toll rose to 55 when an injured man died in hospital.

6 Nov. 1986 (1988): Forty-five people died when a Chinook helicopter ferrying oil workers from the Brent oilfield to Sumburgh crashed into the North Sea two miles off the Shetland Islands: there were only two survivors. **13.** Michael Lush, a television viewer undertaking a Houdini-style stunt for the Noel Edmonds' *Late Breakfast Show* was killed during rehearsals: the B.B.C. cancelled the show and launched an investigation.

2 Nov. 1987 (1989): Two R.A.F. Harrier jets collided near Otterburn, Northumberland, killing both pilots. **18.** A fire broke out at King's Cross underground station in London: the final death toll reached 31. The Prime Minister announced that a public enquiry would be held.

7 July 1988 (1989): The Piper Alpha oil production platform in the North Sea exploded, killing 167 men, including three rescuers. The Government ordered an enquiry into the disaster.

21 Dec. 1988 (1990): A Pan-Am jumbo jet crashed onto the Scottish town of Lockerbie, killing everyone on board and demolishing a street in the town. On **Dec. 23** the death toll was estimated at 276, with at least 17 killed in Lockerbie itself. On **Dec. 28** Ministry of Defence scientists found evidence that the jet was blown up in mid-air by a bomb.

9 Jan. 1989 (1990): A British Midland 737 aircraft suffered engine malfunction on a flight from London to Belfast and crashed on the M1 motorway in Leicestershire, ploughing into the motorway embankment. Forty-four of the 82 people on board were killed.

31 Mar. 1989 (1990): A two-year-old boy was savaged by a chimpanzee at the Port Lympne Zoo Park in Kent.

20 Aug. 1989 (1990): A Thames pleasure boat, *The Marchioness,* sank after being hit by the dredger *Bowbelle:* the death toll was 57. On **Aug. 31** the Transport Secretary (Cecil Parkinson) announced new safety rules for vessels on the Thames.

2 June 2002 (2003): A pilot died after ejecting from a fighter jet when it skidded on landing and crashed into the M11.

7 July 2005 (2006): Four suicide bombings in London killed 52 people and injured 700. The three bombs on London Underground trains exploded at **8.50 a.m.** on a Piccadilly Line train between King's Cross and Russell Square stations and on two Circle Line trains, one between Liverpool Street and Aldgate stations, and the other between Edgware Road and Paddington stations. The fourth bomb exploded on a bus in Tavistock Square at **9.47 a.m.** The transport system was suspended for several hours. A statement claiming responsibility was posted on an Islamist website by 'the Secret Organisation Group of Al-Qaeda of Jihad Organisation in Europe'. Recovery work to remove bodies and clear the tracks of wreckage took several days, especially on the Piccadilly Line, where emergency services were severely hampered by the depth and narrowness of the tunnel, temperatures of 60°C and the risk of the tunnel collapsing.

AVIATION

The date in parentheses indicates the edition each of the following extracts was taken from.

12 Dec. 1881 (1883): Mr. Powell, M.P. for Malmesbury, ascended in a balloon, and lost his life in the channel. [The two other passengers of the balloon Saladin fell out of the basket and Powell was last seen waving his hand as he was swept out to sea.]

19 Sept. 1902 (1903): Mr. Stanley Spencer, the aeronaut, made a journey from the Crystal Palace to Harrow in his airship. [*The Telegraph* reported the height at 27,500ft, only 1,500ft less than the record at the time.]

29 July 1907 (1908): A balloon race for the Grand Prix of the Aero Club of France started from Paris.

5 Oct. 1907 (1908): The British airship Nulli Secundus, after a trial voyage at Aldershot, journeyed to London, and alighted in the grounds of the Crystal Palace; owing to unfavourable weather on the days immediately following the return voyage was delayed, and eventually the airship was partially wrecked in a storm while moored in the Palace grounds.

3 May 1909 (1910): Messrs. Wilbur and Orville Wright arrived in London, and had an interview with Mr. Haldane [Secretary of State for War] at the War Office.

> The American Wright brothers were pioneers of aviation and in 1903 became the first to perform a controlled flight with a heavier-than-air plane. In his autobiography, Lord Haldane dismissed the brothers as "clever empiricists" and stated they were at a disadvantage compared with the Germans who used a foundation of science to establish their air service.

15 Oct. 1909 (1910): In extremely unfavourable weather, the first aviation week to be held in Great Britain was opened at Doncaster. During the following days, a number of successful flights were made by foreign aviators.

30 Oct. 1909 (1910): Mr. J. T. C. Moore-Brabazon won the *Daily Mail* £1,000 prize for a circular mile flight by a British aviator on an all-British aeroplane.

> The 1st Baron Brabazon of Tara was an aviation pioneer and a Conservative politician who served as Minister of Transport and Minister of Aircraft Production during the Second World War. In 1909, he became the first Englishman to make an officially recognised aeroplane flight in England.

6 Dec. 1911 (1913): Mr. Hubert Oxley and a passenger, Mr. Weiss, were killed by falling from an aeroplane at Filey.

2 April 1912 (1913): Gustav Hamel flew from London to Paris with a lady passenger – the first woman to cross the Channel on an aeroplane.

> Gustav Hamel was known for many aviation stunts and firsts. In 1911, Hamel flew a distance of 21 miles between Hendon and Windsor to deliver the first official airmail, including a postcard written on the plane.
>
> When he was 24, Hamel disappeared over the English Channel in 1914 on his return from Paris. No trace of the aircraft was found and his body was not retrieved.

21 April 1912 (1913): Mr. Corbett Wilson flew from Fishguard to Enniscorthy across the St. George's Channel. Mr. D. L. Allen, who attempted a similar flight, was not heard of again after leaving Holyhead.

> The flight occurred a week after the sinking of the *Titanic*, when people began to look for new ways to travel overseas. The feat, which journalists had called "the unthinkable" lasted for 100 minutes. Corbett Wilson was killed in 1915 when serving in the Royal Flying Corps during the First World War, when his aircraft was struck by an enemy shell.

AERONAUTICS IN 1916
As recorded in the 1917 edition

Nothing that has occurred during the past year has been more gratifying to the British nation than the enormous development of its Air Service. It has been one of the wonders of the war, into which we entered the least prepared in respect to fighting and scouting aeroplanes, that our Flying Corps has established a supremacy which has done much towards the gaining of many artillery successes.

On **Sept. 3** during a raid on the northern outskirts of London, in which a number of Zeppelins took part, one of them, the L21, was hit and set on fire by Lieut. Robinson, a young flying man. The Zeppelin fell to earth at Cuffley, near Enfield, a flaming mass, and all the crew, 19 in number, perished in the fire, their bodies being charred. For his daring feat Lieut. Robinson was awarded the Victoria Cross, and he was also the recipient of several large rewards offered by private persons to the first airman or gunner to bring down a Zeppelin.

AERONAUTICS IN 1917
As recorded in the 1918 edition

As might be expected, all developments of aeronautics in the past year were inseparable from military operations. […] Airships of the Zeppelin type were found useful for patrolling the waters around our coasts, acting as scouts for the Navy, and employed in the detection of enemy submarines attacking our mercantile marine. Captive balloons of the "sausage" type were extensively used on the fighting front for spotting enemy batteries and general observation work.

It had at length become recognised that supremacy in the air meant supremacy of the artillery, the most valuable part played by airmen being the taking of photographs of enemy lines, trenches, batteries, and positions.

The output of aeroplanes from our factories was speeded up as much as possible by the Ministry of Munitions, first under Dr. Addison, and then under his successor, Mr. W. S. Churchill.

Daylight aeroplane raids on the South Coast had been frequent in 1916, but it was not till **Nov. 28** of that year that a single enemy machine appeared at mid-day over London and, after dropping its bombs, got clear away.

Of the commercial development of aeronautics, it is impossible yet to do more than speculate. So vast have been the improvements in engines and machines that commercial transport is a certainty of the near future. To visualise a regular aerial service between Great Britain, the Continent, the United States, and Canada is no vain thing. When the war is ended there will be a great boom in this more civilised use of the aeroplane, rendered possible by the improvements effected by the exigencies of war.

THE FIRST NON-STOP TRANSATLANTIC FLIGHT
As recorded in the 1920 edition

The year 1919 will be ever memorable in the history of aeronautics for the fact that the Atlantic was four times crossed by air – twice by heavier than air machines and twice (westward and eastward) by an airship. To a British aeroplane belongs the credit of the first direct flight and to a British airship that of the east and west voyages. The fourth crossing, though first in point of time, was made by an American seaplane by an indirect and convoyed route from Newfoundland to Portugal, with an intermediate landing in the Azores. In all eight different aircraft attempted the crossing – three seaplanes, five aeroplanes, and one airship. Of the five aeroplanes four did not succeed. One of the four, piloted by the famous airman H. G. Hawker, an Australian, fell in mid-Atlantic, the pilot and his navigator being miraculously saved by a Danish tramp steamer, which landed them in the Orkneys nearly a week later. The remaining three aeroplanes ultimately gave up the attempt.

The first direct flight was made on the night of **June 14–15** by Captain John Alcock, D.S.C. (pilot), and Lieut. Arthur Whitten Brown (navigator), flying a Vimy-Rolls-Royce twin-engine aeroplane. They left St. John's, Newfoundland, at 5.13 p.m. (summer time) on Saturday and landed at Clifden on the Galway coast of Ireland at 9.40 a.m. Sunday. The coast to coast flight of 1,880 miles over the sea was accomplished in just under 16 hours. By this achievement the *Daily Mail* prize of £10,000 was won. Both pilot and navigator were subsequently honoured with knighthoods by the King [George V].

THE FIRST WOMAN TO ATTEMPT A TRANSATLANTIC FLIGHT

31 Aug. 1927 (1928): In a Fokker monoplane, Col. F. F. Minchin and Capt. Leslie Hamilton, with Princess Lowenstein-Wertheim as passenger, left Upavon, Wiltshire, on attempt to fly to America. Nothing definite was heard of them after they had left Irish coast.

Aged 63, Princess Anne of Lowenstein-Wertheim-Freudenberg, an English socialite and aviation enthusiast, thus became the first woman to attempt and perish in a transatlantic flight. The Princess had financed Captain Leslie Hamilton's attempt to fly from England to Canada for the first time in history and had decided to partake in the attempt as a passenger against the wishes of her family. The plane they were travelling in, the St. Raphael, is believed to have crashed in the north Atlantic on the 31 August but no trace of the plane or its crew was ever discovered.

---

30 May 1942 (1943): Over 1,000 bombers – Lancasters, Halifaxes, Stirlings, Manchesters, Wellingtons – concentrated on Cologne in biggest R.A.F. raid of the war; 44 of our aircraft were missing from the night's operations, but attack was outstanding success, huge fires being visible from coastline of Holland.

7 Sept. 1946 (1947): Group Captain E. M. Donaldson set up new speed record off Rustington, averaging 616 m.p.h. in four laps in Gloster Meteor jet-propelled fighter, and doing two laps at 623 m.p.h.

9 April 1969 (1970): British-built Concorde 002 supersonic airliner made successful maiden flight from Filton, near Bristol.

21 Jan. 1976 (1977): Two Concordes took-off simultaneously from Heathrow and Charles de Gaulle airport in Paris on their inaugural commercial flights, British Airways plane touching down in Bahrain and Air France's plane arriving at Rio de Janeiro.

SUPERSONIC AIRLINERS
As recorded in the 1970 edition: Science, Discovery and Invention in 1969

The first prototype, Concorde 001, built by the French side of the consortium, made its maiden flight in March, to be followed a few weeks later by 002, the British built prototype. The French prototype made its first supersonic flight during the autumn and 002 was due to follow suit in the early part of 1970. American competition in this field was lagging. The original ambitious plan for a supersonic airliner considerably faster than the planned 1,550 m.p.h. of Concorde, had run into design and cost troubles and was replaced by a less ambitious alternative. The only rival on the scene was the Russian Tu 144, which made its maiden flight on the last day of 1968, went supersonic in the early Spring and was flying around twice the speed of sound in the summer. Confident they would get it into service by the end of 1970, the Russians had laid down a production line and were talking of their hopes of selling it to foreign airlines in two years, but British experts could not see it as a great menace to Concorde's sales prospects.

CRIME

The date in parentheses indicates the edition each of the following extracts was taken from.

24 Aug. 1867 (1869): Horrible murder of a child, Fanny Adams, by Frederick Baker, at Alton, Hampshire.

> This is the first crime report ever recorded in *Whitaker's Almanak*, not only does it document a horrific crime for which Frederick Baker was later hanged, but also the origin of a common phrase.
>
> The expression "Sweet Fanny Adams" or "Sweet F.A." has come to mean "nothing at all". This is due to the fact the girl's body was found with her torso emptied and eyes removed, with organs strewn around. At the same time, British seamen were provided with new rations of tinned mutton, which, unimpressed by, they speculated it to be the butchered remains of Fanny Adams. Thus her name, in addition to the aforementioned meaning, can also be used to describe something as worthless.

THE CLERKENWELL EXPLOSION
13 Dec. 1867 (1869): Terrible explosion at the House of Detention, Clerkenwell, London, caused by Fenians intending to rescue Burke [a senior Fenian arms agent], confined in that prison. A whole street was laid in ruins, many lives were lost, and the surrounding neighbourhood greatly injured. [The Clerkenwell explosion, also known as the Clerkenwell Outrage, killed 12 people.]

12 Mar. 1868 (1869): Attempted assassination of the Duke of Edinburgh [Alfred, the second son of Queen Victoria] by an Irishman named O'Farrell, at a picnic held at Clontarf, near Port Jackson, New South Wales. O'Farrell was tried on **March 31st**, found guilty, and executed **April 21**.

> Henry James O'Farrell, who had briefly been employed by his brother as a law clerk, was an alcoholic who had been released from a lunatic asylum shortly before the assassination attempt. He approached the Prince from behind and shot him with a revolver to the right of the spine. The wounded Prince was treated for the next two weeks but did recover from his injury. He was the first member of the royal family to visit Australia.

10 Jan. 1872 (1873): Trial and conviction of Rev. John Selby Watson for the murder of his wife at Stockwell, on **8th October 1871**; sentenced to death, but afterwards reprieved. [Watson was found unconscious by his servant having taken prussic acid.

He had left a note to his doctor "I have killed my wife in a fit of rage to which she provoked me". He had battered her to death with his pistol butt. Watson pleaded insanity and served life imprisonment.]

29 Feb. 1872 (1873): The Queen, while entering Buckingham Palace Gardens, is attacked by a young man named O'Connor with an unloaded pistol. He was immediately arrested, and on following day examined before the magistrates at Bow Street.

AN INDECENT BOOK
21 June 1877 (1878): Mr. Charles Bradlaugh and Mrs. Annie Besant are condemned in the Court of Queen's Bench for publishing an indecent book. The jury find that the work ("Fruits of Philosophy") was calculated to debase public morals, but the defendants are exonerated from any corrupt motive in publishing it. [Bradlaugh was a political activist and the book, written by the American physician Charles Knowlton, advocated birth control. Bradlaugh attempted to get Charles Darwin to support him in his trial but Darwin refused.]

2 Mar. 1882 (1883): The Queen fired at by Roberick Maclean when leaving Windsor Railway Station. [This was the last of eight attempts over 40 years to kill or assault Queen Victoria. Maclean's motive was supposedly a terse reply to poetry he had sent her.]

11 June 1902 (1903): Arthur Lynch, who had been elected M.P. for Galway City, arrived in England, and was at once arrested on a charge of treason. In South Africa he was known as "Colonel" Lynch, and it was stated that he had fought against this country on the Boer side. [Lynch was tried for treason and sentenced to be hanged, which was changed to a life sentence. He was released a year later, then pardoned in 1907.]

25 Sept. 1902 (1903): Mr. John Kensit, a Paternoster Row bookseller, who had for some time previously made his name notorious by his anti-ritualistic meetings [the Protestant Truth Society which opposed the growing influence of the Oxford Movement over the Church of England], was seriously assaulted by roughs at Birkenhead. A chisel was thrown, hitting him on the head, and he died on **Oct. 8.**

MURDER IN THE NATIONAL PORTRAIT GALLERY
24 Feb. 1909 (1910): An American shot his wife in the National Portrait Gallery and then committed suicide.

> James Milner, the director of the gallery, was returning from lunch when he was told an elderly man had shot himself and a woman in the East Wing. After closing the wing, Mr. Milner found a police sergeant attending to the woman, still alive despite a gunshot wound to the head. The woman was carried on a stretcher through to the front entrance where a stretcher-ambulance was waiting. The director then ordered the floors to be cleaned and the man's body removed to prevent "further disfigurement of the floor". The couple were businessman John Tempest Dawson, aged 70 and his wife Nancy, 58. A coroner's report found Mr. Dawson to have committed the murder-suicide while insane.

DR CRIPPEN
13 July 1910 (1911): Mutilated remains supposed to be those of a former music-hall artiste, Belle Elmore, were discovered buried in the cellar of a house in Hilldrop Crescent, North London. A few days previously her husband, Hawley Harvey Crippen, an American doctor, disappeared in company with his typist, Ethel Le Neve. They were eventually located on an outward-bound Canadian liner, the woman in boy's clothing, and they were arrested on arrival on the Canadian side and brought back to London. After protracted inquiries before the magistrate and the coroner, Crippen was, on **Oct. 22** at the Central Criminal Court, found guilty of the murder of his wife and was sentenced to death. An appeal against the conviction was unsuccessful. His companion in his flight, Miss Le Neve, was, on **Oct. 25**, found not guilty of a charge of being an accessory after the fact and was acquitted. [Dr Crippen was the first criminal to be captured using wireless communication.]

THE SIDNEY STREET SIEGE
16 Dec. 1910 (1912): Suspecting a burglary at a jeweller's shop in Houndsditch, the police forced an entrance and were met immediately by a fusillade of bullets from quick-firing weapons, two sergeants and a constable being killed and two others seriously injured. The miscreants, who were aliens, escaped, but one of them, presumably accidentally shot by an accomplice, was discovered dying in a house in the vicinity a few hours later.

3 Jan. 1911 (1912): A remarkable sequel to the Houndsditch murders occurred at a house in Sidney Street in the East End. Two of the aliens implicated had been traced to the building, but an attempt to arrest them failed after one officer had been seriously wounded by a bullet. For seven hours the house was besieged, a continuous fire being kept up by the defenders, and returned by armed police and picked shots of the Scots Guards. The house finally took fire, and the two inmates perished in the flames. [The incident began a political row over the close involvement of the Home Secretary, Winston Churchill, who had stood in the line of fire.]

14 Feb. 1916 (1917): At the Old Bailey, William Gardiner Rigden, William Fownes Rigden, and Stanley Fownes Rigden, partners in the firm of glove manufacturers, were respectively fined £500, given 12 months' imprisonment, and given four months' imprisonment, and ordered to pay the costs, for trading with the enemy.

THE ILFORD MURDER
4 Oct. 1922 (1924): Percy Thompson, a clerk, was found dying from knife wounds in an Ilford street while on his way home from theatre with his wife. Later the wife, Edith Jessie Thompson, aged 28, and her lover, Edward Francis Bywaters, aged 20, a steward, who admitted killing Thompson, were arrested, and at the Old Bailey on **Dec. 11** both were found guilty of wilful murder and sentenced to death. Appeals failed and they were executed on **Jan. 9, 1923.**

THE CASE OF NEVILLE HEATH
22 June 1946 (1947): Body of Mrs. Margery Gardner found in her room at guest house at Notting Hill Gate, and police began search for South African named Neville George Clevely Heath. On **July 3** Miss Doreen Marshall was missing from Bournemouth hotel in which she was staying and 5 days later her body was found partly buried in Branksome Dean Chine. Meanwhile Heath had been questioned and on **July 8** he was remanded charged with murder of Mrs. Gardner. He was charged with murder of Miss Marshall on **July 29** and was committed for trial on both charges. After three-day trial at Central Criminal Court, Heath was on **Sept. 26** found guilty of murder of Mrs. Gardner and was sentenced to death, the other charge not being proceeded with, although his counsel mentioned it. Heath did not appeal and he was hanged at Pentonville on **Oct. 16.**

THE ACID BATH MURDERER
18 Feb. 1949 (1950): Wealthy widow, Mrs. Olive Durand-Deacon, aged 69, disappeared from London hotel where she had lived. Search by police resulted in discovery at small factory at Crawley of remains of a body practically destroyed by immersion in acid, and on **March 2** John George Haigh, company director, who lived at same hotel as Mrs. Durand-Deacon, was at Horsham charged with her murder. He pleaded insanity at his trial at Lewes Assizes where on **July 19** he was found guilty and sentenced to death, statements being read attributing to him murders of 8 other people. After examination by panel of experts in mental diseases Haigh was hanged on **Aug. 10.**

THE GREAT TRAIN ROBBERY
8 Aug. 1963 (1964): Scotland to London overnight post office express was ambushed and robbed after signals had been tampered with near Cheddington, Buckinghamshire. Sum of £2,626,000 was finally found to have been stolen. On **Aug. 13**, empty mailbags and 3 abandoned vehicles were found at unoccupied farm at Oakley, Buckinghamshire, about 20 miles from Cheddington; on **Aug. 15**, 3 men and 2 women were arrested and charged with offences connected with the robbery, and it was stated that notes to value of £102,000 had been found; on **Aug. 16** further £101,000 was found in wood near Dorking and on **Aug. 21** another £30,000 was discovered concealed in caravan which police moved from site at Box Hill.

8 July 1965 (1966): Ronald Arthur Biggs, who was serving sentence of 30 years' imprisonment for his part in mail train robbery, escaped from Wandsworth Gaol with 3 other prisoners. [15 months after he began his sentence, Biggs used a rope ladder to clamber over the prison walls into a waiting removal van.]

The Great Train Robbery has gone down in history as one of the most infamous robberies of all time. As the train passed south at 3 a.m., the driver, Jack Mills saw a red signal at Sears Crossing. A glove had been stuffed onto the correct signal and a red light activated by attaching it to a six volt battery.

The train stopped and the co-driver, David Whitby, was thrown down the railway embankment after he had gone to investigate the problem. A masked man climbed the train cab and knocked the driver unconscious. The gang's plan was to uncouple most of the carriages and drive the cab and the money a mile further to waiting Land Rovers. The gang's driver realised the diesel train was more complicated to use than trains he had experience with, so Ronnie Biggs roused the driver to assist with the controls.

After eventually being caught, the gang received a total of 307 years' imprisonment. Ronnie Biggs escaped prison in 1965 and lived abroad for 40 years before returning voluntarily to the UK in 2001.

THE KRAY TWINS
5 Mar. 1969 (1970): The Kray twins, Ronald and Reginald, were sentenced at Central Criminal Court to life imprisonment for murder; the judge recommended that they should be detained for minimum of 30 years; Ronald Kray was sentenced for the murders of George Cornell and Jack McVitie, and Reginald Kray for the murder of the latter; Christopher Lambrianou and his brother Anthony, and Ronald Bender were all sentenced to life imprisonment for the murder of McVitie; John Barrie received life imprisonment for the murder of Cornell; and Charles Kray, eldest brother of the twins, Frederick Foreman, Albert Donaghue and Cornelius

Whitehead all received sentences ranging from two years to ten years for being accessories to the murder of McVitie.

24 Apr. 1969 (1970): Ronald and Charles Kray were acquitted, on direction of the judge at Central Criminal Court, of murder of Frank Mitchell, known as the "Mad Axeman", who escaped from Dartmoor Prison in 1966; and on **May 16**, Reginald Kray and Frederick Foreman were also found not guilty of the murder; Foreman, however, was found guilty of plotting Mitchell's escape and was sentenced to five years' imprisonment.

The identical twins were the most notorious criminals of the 1960s, whose criminal activities and obsession with personal power culminated in the operation of a serious protection racket in London. With their gang The Firm, they were involved in numerous crimes including robberies, arson, assaults and murders. The twins were also nightclub owners in the West End, and mixed with the rich and famous such as Frank Sinatra and Diana Dors.

Following their arrest in 1968, they were sentenced to life imprisonment, with Ronnie dying of a heart attack in Broadmoor Hospital in 1995; Reggie was released on compassionate grounds in August 2000, a few weeks before his death from cancer.

EXPLORATION

The date in parentheses indicates the edition each of the following extracts was taken from.

10 Nov. 1871 (1873): Dr. Livingstone discovered at Ujiji, in Central Africa, by Mr. Henry Stanley, an American newspaper correspondent.

> This is the moment in history when Stanley greeted Dr Livingstone with the famous line "Dr Livingstone, I presume?"

27 Aug. 1872 (1873): The Queen presents Mr. Stanley, the discoverer of Dr. Livingstone with a handsome snuffbox, and a letter thanking him for the service rendered.

8 Aug. 1877 (1878): Mr. H. M. Stanley, the African explorer, arrives at the Congo River, on the West Coast of Africa, having traversed the entire continent from east to west, and proving the Lualaba River to be identical with the Congo.

28 June 1909 (1910): Lieut. Shackleton gave an account of his expedition before the Royal Geographic Society, the Prince and Princess of Wales being present.

GEOGRAPHICAL PROGRESS AND TERRITORIAL CHANGES, 1909
As recorded in the 1910 edition

Towards the end of March came the news of the return of Mr. (now Sir E.) Shackleton's Expedition, after a remarkable success had been achieved; the advance into the unknown area around the South Pole, begun by Capt. Scott during the National Antarctic Expedition of 1901–4, having been carried forward at one step no less a distance than 430 miles from the Pole itself. So near an approach to that point was not known to have been previously made by man in either hemisphere. This achievement, performed amidst immense hardships and dangers, was the work of Sir E. Shackleton himself and two companions, who during their dash south early in 1909, having reached the point where the coast of South Victoria Land trends to the east, struck inland into the heart of the Antarctic continent, climbing its mountain fringe until the great plateau, 9,000 to 10,000 feet in altitude, apparently stretching to the Pole itself, was gained. The three explorers only turned in 88° 23' S., when their strength was rapidly failing, and the return to the base was a constant struggle against famine and illness.

SCOTT OF THE ANTARCTIC
As recorded in the 1914 edition

15 Nov. 1912: Capt. Amundsen, the discoverer of the South Pole, gave a lecture upon his expedition before the Royal Geographical Society.

10 Feb. 1913: The news reached London that Capt. Scott and four of his companions had lost their lives in the Antarctic, while returning to their base after having reached the South Pole. Capt. Scott, Lieut. Bowers and Dr. Wilson died from exposure on **March 29**, and Capt. Oates on **March 17**. Petty Officer Evans, it was stated, succumbed from injuries. In his final message Capt. Scott wrote: "I do not think human beings ever came through such a month as we have come through."

The nation was stirred to its depths, in the early part of February, 1913, by the tidings of grievous disaster to the British Antarctic Expedition under Capt. Scott, the leader and four companions have perished from want on their return from the South Pole. The universal grief was, however, mingled with admiration for the inspiring example of fortitude set by the lost heroes. A year before, on the return of Capt. Scott's ship with the news that his last supporting party had left him well on the way to the Pole, confidence was felt that the leader's proved qualities would have carried him through (like his rival, Amundsen, only a month sooner) to the desired goal. That confidence was not misplaced, though the measure of anxiety which could not but be felt also was likewise, unhappily, only too justified. The Pole was reached on **January 18, 1912**, and the records left there by Amundsen were found at his camp. During the return over the high plateau the health of Petty Officer Evans caused anxiety, and progress was thereby delayed. His condition was rendered worse by a fall and injury to his head during the descent of Beardmore glacier, and he succumbed on **February 17**. On the ice-barrier below, the lateness of the season and persistent bad weather, with the breakdown of another of the party, Capt. Oates, more and more reduced the rate of progress, and the supplies became rapidly exhausted. On **March 17**, Capt. Oates, feeling himself but a drag on his companions, walked out into the blizzard and was not seen again. Capt. Scott, with Dr. Wilson and Lieut. Bowers, struggled on to within 11 miles of safety, but, their strength being then exhausted, and the blizzard raging with unabated fury, they awaited their end in the tent with calm fortitude, their bodies being eventually found and buried with due honours by a search party. Capt. Scott spent his last hours in writing a touching appeal to the nation in behalf of the dependents of those who perished – an appeal which found a ready response at home.

SHACKLETON'S EXPEDITION
As recorded in the 1917 edition

The principal event has been the return of Sir E. Shackleton from his daring venture in the Antarctic – unsuccessful as regards his hope of crossing the Antarctic continent from the Weddell to the Ross Sea, but with a record of pluck and endurance which has made the voyage one of the most remarkable in the history of Polar discovery. The *Endurance* left South Georgia on **Dec. 6, 1914**, sighting Coats Land on **Jan. 10, 1915**, and tracing 200 miles of new coast-line to the south. But the abnormal cold of the season made it impossible even to land, the ship being beset in February, and drifted through the ensuing winter at the mercy of the currents of the Weddell Sea. These, after taking the ship S.W. to 77°, set to the N.W. and brought the voyagers into lower latitudes; but the increasingly severe ice-pressure at last resulted in the crushing and forced abandonment of the vessel (**Oct. 27, 1915**). All efforts to advance over the ice proved fruitless, and progress north was only effected by the slow drift of the ice. On **April 8, 1916**, the break-up of the ice forced the party to take to their boats, in which they fought their way through heavy seas and drifting ice to the South Shetlands, where a landing was effected on Elephant Island. Leaving twenty-two men in a precarious position here, the leader, with five volunteers, started on the forlorn hope of reaching South Georgia, across 700 miles of stormy seas, in order to obtain succour. The venture was successful, and on the news reaching England steps were promptly taken to organise a relief expedition. Sir Ernest himself made repeated efforts to succour his men with the means available in the Southern Hemisphere, and after several vain attempts the desired end was achieved by a vessel fitted out for the purpose by the Chilean Government.

CONQUERING EVEREST
2 June 1953 (1954): The Queen on her Coronation Day sent congratulations to Everest expedition on reaching summit.

It was on the **29 May 1953** when the New Zealander Edmund Hillary and the Nepalese Sherpa Tenzing Norgay became the first people to reach the summit of Mount Everest, the highest peak on the planet. News of the achievement did not reach home until **June 2**, the eve of the coronation. Hillary was knighted on his return.

Sir Edmund Hillary died aged 88 in January 2008; Tenzing Norgay in 1986.

MAN'S FIRST LANDING ON THE MOON
As recorded in the 1970 edition

With the words "That's one small step for a man, one giant leap for mankind," American astronaut Neil Armstrong realized an age-old dream of humanity when he took the first step on the surface of the Moon at 3.56 a.m. B.S.T. on Monday, **July 21, 1969**. America's £10,000,000,000 programme for landing a man on the Moon in this current decade had come to success sooner than many would have believed even a short year before. Perhaps the words uttered by Armstrong were a little uncharacteristic of the more laconic comments he made during the nine days in which the world's gaze was fixed, *via* television, on *Apollo 11* and its historic journey. But they did elicit an immediate response from the millions watching the strange shadowy scene as the American foot in the heavy boot of the spaceman's outfit lowered hesitantly to the lunar surface. Armstrong, with his colleagues, Col. Michael Collins and Col. Edwin (Buzz) Aldrin, took off from Cape Kennedy in their spacecraft at the head of a 7,500,000lbs. thrust Saturn V rocket on **July 16**. Two and a half days later they crossed the point at which the Moon's gravitational pull becomes dominant over that of the Earth and four hours after that they were behind the Moon, going into orbit about it. On Sunday, **July 20**, Armstrong and Aldrin entered the lunar landing module, code-named *Eagle,* leaving Collins behind in the command ship, *Columbia,* and descended for the first manned landing on the Moon. Using the landing craft's rocket motors they delicately picked their way between craters, avoiding the spot originally chosen because at the last moment its unsuitability became apparent, to drop the last few feet to a level spot in the Sea of Tranquility. With everything going faultlessly the programme was speeded up for Armstrong to become the first man to set foot on an extra-terrestrial body just over five hours after the landing. He was followed by Aldrin and together they planted the U.S. flag in the dusty surface, collected rock samples and set up scientific experiments. Armstrong spent 2 hours 32 minutes on the lunar surface, Aldrin 1 hour and 43 minutes, before returning to *Eagle* which took off after a stay of 21 hours and 37 minutes. Just under four hours later they had joined up with Collins 69 miles above the Moon's surface ready for the return to Earth. In the official film of the expedition one thing more than any, even more than the footprints in the lunar dust, brought home the immensity of the achievement. That was the view of the cratered and scared surface of the Moon, taken by Collins in the command ship, with the appearance to one side, of a minute pinpoint of light. That light was the Sun reflecting off the ascent stage of *Eagle* as it soared towards the rendezvous in space. That speck grew, the light changed as rocket engines fired and then the module came fully into view, with the sun glinting in innumerable reflections on its insect-like body, a strange man-made object against the stranger lunar background.

Despite forebodings that the operation was directed more towards achieving prestigious ends than scientific ones, as a piece of space one-up-man-ship over the Russians, it appeared afterwards that the scientific rewards of the mission would be considerable. Preliminary examination of the rocks and the first reports of the scientific experiments left behind gave a picture of the Moon and its history entirely different from that of the Earth. The findings were not at all clear but they indicated a present-day Moon uniformly cool throughout, unlike the Earth with its distinct layers of cool crust, warm underlying mantle and molten core. Taking together the findings suggested, said NASA: "The Moon may be like a great shattered brittle ball beneath its crust, fractured into huge rock blocks with fissures and cracks penetrating deep into the interior; the Mascons, the concentrations of mass which make the Moon exert an uneven gravitational pull on orbiting spacecraft, are probably the Moon's maria themselves, rather than some unseen feature beneath them; lunar dust is fully 50 per cent glass in tiny rods and globe shaped particles." The surprisingly abundant glass, the high store of radioactivity in the lunar samples brought back, the high density of the rocks compared to the rest of the lunar surface and the age of the Moon's surface, at least 3,100 million years, all indicated a lunar history surprisingly different from that of Earth.

THE TRANSGLOBE EXPEDITION
As recorded in the 1983 edition

The three-year, 35,000-mile, circumnavigation of the earth, the first to be carried out via the North and South Poles, finally came to an end on **August 29th, 1982** when the British Transglobe expedition ship, *Benjamin Bowring*, returned to Greenwich, whence it had sailed on **September 2nd, 1979**. It was welcomed by thousands lining the banks and the Prince of Wales, patron of the Expedition, took the ship's helm for a brief period during the journey up the Thames.

The explorers, Sir Ranulph Fiennes, Charles Burton and Oliver Sheppard (who had dropped out after the Antarctic for domestic reasons) had crossed the Sahara Desert, in **October 1979**, sailed to Cape Town and arrived in Antarctica on **January 5th, 1980**. They reached the South Pole, almost a year later, on **December 17th**. From New Zealand, in March 1981, and Australia, in April, they sailed to Los Angeles and thence to Vancouver. Following a boat trip down the Yukon River and after entering the North West Passage to attain Ellesmere Island, they reached the North Pole in **April 1982**. Extremes of weather were compounded by misfortune, most disastrously a fire, which destroyed several of the expedition vehicles and seemed at first sight to threaten its whole future.

On **March 15th, 1982**, a plane flew through difficult conditions to deliver emergency equipment and supplies to the explorers after Sir Ranulph's snowmobile had disappeared into a 20-ft ice crevasse. Burton held on to the sinking vehicle until his hands were frozen but long enough for Sir Ranulph to drag two crates of vital supplies onto the ice. By clinging on, Burton saved the expedition's radio gear but a lot of equipment was lost.

The two men spent the night sharing the same sleeping bag with just a tent flysheet and tarpaulin for cover. When the aircraft delivered a replacement snowmobile, the explorers started cutting ice blocks to build a bridge across the biggest crevice to get started again. They were then confronted with an unseasonal rise in temperatures and the ice cracked all around them. They were unable to use their snowmobiles for 36 hours. Subsequently they moved on to another floe after the giant floe on which they had been trapped collided with another. However, conditions eventually eased and on **March 26th** it was reported that the two men were back on course after two days of relatively smooth going.

By **April 9th**, the explorers had only 25 miles to go and then on **April 11th** they reached the Pole itself where they celebrated with a magnum of champagne and flew the Union flag. They were now faced with a 600-mile trek to the edge of the ice-cap to rendezvous with the expedition ship. By **June 17th** they had spent the past six weeks on an ice floe waiting for the pack ice to melt and were some 227 miles from the place where their ship was to pick them up for the last leg to Spitzbergen. The *Benjamin Bowring* made an attempt to reach them in mid-July but had to pull out because of ice closing around it, but on **August 5th** the explorers were aboard the vessel homeward bound, although unfavourable winds slowed the voyage and compacted ice around it.

The expedition, although primarily a test of human endeavour, had a scientific and commercial purpose as well and attracted sponsors in 18 different countries. It was able to test equipment in extremes of heat and cold and valuable export orders were won.

SHIPPING

The date in parentheses indicates the edition each of the following extracts was taken from.

4 Mar. 1872 (1873): Wreck of a ship off Cornwall, with all hands; the wife and child of the captain saved by the sagacity of a Newfoundland dog.

THE SINKING OF THE NORTHFLEET
22 Jan. 1873 (1874): The ship *Northfleet* is cut down and sunk by the Spanish steamer *Murillo*, off Dungeness, with loss of upwards of 300 lives.

4 Nov. 1873 (1874): The steamer *Murillo* is condemned by the High Court of Admiralty, at the suit of the owners of the *Northfleet*, sunk by the former.

The *Northfleet* was a British full-rigged trade ship built in 1853 and spent her career travelling between England and Australia, India and China.

At the time of the sinking, the *Northfleet* had been dispatched carrying labourers, their families and equipment to build a railway line in Tasmania, but bad weather had forced the ship to drop anchor at Dungeness and around 10.30p.m. the Spanish steamship *Murillo* ran her down before disappearing. Two hundred and ninety three people drowned, including the captain but 86 were saved. The *Murillo* was finally stopped off Dover in September 1873.

THE BATTLE OF PACOCHA
29 May 1877 (1878): Engagement between the British ships *Shah* and *Amethyst* and the Peruvian ironclad *Huascar*, off Ylo, on the coast of Peru, for alleged piratical acts against British subjects.

The Battle of Pacocha occurred during an attempted revolution by Nicolás de Piérola in Peru. Piérola had used the ironclad *Huascar* to board British merchant ships, having previously used it for the purpose of sabotage against the Peruvian government. As a consequence, Rear Admiral de Horsey was sent to capture the *Huascar*. With the HMS *Shah* and the HMS *Amethyst*, the British ships fired many times at the enemy but as they did not carry armour-piercing ammunition, the *Huascar* was mostly unharmed. The battle saw the first use in history of a self-propelled torpedo in warfare but the missile failed to hit the *Huascar*, which escaped only to surrender to the Peruvian government two days later.

5 Dec. 1881 (1883): Captain Brownrigg and three men of H.M.S. *London* killed at Pemba, on the Zanzibar coast, while attacking a slave dhow.

5 Oct. 1887 (1888): The P. & O. steamer *Victoria* reached Gibraltar from Plymouth in 69 hours: the fastest run on record.

5 Aug. 1897 (1898): Mr. T. C. Garth's *Hyacinth* won the German Emperor's Cup at Cowes, and H.R.H. the Prince of Wales' *Britannia* won the "Meteor Challenge Shield."

2 Dec. 1901 (1903): H.M. sloop *Condor* sailed from Esquimault for Honolulu. After this date no further definite news of the vessel was ever received, though life-belts, the dinghy, and other articles of her equipment were from time to time picked up on the high seas, and, after a protracted search, the ship was eventually given up as lost.

21 Feb. 1907 (1908): The G. E. Ry. Steamship *Berlin* stranded while trying to enter the waterway of the Maas River, Hook of Holland, and broke in half; the fore part foundered, causing great loss of life, and the remainder stranded with a few survivors, 15 of whom were eventually rescued after terrible privations.

THE SINKING OF THE SS OCEANA
16 Mar. 1912 (1913): The P. & O. Liner *Oceana* sank after collision with the German barque *Pisagua* off Beachy Head, 14 lives being lost through the swamping of one of the liner's boats.

The SS *Oceana* was built in 1888 by Harland and Wolff of Belfast. Originally assigned the task of taking passengers and mail to Australia, later routes took her from the UK to India.

The day prior to the collision, the *Oceana* had finished loading for the voyage to Bombay. It is alleged that on board was £747,110 worth of gold and silver ingots.

Sailing the following day within the Strait of Dover, she was approached by the *Pisagua* who was on her way from Chile to Hamburg. The captain of the German boat burnt a warning flare which was registered by the *Oceana*. However, the manoeuvre of the British steamship was too slow considering the speed of the German vessel and the collision left a 40 foot gash in her side.

A nearby boat, the TSS *Sussex* attended the scene and rescued the 241 survivors. The day following the disaster, divers were sent to recover the bullion in an operation which lasted ten days.

THE TITANIC

10 Apr. 1912 (1913): The new White Star liner *Titanic*, the largest vessel afloat, sailed on her disastrous maiden voyage from Southampton to New York.

14 Apr. 1912 (1913): On her maiden voyage to New York, the White Star liner *Titanic* (45,000 tons) collided with an iceberg, and sank a few hours later. Wireless distress signals were sent out, but the vessels that picked up the messages arrived too late to render assistance. Of the 2,206 persons on board the liner, 703 escaped in boats and some hours later were picked up by the *Carpathia*, the number of victims reaching the appalling total of 1,503. Among the latter were Mr. W. T. Stead [William Thomas Stead, journalist and editor] and Mr. C. M. Hays [Charles Melville Hays], President of the Grand Trunk Railway. The unparalleled disaster was marked by an absence of panic and a maintenance of discipline. World-wide sympathy was expressed and many relief funds were opened for those who had suffered.

> The *Titanic*, which was called "unsinkable" at the time of her construction, resulted in the death of 1,502 people (revised). The disintegrating wreck, which was discovered in 1985, is located 370 miles south east of the coast of Newfoundland and lies at a depth of 12,500 feet.

24 Apr. 1912 (1913): Dissatisfaction with the supply and safety of the boats led to a strike of firemen on board the White Star liner *Olympic*, shortly before its departure from Southampton, and further developments led to the abandonment of the voyage three days later. 53 of the men were subsequently arrested and charged with disobeying the lawful commands of the captain, but the magistrates, although finding the charges fully proved, inflicted no penalties, the exceptional circumstances of the *Titanic* being taken into consideration.

10 Aug. 1912 (1913): The Allan liner *Corsican* struck an iceberg while on a voyage to Liverpool; no damage was done, as the vessel was proceeding slowly.

THE SINKING OF THE LUSITANIA
As recorded in the 1916 edition

7 May 1915: Sinking of the great Cunard liner *Lusitania* by two torpedoes fired by a German submarine off the Old Head of Kinsale; 1,134 lives lost.

Diary of the War
The unarmed Cunard liner *Lusitania* struck by two torpedoes and sunk, with the loss of 1,134 lives by a German submarine off the Old Head of Kinsale. Many distinguished people, of whom a large number were citizens of the United States, were passengers. Among those who were drowned were Mr. A. G. Vanderbilt [Alfred Gwynne Vanderbilt I, a member of the Vanderbilt family of philanthropists],

Mr. A. L. Hopkins [Albert Hopkins, president of a shipbuilding company], and Mr. Charles Frohman, the actor-manager [theatre producer]. [The number who died is now considered to be 1,198.]

THE BATTLE OF JUTLAND
As recorded in the 1917 edition

31 May 1916: A great naval battle took place off the coast of Jutland. The Grand Fleet came into touch with the German High Seas Fleet. The leading ships of the two fleets carried on a vigorous fight. The losses were heavy on both sides, but when the main body of the British Fleet came into contact with the German High Seas Fleet, the latter, who had been severely punished, quickly sought refuge in their protected waters. This manoeuvre was rendered possible by low visibility and mist, no continuous action being possible. The pursuit was continued until the light wholly failed, the British destroyers making a successful attack upon the enemy during the night. Sir John Jellicoe, having driven the enemy into port, returned to his bases, refuelled his fleet, and in the evening of **June 2** was again ready to put to sea. The German losses were the battle-cruiser *Lutzow*, the pre-Dreadnought battleship *Pommern*, 5 light cruisers, 5 torpedo-boat destroyers, 1 submarine (admitted by the Germans, but probably greater: other ships were badly damaged). The British losses were H.M.S. *Queen Mary*, *Indefatigable*, *Invincible*, *Defence*, *Black Prince*, *Warrior*, and 8 torpedo-boat destroyers. Rear-Adm. Sir R. Arbuthnot and Rear-Adm. the Hon. H. Hood went down with their flagships.

> The Battle of Jutland was the largest naval battle of the First World War, which saw many thousands killed, wounded and captured. Both sides claimed victory but the true result was inconclusive. However, although the British press criticised the fleet's failure to win the battle, the British supremacy of the North Sea was preserved.

DUNKIRK EVACUATION
As recorded in the 1941 edition

30 May – 4 June 1940: Announced that Allied retreat had been carried out with great skill and daring and that thousands of men had reached England from Dunkirk with help of Navy and R.A.F. Destroyers *Grafton*, *Grenade* and *Wakeful* and transport *Aboukir* lost in helping B.E.F. [British Expeditionary Force]. Admiralty stated that 222 British naval vessels, and 665 other British craft, mostly small boats, took part in evacuation from Dunkirk. Six destroyers and 24 minor war vessels had been lost. 300 German planes dropped over 1,000 bombs on Paris, causing 900 casualties. [...] Dunkirk abandoned by the Allies. Mr. Churchill told Commons that 335,000 British and French troops had been evacuated and that

British losses were 30,000 killed, wounded and missing, 1,000 guns and all transport and armoured vehicles. In historic speech, Premier declared we should defend our island, whatever the cost. "We shall fight on the beaches, in the fields, in the streets and in the hills. We shall never surrender."

The evacuation of Dunkirk, took place between **27 May** and **4 June** and was codenamed Operation Dynamo. Approximately 900 naval and civilian vessels journeyed across the English Channel and 338,226 people were rescued. A BBC radio announcement was issued to all owners of pleasure craft between 30 feet to 100 feet in length to lend the vessels to the Royal Navy.

Although the German forces captured over one million Allied prisoners in three weeks, the evacuation was a huge boost to British morale in the war effort. Winston Churchill hailed the evacuation as a "miracle of deliverance".

---

10 Dec. 1942 (1943): *Famous Battleships sunk:* Prime Minister in Commons announced that *Prince of Wales* and *Repulse* had been sunk in operations off Malaya. Later news showed losses were caused by torpedoes from aircraft and our warships were without air support. Admiral Sir Tom Phillips, new Commander-in-Chief, was lost; about 130 officers and 2,200 ratings were saved.

SUCCESSFUL LANDINGS IN NORMANDY
6 June 1944 (1945): The greatest operation of its kind began with the landing of Allied Army of Liberation on beaches of Normandy. After 5,000 tons of bombs had been dropped by R.A.F. on enemy coastal batteries, and mass airborne landings behind German lines, British, American and Canadian troops fought their way ashore on broad front east of Cherbourg Peninsula under cover of fighters and warships. […] Over 4,000 ships and thousands of smaller craft were engaged, naval casualties being very light, and thousands of sorties were flown by Allied aircraft to bomb enemy positions and communications.

D-Day: The Normandy Landings, codenamed Operation Neptune, was the largest amphibious invasion in history. The successful attack on five Normandy beaches (codenamed Gold, Juno, Omaha, Sword and Utah) formed the landing operations of the Allied invasion of Normandy, codenamed Operation Overlord.

The invasion resulted in the Allied liberation of western Europe from the control of Nazi Germany and marked the beginning of the end of the war in Europe.

THE BRITISH
EMPIRE

THE BRITISH EMPIRE

The main events relating to the British Empire which feature in *Whitaker's Almanack* (first edition published 1868) are as follows:

1878	Cyprus becomes a British colony
1894	Uganda becomes a British protectorate
1899	The Second Boer War begins
1901	Colonies of New South Wales, Victoria, Queensland, Van Diemen's Land (later Tasmania), South Australia, and Western Australia unite to form the Commonwealth of Australia and gain Dominion status
1907	New Zealand gains Dominion status
1914	[The First World War begins]
	Egypt becomes a British protectorate
1918	[The First World War ends]
1919	German African colonies gained by Britain
1920	British East Africa becomes Kenya
1922	Egypt gains independence
1925	Cyprus becomes a British colony
1930	Indian National Congress issues declaration of independence for India
1939	[The Second World War begins]
1941	Fall of Hong Kong to the Japanese
1942	Fall of Malaya, Singapore and Burma to the Japanese
1944	Burma recaptured from the Japanese
1945	[The Second World War ends]
1947	India granted independence; Pakistan created
1948	Burma and Ceylon granted independence; end of British mandate in Palestine
1949	Ireland leaves the Commonwealth
1952	[Elizabeth II ascends the throne]
1957	Ghana, Gold Coast, and Malayan states become independent
1959	Cyprus joins the Commonwealth
1961	Sierra Leone becomes independent; South Africa leaves the Commonwealth
1962	Jamaica, Trinidad and Tobago, Uganda, and Western Samoa become independent
1963	Kenya and Zanzibar granted independence
1964	Malawi and Malta become independent
1966	Botswana, Gambia and Lesotho granted independence
1970	Fiji and Tonga granted independence
1971	Bahrain and Qatar become independent
1973	The Bahamas become independent
1975	Papua New Guinea becomes independent
1976	Seychelles granted independence
1978	Dominica granted independence
1980	Zimbabwe granted independence
1981	Belize becomes independent
1984	Sino-British agreement on future of Hong Kong
1987	Fiji leaves Commonwealth
1996	South Africa rejoins Commonwealth
1997	Hong Kong becomes Chinese territory, as agreed in 1984

Introduction to 'The British Empire'
As recorded in the 1878 edition

The British Empire is grander than those of Greece or Rome, or any other, and it may be safely asserted that its rule is more beneficent. Wherever the flag of England floats there is freedom. Justice is impartially administered, and no man can be punished except for infringements of the law. Religion is also free. With all its anomalies, the British Empire under its present Sovereign, presents the nearest approach to a true Commonwealth that the world has yet seen.

In the following brief table an abstract is given (approximately) of the area, population, revenue, public debt, and commerce of the British Empire. The figures given are near enough for the purpose, although it is to be regretted that the precise amounts can not be procured.

Name of Country	Area Sq. miles	Population thousands	Revenue £ thousands	Public Debt £ thousands	Imports and Exports £ thousands
Great Britain and Ireland	121,155	33,000	80,000	730,000	632,000
Indian Possessions, etc.	1,558,254	240,000	50,000	131,000	100,000
Other Eastern Possessions	25,268	3,200	2,200	1,800	35,000
Australasia	3,087,000	2,500	11,000	45,000	80,000
North America	3,620,500	4,000	4,500	23,000	48,000
Guiana, etc.	100,000	200	375	500	4,000
Africa	250,000	1,500	1,000	1,600	8,000
West Indies, etc.	12,707	1,100	110	1,000	10,000
European Possessions	120	160	210	250	20,000
Various Settlements	96,171	200	550	650	2,000
Totals	**8,871,135**	**285,860**	**149,945**	**934,800**	**939,000**

The following is part of an essay, as recorded in the 1897 edition, on the sixtieth anniversary of Queen Victoria's Reign:

On the 20th of June, 1897, Her Majesty Queen Victoria will have completed the sixtieth year of her reign, a reign which is now the longest in the history of the English people. It will therefore be fitting to give a short summary of the leading events which have taken place during this long period, and to set before the reader in the briefest possible fashion, a general outline of the changes, political and social, which have marked out the Victorian era, and have given it the pre-eminent importance which it must necessarily claim in all future histories of the English nation.

To describe in detail the enlargement and expansion of our Indian and Colonial Empire during this period would take up more space than we can spare, but even the bare outline of the territories which have been added to British rule far surpass the conquests of any previous reign. It would not be accurate to say that the whole of India has been added to the Empire, though as a matter of fact, before the year 1858 the then British territories in India were governed, not by the Queen, but by the East India Company. Between 1837 and that date, however, the territories of Scind, of the Sikhs, Tanjore, the seaboard provinces of Burma, Sattara, Jhansi, Nagpur, and lastly Oude, had been brought under English dominion. Since 1858 annexation has been less busy, but in 1884–88 Upper Burma and the Shan States were added, and the frontier of Afghanistan defined; in 1891 the small State of Manipur was absorbed, and last year it was decided to annex the province of Chitral, which has for some time been the scene of disturbances which were finally put down by the gallant efforts of Sir Robert Low and Colonel Kelly.

In the Southern Hemisphere it may almost be said that the growth of our vast Australian dominion has been contemporary with the Queen's reign, for the various colonies before that date had scarcely been commenced, and were hardly more than penal settlements. Of the seven separate colonies into which the Australian continent is now divided, New South Wales, Victoria, South Australia, Queensland, West Australia, New Zealand and Tasmania, only New South Wales and Tasmania had a separate colonial existence when the Queen ascended the throne. Since then New Zealand in 1841, Victoria in 1851, South Australia in 1856, Queensland in 1859, and West Australia in 1890 respectively, have been constituted separate colonies, and New South Wales received in 1855 the constitution under which it is at present governed. In 1837 the population of the whole of Australia can hardly have exceeded a few thousands; according to the latest returns now available, it reaches the total of 3,400,000 in round numbers, the vast majority of whom are of British descent. Besides this wonderful development of our Australian possessions, in 1881 the island of Fiji was annexed, and in 1884 British New Guinea, while the

English flag also waves over several islands in the Western Pacific under the charge of the Governor of Fiji.

In North America, the territorial extent of our Empire remains much the same as at the beginning of the Queen's reign, though in population, wealth and general development, the progress made during the past sixty years is almost as great as that in other parts of the British possessions. In 1841 the population is stated at about one-and-a-half millions, in 1891 it was nearly five millions, an increase of more than threefold. During the past twenty years, for example, the population of Winnipeg, in Manitoba, has increased from 241 in 1871 to 25,642 in 1891, while the city of Vancouver, in British Columbia, which in 1885 had no existence, six years later had a population of 13,685.

In South and Eastern Africa, the expansion of British influence has been equally marked, particularly during the last decade, and there is every prospect that progress in the immediate future will be even greater. Since 1837, when Cape Town was our only possession in South Africa, we have added to our colonies Natal in 1843, Basutoland in 1884, Bechuanaland in 1885, and Zululand in 1887. In 1889 the British South Africa Company received a Royal Charter entrusting it with the development of the immense territory lying to the South of the Zambesi, which in 1888 had been assigned to British rule. In May, 1891, the sphere of the Company was extended to the north of the Zambesi, and now includes the whole of British South Africa from Mafeking to Tanganyika, an area of 750,000 square miles.

In East Africa the "British East African Protectorate" extends British influence over some 468,000 square miles from the eastern coast to the Congo State on the west, and from the German sphere on the south indefinitely towards Khartoum and Egypt on the north. Zanzibar also is now under British control and has been a British Protectorate since 1890.

On the West Coast the influence of Britain is maintained by the Niger Coast Protectorate, which in 1891 was placed under an Imperial Commissioner, and includes the whole maritime region lying between Lagos and the Rio del Rey. The Royal Niger Company, which received its charter in 1886, under the control of the Secretary of State, maintains 44 stations on the Niger, and promises larger and extensive developments. In other parts of the West Coast, the settlements of the Gold Coast, Lagos and Gambia were separated from the government of Sierra Leone in 1874, 1886, and 1888 respectively.

ACQUISITION OF CYPRUS IN 1878
As recorded in the 1879 edition

The latest acquisition of the British Crown is an island of the Levant, situated at the eastern end of the Mediterranean Sea, between N. lat. 34° 30' and 35° 45', E. long. 32° 15' and 34° 40'; about 50 miles distant from the coast of Asia Minor, and 60 miles from its N. E. extremity to the port of Latakia on the Syrian coast, with which it is connected by a submarine telegraph cable; the distance to Port Said, at the entrance to the Suez Canal, is 240 miles.

> "High and Low are delighted..." wrote Queen Victoria to Prime Minister Benjamin Disraeli, of public reaction to his acquisition of Cyprus from the Ottoman Empire in 1878. The Sultan of Turkey agreed to lease the island to Britain as a reserve *place d'armes,* a base from which Britain could help to defend Turkey's Asian provinces against Russian encroachment but its more obvious, if unmentioned role, was defence of the Suez Canal, in which Britain had acquired an interest. Once Britain was established in Egypt, however, Cyprus was no longer such a strategic outpost.

The larger part of the island is an irregular parallelogram, 90 miles in length, with an average breadth of 40 miles; extended N. E. by a narrow hornlike projection 45 miles long. The area is calculated to be about 4,000 square miles. A narrow range of mountains skirts the N. coast, the central and southern portions of the island being occupied by a much more extensive range and its offshoots, the highest points, Mt. Troodos (Olympus), rising to 6,590 feet above the sea. Between these lies the great plain of Messaria, stretching across the island from E. to W., on which the capital is situated. The rivers are mere mountain torrents, the largest being the Pidias, which rises in the southern mountains, and flowing E., through the plain, discharges its waters into the plain of Famagusta, near the ancient port of Salamis. The soil is rich and fertile, but owing to bad administration, many districts are uncultivated. The principal productions are cotton of fine quality, excellent wine, the best of which is produced near Limasol, and all kinds of fruits. The climate varies in different localities; in the central plain and about Larnaka the summer heat is very great, but is tempered by cool sea-breezes till about the middle of September, between which time and the end of October is the hottest period. The winter is short and cold; snow, however, being of rare occurrence, except on the highest peaks. Fevers are prevalent during the warm months, but are seldom fatal; the cause of unhealthiness is in many places quite local, and may be easily removed. Cyprus was in older times famous for its mineral wealth, its copper being superior to any other; but the mines are now abandoned. Recent accounts state that gold and coal have also been found, and only need sufficient enterprise in working, to prove highly remunerative. Large quantities of salt are obtained from salt lakes near Larnaka.

The capital of Cyprus is Nikosia (Lefkosia) near the centre of the island, with a population of 16,000; it is about 3 miles in circuit, and once contained many handsome buildings, but is now in a dilapidated state. The other principal towns are Famagusta, Larnaka and Limasol, all on the south-east coast. The chief exports are cotton, wine, salt, locust-beans, wheat, barley, wool and madder, amounting in 1873 to about £55,000.

The island was early colonised by the Phoenicians, and afterwards successively possessed by the Egyptians, Greeks, Romans, and Byzantines; it eventually passed to the Venetians, from whom it was taken by the Turks in 1571. On June 4th, 1878, a convention was concluded between England and Turkey, by which the Sultan accorded to Great Britain the right to occupy Cyprus, as a guarantee against further Russian aggression in Asia Minor; and the island was formally taken possession of in the name of the Queen, by Vice-Admiral Lord John Hay, C.B., on July 13th, 1878.

THE SECOND BOER WAR (1899–1902)

As recorded in the 1902 edition

The long and patient efforts of the British Government to secure by negotiation with the Government of the South African Republic the equitable treatment of the very large population of "Outlanders," principally British, resident within the South African Republic, came to an unsuccessful conclusion in October, 1899. Earlier in the year it had been found necessary to provide for possible eventualities by strengthening the British forces at Cape and in Natal. On October 7th the Reserves were called out; on the 10th an Ultimatum was received from the Transvaal Government demanding the recall of the British troops stationed near their frontiers, and also of any that were at that date on the way to South Africa. The period fixed for the acceptance of the terms of this communication having expired, a state of war began at **5 p.m.**, Transvaal time, on **October 11th**.

On the following day Natal was invaded by the South African Republic Boers, acting in co-operation with the Boers of the Orange Free State, the Government of which had a short time previously notified their intention of throwing in their lot with their neighbours on the North. Very shortly after the opening of hostilities an Army Corps, under the command of General Sir Redvers Buller, VC, was despatched to the scene of action, and at the close of December, 1899, the operations had assumed such extensive proportions that Field Marshal Lord Roberts of Kandahar, VC, was sent out in chief command of the considerably enlarged forces, which eventually exceeded 250,000. The Commander-in-Chief despatched General French to the relief of Kimberley, which had been closely invested. The relief was effected on **15th February 1900**, almost the whole of the investing force being captured. General Buller relieved Ladysmith, sorely pressed by a siege of 120 days, on 28th February, and on 17th May, a flying column under Col. Mahon, D.S.O., broke through the cordon surrounding Mafeking, where Col. Baden-Powell with a small mixed garrison had defied all hostile efforts since 15th December, 1899.

On **18th March, 1900,** Bloemfontein was occupied, the Orange Free State being annexed by Proclamation, 28th May, 1900, under the title of the Orange River Colony; and on 31st May and 5th June, Lord Roberts entered Johannesburg and Pretoria in the South African Republic, which territory was formally annexed as the Transvaal Colony on 25th October, 1900. Ex-President Kruger of the South African Republic has found an asylum in Europe, and ex-President Steyn of the Orange Free State leads a nomadic life in the Orange River Colony. Lord Roberts left South Africa at the close of 1900 in order to assume the post of Commander-in-Chief in London, and General Lord Kitchener, who had acted as Chief of the Staff to Lord Roberts, was left in supreme command.

By Proclamation in August, 1901, **September, 15, 1901**, was fixed as the latest date for the voluntary submission of the Boer leaders; the results of this offer were very small, and in accordance with the terms of the Proclamation all leaders are banished for life from the country when captured, and the cost of maintenance of Boer families in the refugee camps is to be exacted from the property of the militant Boers. The whole of the railway and all the towns and principal strongholds are effectively occupied, and the roving bands are gradually being lessened by the pursuing forces, the total number of Boer prisoners amounting to over 36,000 at the end of October, 1901. Already a recovery has taken place in the loyal colony of Natal, and there is every prospect of a united and loyal South Africa in the near future, directed to that end by the preparations of the General Lord Kitchener and statesmanship of the High Commissioner, Lord Milner.

THE UNION OF SOUTH AFRICA (1910)
As recorded in the 1911 edition

The Union of South Africa was established as a Dominion of the British Empire on 31 May 1910. The precursor to the current Republic of South Africa, it was formed through the unification of four separate British colonies: Cape Colony, Natal Colony, Transvaal Colony and Orange River Colony.

The Union of South Africa is constituted under the South Africa Act 1909 (9 Edw. VII., cap. 9), passed by the Parliament of the United Kingdom on September 20, 1909. In terms of that Act the self-governing Colonies of the Cape of Good Hope, Natal, the Transvaal, and the Orange River Colony became united on May 31, 1910, in a legislative Union under one Government under the name of the Union of South Africa, those colonies becoming original Provinces of the Union under the names of the Cape of Good Hope, Natal, the Transvaal, and the Orange Free State, respectively.

The Act constituting the Union provides for the appointment by the Sovereign of a Governor-General, who, with an Executive Council (of which the members are chosen and summoned by him), administers the executive government of the Union as the Governor-General in Council. Departments of State are established by the Governor-General in Council, the Governor-General appointing not more than ten officers to administer them. Such officers are King's Ministers of State for the Union and members of the Executive Council. Justice is administered by a Supreme Court and by lesser Courts.

The Senate consists of 40 members. For ten years after the establishment of Union eight are nominated by the Governor-General in Council and 32 are elected, eight for each Province. The first election was made prior to the establishment of the Union by the two Houses of each of the Colonial Legislatures sitting as one body, and a vacancy will be filled by the choice of the Provincial Council in respect of whose Province a vacancy occurs.

The House of Assembly consists of 121 elected members, 51 of whom represent the Cape of Good Hope, 17 Natal, 36 Transvaal, and 17 the Orange Free State. Members of both Houses must be British subjects of European descent.

A Provincial Council in each Province has power to legislate by ordinance on certain subjects specified in the Act, and on such other subjects as may be delegated to it. All ordinances passed by a Provincial Council are subject to the veto of the Governor-General in Council. Members of the Provincial Council are elected on the same system as members of Parliament, but the restriction as to European descent does not apply. The number of members in each Provincial Council are as follows: Cape of Good Hope, 51; Natal, 25; Transvaal, 36; Orange Free State, 25.

The Union Government is seized of all State property, and the Railways, Ports, Harbours, and Customs are administered by Union Commissioners for the benefit of a Consolidated Revenue Fund. The former debts of the Provinces are administered by and form a first charge upon the funds of the Union. Provision is made in the Act of 1909 for the admission to the Union of Rhodesia, and for the transfer to the Union Government of the administration of protected and other native territories. The Union was inaugurated by H.R.H. the Duke of Connaught, K.G., in 1910.

THE FOUNDATION OF THE COMMONWEALTH

After the end of World War I, the Dominions of the British Empire pressed for greater independence from Great Britain. Their status in relation to Great Britain evolved through a series of Imperial Conferences, held in London in 1921, 1923 and 1926.

The Imperial Conference and the Balfour Declaration (1926)
As recorded in the 1927 edition

After an interval of three years, the Imperial Conference again assembled in London in the autumn of 1926, the delegates including the Prime Ministers of six of the Dominions – Canada, Australia, New Zealand, South Africa, the Irish Free State and Newfoundland – as well as representatives of India. Speaking of the proceedings at the Guildhall Banquet, Mr. Baldwin, who presided over the main deliberations, said there could never have been a conference in which a better and more harmonious spirit had been manifest, and in which there had been a more genuine desire to solve many difficult problems, to bring unity to their councils, and to pave the way for further and more rapid progress in the future than had been hitherto achieved. The Conference considered the main questions, such as foreign policy, Imperial defence and Empire trade, at plenary sessions, but a great part of the work was first dealt with by committees, which made recommendations for adoption by the full Conference, a large number of subjects securing exhaustive attention in this way.

STATUS OF THE DOMINIONS
One of the most important committees set up – with the Earl of Balfour as chairman – considered the subject of inter-Imperial relations and made recommendations of far-reaching significance, which were adopted unanimously by the full Conference. Without laying down a Constitution for the British Empire, the report of this Committee emphasised that Great Britain and her self-governing Dominions are "autonomous Communities within the British Empire, equal in status, in no way subordinate one to another in any aspect of their domestic or external affairs, though united by a common allegiance to the Crown, and freely associated as members of the British Commonwealth of Nations."

The Statute of Westminster (1931)

The following is an extract from the 1933 edition detailing the Statute of Westminster Bill:

Early in the Session [December 1931], the Statute of Westminster Bill, designed to make clear the powers of Dominion Parliaments and to promote the spirit of free co-operation among members of the British Commonwealth of Nations, received the Royal Assent. The Bill, which was an attempt to define Dominion status, was introduced in conformity with a decision of the Imperial Conference of 1930, and Mr. J. H. Thomas [Secretary of State for the Colonies 1924; 1931; 1935–1936], during the second reading debate on **Nov. 20**, explained that the condition that each of the Dominions should ask for its passage had been complied with. Mr. Thomas said that the Bill merely expressed that equality of status between the Dominions and the United Kingdom which had been acknowledged by all British statesmen since the Imperial Conference of 1921 and confirmed at every subsequent Conference. He hoped that its passage, by removing grounds for controversy in the political field, would be the prelude to increased co-operation in the economic field between the several parts of the British Empire. Mr. Churchill [Conservative MP and former Secretary of State for the Colonies, 1921–1922] expressed doubts regarding the Irish Free State Agreement Act of 1922, which he suggested should be added to the North America Acts of 1867–1930 as a measure not affected by the Statute. In committee on **Nov. 24** an amendment was rejected by 350 to 50 providing that nothing should be done to authorise the Irish Free State legislature to repeal, amend or alter the agreement of 1922. Mr. Thomas read a letter from Mr. Cosgrave [first Prime Minister of the Irish Free State, 1922–1932] reaffirming that the Treaty could be altered only by consent, that good relations must rest upon reciprocal credit for good faith, and that any attempt to insist upon good faith by statute would cause the Irish people to disbelieve in the sanctity of the Treaty. The remaining stages were quickly secured.

The Statute of Westminster was an Act of Parliament which gave the Dominions of the British Empire control over their own legislation, by removing the ability of the British Parliament to impose ordinary laws unless specifically requested by the government of that Dominion. It formalised the Balfour Declaration and certain other political resolutions passed by the Imperial Conferences of 1926 and 1930.

The statute applied immediately to Canada, the Irish Free State, and the Union of South Africa without it having to be ratified specifically. The parliaments of the other three Dominions – Australia, New Zealand, and Newfoundland – were required to adopt the statute before it would apply to them as part of their domestic laws.

Although the structure and role of the Commonwealth has changed significantly since 1931, the Statute of Westminster remains the basis for the relationship between Great Britain and the Commonwealth realms – countries including Canada, Australia and New Zealand which have Elizabeth II as their monarch and Head of State.

IRISH INDEPENDENCE

The Anglo-Irish Treaty (1922)
As recorded in the 1923 edition

The demand for a separate Parliament for Ireland was first advanced at Westminster by an Irish Party under the leadership of *Isaac Butt* (born 1813, died 1879), who was succeeded by *Charles Stewart Parnell* (born 1846, died 1891) by whose efforts the necessity of granting a measure of Home Rule to Ireland was impressed upon one of the great political parties of Great Britain. After many failures to pass a Bill through both Houses of Parliament a Home Rule Bill was eventually placed on the Statute Book in 1914, with a suspensory clause for the duration of the War. In the later stages of the War, however, the extreme party of Irish politicians developed their organization under the name of *Sinn Fein* ("Ourselves Alone") and demanded complete severance from Great Britain and the recognition of an Irish Republic, and of its selected legislature *(Dail Eireann)*. Various efforts were made by the Cabinet of the United Kingdom to arrive at a solution of the Irish problem, which was complicated by the separatist demands of the extremists (in open rebellion against the Government), and the desire of the Protestants of Ulster to remain united with Great Britain, with the additional problem of the minorities of Protestants in the Southern counties. The *Government of Ireland Act*, 1920, superseded the Act of 1914 and established two governments in Ireland, with an executive and legislature of two chambers in Southern Ireland and in Northern Ireland, and a Council of Ireland to co-ordinate the work of the two legislatures. This Act was accepted and was brought into operation in Northern Ireland, the Northern House of Commons being duly elected and the Senate formed, Sir James Craig becoming the first Prime Minister of Northern Ireland. The Republicans *(Sinn Fein)* of Southern Ireland refused to accept the Act, and lengthy negotiations took place between Sinn Fein representatives and the Cabinet of the United Kingdom, resulting ultimately in the signing of a "Peace Treaty," Dec. 6, 1921, which was ratified by *Dail Eireann*, Jan. 7. 1922.

THE IRISH FREE STATE
Under this treaty there was set up in Southern Ireland the *Irish Free State* (*Saorstat Eireann*), "a co-equal member of the Community of Nations forming the British Commonwealth of Nations," the Constitution being defined in the *Irish Free State (Agreement) Act* of 1922.

Formation of the Republic Of Ireland (1949)
As recorded in the 1950 edition

> After the establishment of the *Irish Free State* in 1922, a new constitution and the name of 'Ireland' was adopted in 1937. In 1949 the remaining duties of the British monarch were removed and Ireland was declared a republic, with the description *Republic of Ireland*.

As a result of the decision of the Government of Eire to create the Republic of Ireland and to secede from the Commonwealth, a Bill to remove legislative anomalies and to confirm the constitutional position of Northern Ireland was presented to the House of Commons on **May 3** and speedily placed on the Statute Book. It recognized the secession from His Majesty's Dominions, provided that the new Republic was not a foreign country for the purpose of our laws and confirmed citizens of the Republic in all the rights they enjoyed in the United Kingdom while Eire was a member of the Commonwealth. One clause was designed to remove any doubts about the right of Eire citizens to claim to remain British subjects under the British Nationality Act or to apply for registration as citizens of the United Kingdom. Citizens of the Republic domiciled in Great Britain would become liable to military service in the same way as Eire citizens had been liable in the past. The clause relating to Northern Ireland, which aroused considerable criticism in the new Republic, declared that Northern Ireland remained part of His Majesty's Dominions and of the United Kingdom, and affirmed that "in no event will Northern Ireland or any part thereof cease to be part of His Majesty's Dominions and of the United Kingdom without the consent of the Parliament of Northern Ireland." A special residence qualification of three months for electors in Northern Ireland constituencies for the United Kingdom Parliament was provided, to prevent persons coming over the border from the Republic and voting in those elections after only a brief residence. The Prime Minister, moving the second reading on **May 11**, pointed out in reply to speeches in the Dail that the initiative for tightening the ligature fastened round the body of Ireland came from the Government of the Republic of Ireland and not from the Government of the United Kingdom. It was the act of the Eire Government itself in deciding to leave the Commonwealth which had made inevitable the declaration as to that part of Ireland which was continuing in the Commonwealth. It was quite impossible that we should take up a position which would suggest that Northern Ireland should be excluded from the Commonwealth against its will. We recognized the right of the Parliament of Northern Ireland to decide on the part of the people of Northern Ireland to stay in or leave the United Kingdom and Commonwealth. Mr. Eden, supporting the Bill, emphasized the privilege conferred on an Eire citizen of remaining entitled to the rights of British subjects, and he suggested that reciprocity should be given. A motion for rejection by Mr. J. Beattie, Labour member for Belfast West, was defeated by 317 to 12, and the Bill was read a second time. It passed through Committee on **May 16** after several attempts to alter the position of Northern Ireland had been negatived and on the following day received its third reading without a division, the Home Secretary stating that if ever the Republic of Ireland desired to re-enter the Commonwealth she would find that the door was open. When the Lords gave the Bill a second reading, Lord Salisbury agreed that something had to be done to clarify the position, but said that what caused anxiety was the nature of the settlement proposed in the Bill. It conferred no very remarkable advantages on us, but it enabled the Irish people in matters of trade to enjoy all the advantages available to members of the Commonwealth. In Committee, as a result of an amendment moved by Lord Simon, the Upper House on **May 31** accepted an agreed amendment to regularize the position of British subjects born before Dec. 6, 1922, in the Republic of Ireland. This was accepted by the Commons and the Bill received the Royal Assent on **June 2**.

THE ROYAL TOUR 1953-1954
As recorded in the 1955 edition

> The Queen's reign commenced with her longest ever Commonwealth tour. It lasted from November 1953 until May 1954, encompassed 13 countries in the West Indies, Australasia, Asia, and Africa, and covered 40,000 miles.

(1953) Nov. 23. The Queen and the Duke of Edinburgh left London Airport in stratocruiser *Canopus* on their Commonwealth tour, and were given great send-off by large crowds on their journey from Buckingham Palace and at the airport, where the Queen Mother, Princess Margaret, Sir Winston Churchill and other members of the Cabinet wished them God-speed. **24.** After making detour to avoid storm, *Canopus* arrived in Bermuda, and the Queen and the Duke drove through cheering crowds to St. George and Hamilton, where Her Majesty replied to address from House of Assembly, and then toured the island, afterwards attending garden party. **25.** The Queen and the Duke flew to Jamaica, where delegates from Legislatures from other West Indian colonies were presented to Her Majesty at Montego Bay before she crossed the island to Kingston, being everywhere welcomed with enthusiasm. **26.** Addressing joint session of Legislative Assembly, the Queen thanked Jamaica and rest of West Indies for their welcome; she and the Duke attended great gathering of children on Kingston cricket ground. **27.** Her Majesty held investiture and visited University College, and later with the Duke left on the liner *Gothic,* escorted by H.M.S. *Sheffield.* **29.** *Gothic* began passage of Panama Canal, the Queen and the Duke disembarking at Cristobal and driving with the President to Colon through cheering people. Later they entered Canal Zone and in evening attended reception and banquet in Panama City. **30.** They left Balboa in *Gothica* for Pacific crossing.

Dec. 11. New Zealand cruiser *Black Prince* took over escort duties. **16.** *Gothica* arrived off Fiji and the Queen and Duke landed at Suva, where chiefs paid their homage with ritual and dancing. **17.** They attended state ball, being escorted by two lines of running torch-bearers. **18.** Loyal address was presented to Her Majesty by Legislative Council, and she held investiture and attended sports meeting. **19.** The Queen and the Duke left Suva by flying boat for Tonga and were warmly welcomed by Queen Salote and Crown Prince and later by thousands of Tongans. **20.** They attended divine service at Wesleyan Church, the Duke reading the lesson, and were entertained to luncheon at Queen Salote's country estate before sailing for New Zealand in *Gothic.* **23.** Her Majesty and the Duke arrived at Auckland and after being welcomed on board *Gothic* by Governor-General of New Zealand were given enthusiastic reception on landing and again at civic reception despite unexpected rain. **24.** They visited Auckland Hospital, school children's rally and naval base and attended reception at Government House. **25.** The Queen made her Christmas Day broadcast from her suite at Government House and declared that she found herself "completely and most happily at home". She said how deeply impressed she was with the achievement and the opportunity which the modern Commonwealth presented, built on friendship, loyalty and the desire for freedom and peace. Finally, Her Majesty sent a message of sympathy to those who mourned as a result of the railway accident at Tangiwai. With the Duke, she attended service at St. Mary's Cathedral and stood with congregation in silent prayer for the bereaved. **27.** The Queen and the Duke attended race meeting, and on return journey visited family of survivors from the train disaster. **28.** They were greeted at Waitangi by number of Maori people and their chiefs, who repeated pledges of allegiance given to Queen Victoria on the same spot. **29.** After long drive in country, welcomed by cheering crowds, the Queen held investiture in Auckland. **30.** Royal visitors concluded stay at Auckland and visited domain of another group of Maoris before going to Hamilton. **31.** The Duke flew to Wellington and attended funeral of unidentified victims of the railway disaster.

(1954) Jan. 2. The Queen and the Duke were made paramount chiefs at Maori ceremony at Rotorua. **6.** After few days' rest they flew to Napier and were cheered by thousands of holidaymakers. **7.** They made journey by train, waving from observation platform to many gatherings and alighting for few minutes at other places. **8.** After making six further stops they arrived at New Plymouth. **9.** The Queen and the Duke flew to Wellington. **11.** Warmly greeted by great crowds, they attended State luncheon and civic reception and visited industrial plant. **12.** Her Majesty opened special session of New Zealand parliament and held investiture. **13.** She held Privy Council at Government House, first meeting outside Britain, and presided over meeting of executive council of New Zealand. **16.** The Queen and the Duke flew to South Island, landing at Blenheim and going on to Nelson. **17.** They flew further down west coast to Greymouth. **18.** By train they crossed the Alps for stay at Christchurch where they were greeted with enthusiasm. **19.** Royal visitors were given civic reception, visited hospital and attended civic banquet. **20.** Her Majesty held investiture and with the Duke attended garden party. **21.** They received great ovation at trotting meeting near Christchurch. **22.** Royal visitors were given wonderful send-off when they left Christchurch to spend quiet week-end at farm-mansion. **25.** By car and train they arrived at Dunedin. **26.** They attended children's rally, sports meeting and concert. **28.** They motored to Invercargill. **29.** From there the Queen broadcast message of thanks to New Zealand and to its "great and united people". **30.** The Queen and the Duke left New Zealand in *Gothic.*

Feb 3. They arrived at Sydney and were given tumultuous welcome by hundreds of craft in the harbour and by over a million people as they drove through the city to Government House. **4.** The Queen opened State Parliament and with the Duke attended State banquet at which Her Majesty spoke of great kindness shown by the people. **5.** They attended rallies of 120,000 children and of ex-service men, visited hospital and went to Lord Mayor's ball, boisterously welcomed everywhere by crowds who delayed progress of royal car. **6.** They were present at race meeting, saw surf carnival and Queen held investiture. **9.** Her Majesty and the Duke visited Broken Hill iron and steel works at Newcastle and went to Lismore. **10.** They returned to Sydney after receptions at Lismore and visit to agricultural show at Dubbo. **12.** As royal train returned to Sydney from Bathurst, crowds swarmed on to railway, dislocating other traffic and causing royal train to reduce speed. **13.** The royal couple flew to Wagga Wagga and thence to Canberra, where they received civic welcome. **15.** Her Majesty opened Federal Parliament, addressing senators and representatives as "my colleagues, friends and advisers" and declaring her resolve not only to rule but to serve. She held investiture and reviewed detachments from Australian territories. **16.** The Queen unveiled near Canberra Australia's memorial to the United States for help in the Pacific, presided over meeting of Executive Council, and, with the Duke, attended State banquet. **17.** Her Majesty presided over meeting of Privy Council and visit to Canberra ended with garden party and State ball. **18.** The Queen and the Duke flew to Sydney and left in *Gothic* for Tasmania. **20.** They arrived in Hobart, where the Queen unveiled memorial to its founder, Col. David Collins. **22.** Her Majesty opened Tasmanian Parliament and attended garden party and State ball. **24.** After brief visit to Launceston, the Queen and the Duke flew to Melbourne, where, as they drove to Government House, a million people roared a welcome. **25.** Her Majesty opened Parliament of Victoria and attended rally of ex-service men and State ball. **26.** Announced that while at Canberra the Queen and the Duke were inoculated against poliomyelitis. **27.** They saw race meeting at Flemington and attended State banquet. **28.** After attending service at Melbourne Cathedral, the Queen dedicated memorial forecourt at the Shrine of Remembrance.

March 4. They left Melbourne on two-day tour of northern districts of Victoria after attending rally of 17,000 children and investiture by the Queen. **7.** They spent quiet week-end at châlet near Warburton. **9.** The Queen and her husband flew to Brisbane and were accorded another enthusiastic welcome as they drove to civic reception. **10.** Her Majesty presided over meeting of Queensland Executive Council and with the Duke attended children's rally and Lord Mayor's ball. **11.** They flew to Bundaberg and Toowoomba, where they watched display of tribal dancing by aborigines. **14.** After visits to Townsville and Cairns, the Queen and the Duke inspected from the *Gothic* parts of Great Barrier Reef. **15.** They flew back to Brisbane. **17.** The Queen attended women's welcome meeting and with the Duke saw rally of 17,000 ex-servicemen. **18.** They flew to Adelaide, calling at Broken Hill to inspect "flying doctor" base. **20.** Visiting Whyalla they watched display of corroboree dances by aborigines. **22.** The Duke of Edinburgh flew to Woomera, venue of atomic explosions, and watched launching of controlled rocket. **23.** The

Queen opened special session of South Australian Parliament, and, with the Duke, attended children's rally and Parliamentary banquet, at which Her Majesty was presented with diamond and opal necklet and earrings. **24.** The Queen held investiture and attended women's reception and the royal visitors were present at garden party and music festival. **25.** They visited fruit and wine-growing centres. **26.** They flew to Kalgoorlie goldfields and on to Perth, and went on board *Gothic* at Fremantle as precaution because of epidemic of poliomyelitis, handshakes being omitted for same reason. **27.** They attended parliamentary reception in grounds of Parliament House at Perth instead of banquet. **30.** Last royal ball of Australian visit took place in grounds of Perth University after the Queen and the Duke had flown to Albany and back. **31.** They went by royal barge to Perth and motored to Northam and York.

April 1. Royal visitors left Australia on the *Gothic* from which Queen broadcast farewell to the Commonwealth, thanking the people for their welcome, hospitality and loyalty. **5.** The Queen and the Duke landed on Cocos-Keeling Islands and were warmly greeted during 90 minutes stay. **10.** They arrived at Colombo and attended civic reception; they attended ball given by Governor-General. **12.** Her Majesty opened Parliament of Ceylon, thousands watching royal party drive to and from the ceremony and when they later attended race meeting. **14.** The Queen and the Duke went to ruins of ancient city of Polonnaruwa and examined remains of old Buddhist monastery. **18.** After spending part of Easter at Nuwara Eliya they drove to Kandy and were joyfully greeted. **19.** They visited famous Buddhist church and shrine and witnessed traditional procession, receiving assurances of devotion from the Kandyan chiefs. **20.** The Duke formally opened University of Ceylon at Kandy before he and the Queen returned to Colombo. **21.** They sailed for Aden on the *Gothic* after Her Majesty had inspected military detachments on her birthday and held a Council. **27.** They were welcomed on arrival in Aden, where the Queen inspected troops and replied to loyal addresses. **28.** They flew to Entebbe for the reduced programme in Uganda, decided upon because of recent trouble in Buganda, and were warmly greeted by European community. **29.** Her Majesty inaugurated Owen Falls dam controlling the source of the Nile. **30.** The Queen and the Duke left Entebbe by air.

May 1. They arrived at Tobruk, and, after being received by King Idris and exchanging presents with him, went on board *Britannia* and greeted their children, royal yacht leaving for Malta. **3.** They arrived at Malta, the Queen and the Duke being given warm welcome on landing. Her Majesty unveiled memorial to Commonwealth airmen lost in the war and received address from Prime Minister of the island. **4.** The Queen reviewed parade of the services, watched by her children, and opened teachers' training centres. **7.** Royal Family left Malta in *Britannia* amid cheers of the people. **10.** They were given enthusiastic welcome at Gibraltar, where the Queen reviewed the combined services and attended civic luncheon, the children being taken to see the rock apes. **11.** They again saw the apes, as did the Queen and the Duke, and Her Majesty held investiture on board *Britannia,* which later left "The Rock" amid roar of farewell cheers. **13.** *Britannia* dropped anchor for the night in St. Austell Bay, Cornwall. **14.** Royal yacht sailed up English Channel, escorted by ships of Home Fleet and greeted by little vessels; at the Queen's invitation Sir Winston Churchill went on *Britannia* off Isle of Wight and stayed on board for the night. **15.** London gave the Queen and the Duke a royal welcome home. *Britannia* passed under Tower Bridge and when she was moored the Queen Mother and Princess Margaret went on board to greet royal travellers. After investiture, the party embarked on Royal barge and to cheers of great crowd on Embankment landed at Westminster, where other members of Royal Family welcomed them. Drive to Buckingham Palace was made in State landaus amid roar of cheers from vast crowd. At night the Queen and the Duke and their children made four appearances on Palace balcony in response to calls of huge concourse of cheering people. **16.** Crowds again assembled outside the Palace and cheered Her Majesty and the Duke when they left to attend morning service. **17.** House of Commons unanimously adopted motion to present address of loyal and affectionate welcome to the Queen and Duke of Edinburgh. Her Majesty gave sherry party for members of the Cabinet, guests including also Opposition leaders. **18.** House of Lords adopted similar address of welcome. **19.** The Queen and Duke of Edinburgh were given "welcome home" luncheon by City of London at Mansion House, Her Majesty emphasizing in her reply that Britain would never lack the friendly cooperation of the Commonwealth.

THE INDIAN INDEPENDENCE ACT (1947)

As recorded in the 1948 edition

The *Indian Independence Act, 1947*, which received the Royal Assent on July 18, 1947, brought to an end the whole structure of British Government in India and the handing over of power was completed on August 15, 1947. The Indian Empire, which extended over a territory larger than the Continent of Europe without Russia, is represented from that date by the *Dominion of India,* the *Dominion of Pakistan,* and Territories of Indian Rulers formerly under the suzerainty of the King-Emperor. Certain tracts of Tribal Territory on the North West and North East Frontiers are under the political influence, though not under the administrative rule, of the Dominion Governments.

Except where otherwise stated herein "India" includes the Dominion of India, the Dominion of Pakistan, the States of India and Tribal Areas.

A Cabinet statement on Indian policy (Cmd. 7136) issued on **June 3, 1947**, explained that no agreement other than by partition having proved acceptable, the plan evolved by Viscount Mountbatten of Burma and agreed to by Indian political leaders would be proceeded with. This involved a decision of the two Indian parties as to whether there should be a partition of India and if partition was decided then two Constitutional Assemblies would determine the future constitution of each of these divisions. The Constituent Assembly for India held its first meeting on **December 9, 1946,** and that for Pakistan on **August 10, 1947**.

The United Kingdom Cabinet statement anticipated the date of **June, 1948**, for the handing over of power and His Majesty's Government proposed to introduce legislation for the transfer of power in 1947 on a Dominion Status basis to one or two authorities, according to the decisions taken as a result of the announcement. This did not prejudice the right of Indian Continent Assemblies to decide in due course whether or not the part of India in respect of which they had authority would remain within the British Commonwealth.

The *Indian Independence Act,* which became law on **July 18, 1947**, made provision for the setting up of a Dominion of India and a Dominion of Pakistan. It defined the territories of each, abolished the existing Provinces of Bengal and Punjab and subject to the decisions of a boundary commission allotted to each new Provinces of East and West Bengal and East and West Punjab. As a result of a referendum the district of Sylhet in Assam (less four thanas) was included in Pakistan.

The Act eliminated the words *Indiæ Imperator* and "Emperor of India" from the Royal Styles and Titles and provided for the appointment by the King of a Governor-General to each of the new Dominions. Paramountcy over the Indian States was allowed to lapse and the functions of the India Office were transferred to the Commonwealth Relations Department.

By the adaptation of the Government of India Act, 1935, and by Orders temporarily passed and valid until **March 31, 1948**, powers were vested in the Governor-General mainly for the purpose of the transfer of powers, rights, property, duties and liabilities of the existing Central Government.

The existing rights of members of the former Secretary of State's Services and of judges who elected to serve in either of the new Dominions were guaranteed. The authority of His Majesty's Government in relation to British forces who might remain in India or Pakistan was unaffected by the Act.

The Central Government and Legislatures came to an end on **August 15, 1947**, and the responsibility of the British Government for the government of former British India ceased.

END OF THE BRITISH MANDATE IN PALESTINE (1948)

As recorded in the 1949 edition

THE TREATY OF LAUSANNE

After the end of the First World War, it was not until the Treaty of Lausanne (signed in Lausanne, Switzerland on 24 July 1923) that the state of war between the Allies and Turkey officially ended. Under the terms of the Treaty, the Allied powers agreed to recognise Turkish sovereignty within its new borders while Turkey abandoned claims to territories formerly held under the Ottoman Empire.

Before this a system of League of Nations mandates had been agreed by which former German and Ottoman territories would be administered by the Allied powers. The British Mandate for Palestine, formally confirmed by the Council of the League of Nations on 24 July 1922, placed the territories of Nablus, Acre, Jerusalem and the southern portion of the Beirut Vilayet under direct British control. The mandate came into effect on 29 September 1923, and came to an end at midnight on 14 May 1948.

The necessary legislation to sanction the end of the British mandate in Palestine was contained in the Palestine Bill, which received the Royal Assent on **April 29 [1948]** after being quickly passed. It provided that on the day the mandate was relinquished, subsequently named as **May 15**, British jurisdiction should be ended and the Government should cease to be responsible for the government of Palestine. Any appeal to the Privy Council pending from a court in Palestine other than a prize court would abate on the relinquishment of the mandate, and actions in respect of good faith and in the course of duty were prohibited. Mr. Creech Jones, the Colonial Secretary, moving the second reading on Mch. 10, defended the Government's policy and said that from **May 15** the authority for administration would be the United Nations Palestine Commission. The situation, he said, had tragically deteriorated since the United Nations Assembly resolution, and the plan had in many respects proved impracticable and unworkable. The immediate prospects in Palestine were not bright, and it was now for others to find and implement the solution which had eluded us. Mr. Butler [MP for Saffron Walden, 1929–1965] said that although the Opposition supported the second reading it was with heavy hearts and in the knowledge that no other course would be wise. A group of Labour members moved an amendment to reject the Bill, but this was defeated by 240 to 30, the Conservatives and Liberal Nationals abstaining. In Committee on Mch. 23 Mr. Ernest Bevin [Secretary of State for Foreign Affairs. 1945–1951] said the Government had not changed their policy and could not do so because some other State made a proposition, an allusion to the withdrawal of United States support for the partition plan. The Government, he said, would not take part in enforcing anything, whether trusteeship or anything else. "We were blamed because we did not do the right thing in Palestine when we were responsible; we were blamed when we were trying to get out; we were blamed for what is happening when we are going out. I say the sooner we are out the better." The remaining stages were quickly passed.

SUEZ CANAL CRISIS (1956–1957)
As recorded in the 1958 edition

The Suez Canal was opened in 1869 following ten years of work financed by the French and Egyptian governments. The canal was operated by the Universal Company of the Suez Maritime Canal, an Egyptian-chartered company; the area surrounding the canal remained sovereign Egyptian territory and the only land-bridge between Africa and Asia.

The canal instantly became strategically important; it provided the shortest ocean link between the Mediterranean and the Indian Ocean. The canal eased commerce for trading nations and particularly helped European colonial powers to gain and govern their colonies. Later, following the Second World War it became extremely important as a major route for the shipment of oil.

In 1875, as a result of debt and financial crisis, the Egyptian ruler, Isma'il Pasha, was forced to sell his shares (44 per cent) in the canal operating company to the British government of Benjamin Disraeli.

July 26. [1956] President Nasser announced that Egypt was taking over the Suez Canal forthwith and would use the revenue from it to build the Aswan High Dam. He said that the Canal company had been "nationalized", and the Egyptian Government officials had already moved into the company's installations and offices in Egypt. **27.** Egypt rejected a British Note protesting against the nationalization of the Canal. The Egyptian Government confiscated £2,050,000 from the Canal company's account with the Ottoman Bank in Cairo. **28.** Mr. Macmillan [Secretary of State for Foreign Affairs, Apr.–Dec. 1955] signed statutory instruments forbidding transfer of cash, securities or gold belonging to the Canal company in the U.K., and transfers into or out of Egyptian sterling accounts in U.K. without Treasury's permission. **29.** M. Pineau [French Foreign Affairs Minister] flew to London, and with British and U.S. representatives discussed the situation. **30.** Prime Minister [Sir Anthony Eden] stated in House of Commons that all exports of war material to Egypt had been stopped. He said that no arrangements for future of Canal would be acceptable to H.M. Government which would leave it in unfettered control of a single power. Canal company stated that its employees were cut off from the company's authority and subjected to compulsory work under penalty of imprisonment in a zone under martial law. **31.** Admiralty and War Office announced that certain naval movements and precautionary military measures had been ordered.

Aug. 1. Mr. Dulles [United States Secretary of State] joined three-power discussions in London, at which it was agreed that a draft scheme for making Canal an internationally controlled thoroughfare should be presented to a conference of interested nations. **2.** It was announced that the international conference would meet in London on Aug. 16. The Air Ministry ordered a number of Canberra twin-jet bomber squadrons to fly to Malta, and the Admiralty said that tank-landing craft were being brought from reserve and made ready for service. The French Mediterranean Fleet was officially stated to be assembling at Toulon for an undisclosed destination. **3.** The Queen, at a Council held at Arundel Castle, issued a Proclamation for calling up the Army Reserve. The Ministry of Supply announced that a number of merchant ships would be requisitioned. Mr. Dulles, in a broadcast from the White House, said that it was inadmissible for the Canal to be exploited by one country for highly selfish purposes. **5.** War Office announced suspension of discharge of regular soldiers and said that delays in release of National Servicemen serving overseas was possible. Parachute brigade group embarked at Portsmouth for the Mediterranean. Egypt ordered partial mobilization of the National Guard. **8.** Sir Anthony Eden said in a broadcast that the oil route through the Canal was "a matter of life and death to us all", but that he was confident that the London conference could produce a workable scheme for the future of the Canal. **9.** Soviet Government stated that it would send a representative to the London conference, though the conference was incompetent to deal with Suez Canal problem and nationalization of the Canal by Egypt was a fully legal act. **10.** Two British oil company employees expelled from Egypt. **12.** Colonel Nasser announced that the Egyptian Government would not attend the London Conference. The Greek Government also refused to attend. President Eisenhower invited leaders of both political parties to the White House, where he and Mr. Dulles addressed them on the implications of the Suez crisis. Two troopships with soldiers and airmen left Southampton for the Mediterranean. **13.** Airlift of troops to the Mediterranean continued. **14.** Mr. Gaitskell, on behalf of Opposition, asked the Prime Minister to recall Parliament immediately after the conclusion of the Suez Canal Conference. Canal Company announced that nearly all its non-Egyptian employees in Egypt had expressed their loyalty to the company and their desire to be repatriated rather than to continue working for the Egyptian authorities. **16.** Suez Canal Conference opened at Lancaster House with speech of welcome by Sir Anthony Eden. Mr. Selwyn Lloyd [Foreign Secretary] was elected Chairman of the Conference. **17.** Mr. Shepilov, Soviet delegate to the Conference, said that new international convention to replace 1888 Convention was required and suggested that if the Conference reached agreement on principles, they should be put to a fuller and wider conference.

> The 1888 Convention, or the Convention of Constantinople, was a treaty signed by the United Kingdom, Germany, Austro-Hungary, Spain, France, Italy, the Netherlands, Russia and the Ottoman Empire on 29 October 1888, which guaranteed passage to all ships during war and peace.

20. Mr. Dulles proposed to the Conference an international board to control the Canal, and Mr. Krishna Menon [Indian Ambassador to the United Nations] suggested a board with consultative and advisory powers only. **21.** Seventeen countries showed themselves in favour of Mr. Dulles' plan, after minor amendments to it, proposed by Pakistan, had been accepted. Russia, Indonesia and Ceylon supported the Indian plan. **22.** Egyptian spokesman said that if British and French pilots ceased to work in Canal, French and British ships would only be taken through after ships of all other nationalities. **23.** London Conference ended after it had been agreed by the nations forming the majority that a committee with Mr. Menzies [Australian Prime Minister] as chairman, and representatives of the U.S.A., Persia, Ethiopia and Sweden should approach the Egyptian Government and initiate discussions. Admiralty announced that R.N. ratings and R.M. other ranks whose seven-year engagements were due to end on or after Sept. 1 would be temporarily retained. **27.** Two Britons arrested in Cairo on charges of espionage. **28.** Col. Nasser agreed to meet the 5-power Committee in Cairo. Egyptian Government requested the withdrawal of two members of British Embassy staff whom it alleged were implicated in "espionage ring". Mr. Dulles said at Press Conference that Suez Canal was given international status by 1888 Convention. **29.** Foreign Office said that British Government had agreed that contingent of French troops should be temporarily stationed in Cyprus. Third British subject arrested in Cairo. **30.** Two members of Egyptian Embassy in London asked to leave within 72 hours. French troops begin to arrive in Cyprus by air.

Sept. 2. Col. Nasser said that he was not prepared to compromise on question of operational control of Canal. **3.** Discussions between 5-power committee and Col. Nasser opened in Cairo. Fourth British subject, a member of an insurance company's Egyptian staff arrested. Thirty persons of different nationalities now stated to be detained as spies. Egyptian War Minister said that Egypt had completed military preparation and was ready to meet any attack. **6.** Statement from 10 Downing Street said that Cabinet had decided to ask Chancellor and Speaker to recall Parliament on Sept. 12. **9.** Discussions in Cairo ended; documents published showed complete lack of agreement. Mr. Menzies described the situation as "very, very grave." **10.** British and French Prime Ministers and Foreign Ministers conferred in London. Col. Nasser proposed new Conference of all states using Suez Canal. **11.** Canal Company authorised its non-Egyptian employees in Egypt to cease work at the end of the week and to prepare to return home at once. **12.** Houses of Parliament met for special session. Prime Minister told Commons that Government, in conjunction with U.S.A. and France, would set up association of users of the Canal, which would employ its own pilots and to which dues could be paid. After Opposition criticism, Government tabled a motion of confidence, to which Opposition proposed an amendment tantamount to censure. Foreign pilots informed Egyptian authority of their desire to leave their posts. **13.** Opposition amendment defeated in the

Commons by 321 to 251, after Sir Anthony Eden had said that the Government must be the judges of the best moment to have recourse to the Security Council. In Lords Opposition amendment was defeated by 145 to 18. Mr. Dulles said that America would assist Europe if passage through the Canal was denied. He said that the U.S. would not give military support to the use of force. **14.** Further London conference of 18 countries arranged. **17.** Mr. Dulles reaffirmed U.S. offer to finance American oil exports to Western Europe if progress through the Canal became impracticable. Mr. Krishna Menon visited Col. Nasser. Egypt asked the U.N. Security Council to keep a "vigilant eye" on the Suez Canal crisis, and accused Britain and France of "shocking acts" in violation of U.N. Charter. **19.** Eighteen-power Conference opened in London, Mr. Dulles elaborating his views on Canal Users' Association, which were opposed by representatives of Denmark and Pakistan. Moscow Radio broadcast suggestion by Marshal Bulganin [Premier of the Soviet Union] for meeting of heads of Governments of U.K., U.S.A., U.S.S.R., Egypt, India and France. **21.** London Conference closed with declaration in favour of establishment of users' association. France expressed reserve. **23.** Britain and France announced that they had instructed their permanent representatives at the United Nations to ask the President of the Security Council to call a meeting to consider the situation created by the unilateral action of the Egyptian Government. M. Mollet [Prime Minister of France], speaking at Lens, said that France felt bitterness and anxiety at the lack of support from some of her friends and allies. **24.** Colonel Nasser, the King of Saudi Arabia and the President of Syria, after three meetings in Saudi Arabia, issued a joint statement that they were completely unanimous on the Suez issue. **26.** Sir Anthony Eden and Mr. Selwyn Lloyd arrived in Paris for discussions with the French Ministers. Security Council agreed to debate Anglo-French protest against Egypt and Egyptian counter-complaint against Western nations.

Oct. 5. U.N. Security Council met to discuss Suez crisis. M. Pineau and Mr. Selwyn Lloyd put Western Powers' case, and latter suggested a secret session of the Council. **8.** U.S.S.R. and Egypt presented joint case to Security Council. **9.** Statement from 10 Downing Street said that it was still necessary to retain Army Reservists on active service. **10.** Heavy fighting took place on Israel-Jordan frontier near Kalkilyia. **12.** Mr. Hammarskjöld [Secretary-General of the United Nations] announced that six principles for operation of the Canal had been agreed, including free and open transit without discrimination, respect for Egypt's sovereignty, agreement on manner of fixing charges between Egypt and the users, a fair proportion of dues to be allotted for development, and arbitration in case of disagreement. **14.** Pre-amble to Anglo-French resolution embodying the six principles passed unanimously by the Security Council, but main part of resolution was vetoed by Russia. **16.** Sir Anthony Eden and Mr. Selwyn Lloyd visited Paris to discuss with French Ministers the common policy of the two Governments over Suez question. **28.** Israel ordered partial mobilisation. **29.** Israel forces penetrated 50 miles into Egyptian territory in Sinai Peninsula. **30.** Britain and France called on Egyptian and Israel Governments to stop all warlike action, to withdraw to distance of 10 miles from Suez Canal and to agree that Anglo-French forces should move temporarily into key positions at Port Said, Ismailia and Suez; if, after 12 hours, one or both parties had not undertaken to comply, British and French forces would intervene. Israel accepted the conditions on the assumption that Egypt would also do so, but Egypt rejected them. The Admiralty advised merchant shipping to keep clear of the Canal and of Egyptian and Israel waters until further notice. At urgently-called meeting of Security Council, the United States sponsored a resolution calling on Israel to withdraw her forces and urging all United Nations members to refrain from use or threat of force in the area. The resolution was vetoed by the U.K. and France, this being the first occasion that Britain had exercised her veto at the Security Council. In the House of Commons the Government's action was approved on a division by 270 to 218, and in the French National Assembly M. Mollet obtained support by 390 to 191. **31.** British and French Governments appointed Gen. Sir Charles Keightley Commander-in-Chief, with the French Vice-Admiral Barjot as deputy, of the forces which were to intervene to secure compliance with Anglo-French requirements. Repeated warnings were broadcast to Egyptian civilians to keep away from all airfields. Later, a statement from the newly-formed Allied Forces headquarters in Cyprus said that a bomber offensive had been launched against military targets in Egypt. Egyptian destroyer *Ibrahim Awal,* formerly H.M.S. *Cottesmore,* which had been shelling Israel coast, surrendered to Israel warships and aircraft and was towed into Haifa. The Air Ministry advised all civil aircraft to avoid a large area in Eastern Mediterranean.

Nov. 1. *Communiqués* from Allied Force headquarters said that it was believed that over 50 Egyptian aircraft had been destroyed on nine airfields, and at least 40 more seriously damaged, and that reconnaissance photographs had shown extensive damage to installations. French naval aircraft had attacked and set on fire an Egyptian destroyer of Russian *Skoryi* class off Alexandria. Egypt broke off diplomatic relations with Britain and Egyptian Government seized all British and French property in Egypt. In House of Commons, after noisy scenes which compelled Speaker to suspend session for half an hour, Opposition motion of censure was defeated by 324 to 255. **2.** Military targets in Egypt were bombed, and Cairo radio station, in the desert seven miles from Cairo, was silenced. The Egyptian Air Force was virtually put out of action. Allied Headquarters stated that Egypt had blocked the Suez Canal by sinking ships. Gaza surrendered to Israel troops, and Israel armoured forces also advanced towards south of Sinai Peninsula. It was claimed that they had taken 15,000 Egyptian prisoners and 100 tanks since fighting had begun. **3.** At special Saturday sitting of House of Commons, Sir Anthony Eden said that he had informed United Nations that Britain and France would most willingly stop military action as soon as three conditions were fulfilled. They were that Israel and Egypt accepted a United Nations police force, that such a force should be maintained until there was agreement on an Arab-Israel settlement and on Suez Canal and that meanwhile Israel and Egypt should accept limited detachments of Anglo-French troops to be stationed between the combatants. **4.** In an all-night extraordinary session U.N. General Assembly passed Canadian resolution requesting Secretary-General to submit within 48 hours a plan to set up, with consent of nations concerned, an emergency international United Nations force to secure and supervise cessation of hostilities. Anglo-French *communiqué* said that British Seahawks had attacked Egyptian E-boats near Alexandria, blowing up one boat, setting two on fire and damaging others. Reconnaissance showed that Egyptians had blown up supports of El Firdan bridge, south of Port Said on the Canal. **5.** British airborne troops dropped into Egypt at dawn and captured Gamel airfield five miles west of Port Said. French airborne troops seized two bridges spanning the Canal backwaters south of Port Said. Another French parachute force was dropped near Port Fuad. Israel announced that fighting had ended in Sinai Peninsula and cease-fire orders had been issued to all Israeli troops. Marshal Bulganin proposed to President Eisenhower that U.S.A. and U.S.S.R. should combine to halt Anglo-French "aggression" in Egypt. He also sent messages to Great Britain, France and Israel warning them of Russia's "determination to stop aggression" and announced that Soviet Ambassador in Tel Aviv was being recalled. Official White House statement in reply said that suggestion that U.S. and Soviet forces should intervene was unthinkable. **6.** British and French commando units landed. Port Said and Port Fuad were captured and troops advanced south along the Canal. Sir Anthony Eden told Commons that Allies had ordered a cease-fire at midnight, and that he had informed Mr. Hammarskjöld that Britain was willing to stop operations if Egypt and Israel accepted unconditional cease-fire and a competent international force could be set up. Allied *communiqué* reported that technicians had already begun work of clearing Canal. Later, it was reported that Egypt had rejected outright the terms upon which Anglo-French cease-fire had been ordered. Saudi Arabia informed United Nations that she had severed diplomatic relations with England and France. **7.** Sir Anthony Eden said that there was no question of withdrawal by U.K. or France unless and until there was a United Nations force to take over. U.N. General Assembly passed two resolutions, the first in favour of a United Nations emergency force and the second calling on Britain, France and Israel to withdraw from Egyptian territory immediately. Sir Pierson Dixon [Permanent Representative of the United Kingdom to the United Nations] said that this demand was unacceptable to Britain. Several nations expressed willingness to take part in an international force and U.S.A. said that she was ready to assist with airlifts, shipping, transport and supplies. **8.** Mr. Ben-Gurion [Prime Minister of Israel] said in reply to an appeal from President Eisenhower that Israel was ready to withdraw from the Sinai Peninsula after the entry of an international force into the Canal Zone. **9.** Sir Anthony Eden said that assault units would be withdrawn from Egypt and replaced by infantry battalions and that an additional infantry reserve would be held in Cyprus. **11.** The British Government gave particulars of the large amount of aircraft, tanks and military equipment provided by Russia to Egypt and Syria during the preceding year. **12.** Col. Nasser agreed to entry of U.N. force into Egypt, subject to certain reservations. **14.** Mr. Hammarskjöld left New York by air for Cairo after instructing Maj.-Gen. Burns to start moving first U.N. units into Egypt. Allied H.Q. in Cyprus gave figures of casualties in Egyptian operations as: British, killed 22, wounded 96. French, killed 10, wounded 33, missing, 1. It was also stated that 8 British and 2 French aircraft had been lost. **21.** Norwegian contingent arrived in Port Said. Mr. Hammarskjöld said that work of clearing Canal would not begin until after withdrawal of Allied troops. **22.** Mr. Butler [MP for Saffron Walden, later (1957–62) Home Secretary] told House of Commons that Britain and France would not withdraw forces from Port Said area until they were satisfied that U.N. police force was competent to discharge tasks allotted to it.

Dec. 3. Mr. Selwyn Lloyd said that British and French troops would be withdrawn immediately and that their salvage resources would be left at disposal of U.N. **7.** Admiralty and War Office stated that bodies of servicemen killed in Egypt were being brought back to U.K. in view of reports of desecration of British graves of the last war in Egypt. British troops were withdrawn from forward positions at El Cap and their place taken by an Indian battalion. **11.** General Wheeler (U.S.A.) who had been appointed to command U.N. salvage operations, said in Cairo that he would investigate possibility of using British salvage equipment, but without British crews. Lord Hailsham [First Lord of the Admiralty, 1956–7], speaking in Malta, said that British salvage ships would emphatically not be used by U.N. unless they took their crews with them. Egyptians kidnapped a British officer, Lieut. Moorhouse, in Port Said. **15.** During continued Egyptian firing in Port Said on Allied and U.N. troops, a British officer was killed. **16.** British troops withdrew into beach-head round Port Said harbour. **18.** Agreements reached between Allied naval authorities in Port Said and Generals Wheeler and Burns whereby, if their safety were guaranteed, Allied salvage crews would remain with their ships, wearing civilian dress and under U.N. command. **23.** Last Allied troops withdrew from Egypt. **27.** Moscow Radio said that Col. Nasser had expressed his profound gratitude to the Russian people for their help to Egypt. **31.** Salvage operations began at Kantara.

Jan. 1. [1956] Egypt informed U.N. authorities that Lieut. Moorhouse had died of suffocation after being left in a small metal cupboard for two days. Egyptian Government abrogated Anglo-Egyptian treaty of 1954. **2.** Body of Lieut. Moorhouse handed over to U.N. officials. British salvage vessel *Dalrymple* left Port Said after being notified by Gen. Wheeler that she was no longer needed. Foreign Office spokesman said that Britain did not recognize right of Egypt to abrogate 1954 treaty unilaterally. **3.** Egyptian and U.N. officials initialled agreement allowing U.N.

salvage fleet to clear the Canal. **6.** President Nasser said that he would not allow British and French troops to pass through the Canal until Israel had evacuated the Gaza strip, that he would not negotiate with the existing British and French Prime Ministers and that in future all ships passing through the Canal would have to pay transit dues direct to Egypt. The body of Lieut. Moorhouse was flown home from Naples in an R.A.F. aircraft. **7.** Foreign Office said, in reply to President Nasser, that before Anglo-French forces had left Port Said, Egyptian Government had given assurances to Mr. Hammarskjöld that there would be no discrimination against British and French shipping in Canal. **8.** Thirteen ships trapped in the Canal since October reached Port Said. **11.** Saudi Arabian batteries attacked an Israel ship cruising near Eilat. **15.** Israel forces withdrew from El Arish, which was occupied by a Yugoslav contingent of the U.N. force. **20.** United Nations passed resolution regretting Israel's non-compliance with previous resolutions requesting her to withdraw from Egyptian territory. Only France supported Israel in opposition to the resolution. **21.** Israel handed over 500 Egyptian prisoners to U.N. forces. **22.** Israel forces withdrew from north Sinai, with exception of the Gaza strip. **23.** Mr. Ben-Gurion announced terms on which Israel would accept U.N. proposals. They included continuance of civil administration of Gaza strip by Israel, who would be responsible for its security, freedom of shipping in Gulf of Akaba, demilitarization of Sinai Peninsula and freedom of passage for Israel ships through Suez Canal. **24.** United Nations dispensed with services of remainder of Anglo-French salvage fleet which sailed for home. **25.** In report of Gen. Wheeler to United Nations, it was disclosed that only 2 out of 19 wrecks in the southern section of the Canal had been moved and that some had not been surveyed. **30.** Two Israelis wounded by mines laid on Israel territory by newly-returned terrorists.

Feb. 3. U.N. General Assembly again called on Israel to complete withdrawal behind armistice line. Israel Cabinet issued statement adhering to its position. **10.** Demonstrations throughout Israel in support of Government's policy. **11.** General Wheeler said that Egypt had still not given him permission to work on two major obstructions. **14.** Four Britons, 11 Egyptians and a Yugoslav brought before a Cairo court on charges of spying for Britain. **20.** In nation-wide sound and television broadcast, President Eisenhower said that United Nations had no choice but to exert pressure on Israel.

March 1. Mrs. Meir, the Israel Foreign Minister, told U.N. General Assembly that Israel would withdraw from Gulf of Akaba and Gaza strip on the assumption that U.N. would take over complete control in the Gaza strip and that Israel reserved her freedom of defence if the situation deteriorated. Mr. Lodge [United States Ambassador to the United Nations] said that in the United States view these assumptions did not make the withdrawal conditional and Mr. Dulles told representatives of 9 Arab nations that it would involve no promises nor concessions whatsoever to Israel by the United States. **3.** Two parties in Israel Government coalition decided not to support withdrawal. **4.** Mr. Ben-Gurion ordered full and prompt withdrawal from Gulf of Akaba and Gaza strip. U.S. State Department said that it had given no private undertaking to Israel in any form. The defendants in the Cairo espionage case were sent to trial. **5.** In defending his action to the Knesset, Mr. Ben-Gurion met with noisy opposition. General Wheeler said that Egyptian consent had still not been given to the beginning of work on two wrecks in the Canal which were said to contain explosives. **6.** Mr. Ben-Gurion won vote for his policy in the Knesset. Israel troops began withdrawal from Gaza strip. Arab terrorists in the area killed two people. **7.** Withdrawal of Israelis from Gaza strip completed. Egyptian Canal authority issued circular to shipping companies saying that the Canal would now be open in daytime to ships up to 500 tons on payment of tolls to Egypt. **10.** Col. Nasser rejected proposal for interim payment of half Canal dues to the World Bank and half to Egypt pending settlement. Guards at U.N. headquarters at Gaza fired over heads of Arab demonstrators who attempted to enter the building. **11.** Egyptian Government announced that it had decided to resume administration of Gaza strip immediately. Egypt also rejected a request by Gen. Burns that Canadian reinforcements should be permitted to land. **13.** Dr. Bunche, representing United Nations, said that U.N. force was prepared to offer full co-operation to Egyptian administration in Gaza strip, and that it was for Egypt to announce when administrative take-over would occur. Arabs blew up Gaza-Israel link carrying supplies to refugees. **14.** Egyptian spokesman said that complete co-operation existed between Egypt and U.N. force. **19.** Egyptian Government, in Note to diplomatic missions in Cairo, said that Canal dues must be paid in advance to Egyptian Canal authority or its authorized agents. **26.** Canal stated to be open to ships up to 10,000 tons. **31.** Col. Nasser said that Egypt would resist passage of Israel ships through the Canal until Arab refugee problem was settled.

April 2. Mr. Dulles said American boycott of Canal was not contemplated. Mrs. Meir told Knesset that Israel would if necessary exercise her right to freedom of navigation through Canal and Gulf of Akaba. **6.** American oil tanker sailed unmolested up Gulf of Akaba to Israel port of Eilat. **8.** Clearance of the Canal stated to be complete. **19.** Hong Kong freighter under charter to Chinese firm passed through Canal, being first British ship to do so since October. **24.** Egyptian Government published its terms for operation of Canal, saying that this would be done by Egyptian Canal authority, but that disputes might be referred to arbitration. **26.** Security Council met at request of United States to continue discussion of Canal dispute, but after full day's debate adjourned *sine die* without making any recommendations.

May 12. Espionage trial opened in Cairo. Two of the four Britons refused to plead because they had not been informed of the charges against them. The other two pleaded Not Guilty. It was disclosed that unofficial conversations had been opened between Britain and Egypt aiming at resumption of trade relations. **13.** Mr.

Macmillan [Prime Minister, 1957–1963] told House of Commons that Government could no longer advise British ship owners to refrain from using Suez Canal. **15.** After first offering his resignation to the French President, who refused to accept it, M. Mollet announced that he intended to demand that the Security Council should ask Egypt to conform to its principles laid down in October, 1956. **18.** Statement by King Faisal and King Saud, after conversations in Baghdad, said that Iraq and Saudi Arabia would support Egypt in excluding Israel shipping from the Canal. **20.** Security Council met at request of France to resume discussion of Canal situation. **21.** After two-day debate, Security Council adjourned without decision; Mr. Lodge said that U.S.A. reserved judgment on Egyptian policy. Three attacks were made on Israel vehicles in the Negev with loss of life. **30.** Anglo-Egyptian financial talks in Rome needed. Statement issued later said that Britain had agreed to release certain of Egypt's frozen sterling balances.

June 9. Egyptian Government approved French request to accept convertible sterling for payment of tolls by French ships using the Canal. **13.** French Government agreed to French ships using the Canal. King Saud and King Faisal, after meeting in Amman, issued statement claiming Gulf of Akaba as Arab territorial waters. **18.** Official Egyptian sources said that 3 submarines purchased from U.S.S.R. had arrived in Egypt. **23.** Two British subjects, Mr. Zarb and Mr. Swinburn, received sentences of 10 and 5 years' imprisonment respectively in Cairo spy trial. Two others were acquitted. **July 18.** Egyptian Government said that former ministers and others who had engaged in a plot against Col. Nasser in April would be put on trial.

BRITISH HOLIDAY AND
HEALTH RESORTS

BRITISH HOLIDAY AND HEALTH RESORTS

Introduction
From the 1905 edition

Everybody, however good his constitution, needs more than ever in these wear-and-tear times to periodically renew his health-springs by a holiday amidst fresh scenes and congenial surroundings.

The sick and the fragile frequently restore their impaired health or lengthen their lives in some cheerful haven enriched by Nature with genial climatic advantages, supplemented by public or private enterprise with modern conveniences and amusements.

The choice of a suitable resort for leisure or heath, recreation or repose, is often difficult; there are so many places to select from in England, Scotland, Ireland and Wales whose claims are as evenly balanced as their attractions are diversified.

Cheap railway fares, steamboats, motor cars, and bicycles have all contributed to largely extend the area within reach of every holidaymaker from which to choose a fresh source of interest.

Individual tastes and temperaments greatly vary, but the love of change is universal; its gratification is Nature's best tonic for mind and body, beneficial to those tired of their toil and to others no less weary of monotony.

Some local authorities are keenly alive to the benefits derived from making widely known the advantages of their respective resorts; others are slowly awakening to the necessity of either following the example of their progressive competitors or falling behind in importance.

To enable an opinion to be formed with as little trouble as possible regarding the resorts which have furnished authentic particulars for this article, a uniform method of presenting the chief characteristics of each place has been adopted.

'How to get there' nowadays, when once 'where to go' has been settled, is a simple matter.

All the railways concerned foster their growing holiday traffic with special fares, travelling conveniences, and shorter journeys. On this occasion space only permitted outlining the systems of the largest lines, which, with their connections, render accessible from the Metropolis the most distant resorts within the British Isles.

The excellent arrangements now made by all the lines to facilitate travelling will do much to stimulate the British public, 'in spite of all temptations to visit other nations,' to first become acquainted with the natural beauty spots throughout their own native country – near-at-hand shrines towards which tourists from every quarter of the globe turn in ever-increasing numbers with ever-increasing zest.

A Selection of Holiday Destination Recommendations

The following is taken from editions of *Whitaker's Almanack* dating from 1905 to 1930. The date given in parentheses specifies the edition the extract was taken from.

BARRY (1906), Glamorgan. Urban District Council. Pop. 28,000, *Means of access:* Barry Railway (from London, G. W. Ry.). *Location:* 8m. from Cardiff. At the end of a peninsula formed by the curve in the Bristol Channel, surrounded by sea to the west, the south, and the east. *Drainage:* Excellent. *Water Supply:* Constant. *Bathing:* Safe, with fine stretch of sand. *Excursions:* Fine steamers ply daily to Weston-super-Mare, Lynmouth, Minehead, and Ilfracombe. Golf, cricket, and boating.

BATH (1905), Somersetshire. County Borough. Episcopal city. Pop. 49,817. *Means of Access:* 107m. from Paddington, G.W. Ry.; also western main line, Midland Ry. *Location:* 11m. from Bristol, on N. bank of River Avon. *Elevation:* 60 to 550 feet above sea-level. *Neighbourhood:* Woodland, hills, and diversified country. *Climate:* Mild, equable, varies according to elevation and aspect. *Sunshine:* 1,391 hrs., 1903. *Water Supply:* Constant. *Drainage:* Modern. *Soil:* Oolithic limestone, clays and sands. *Baths:* Luxuriously appointed, with every scientific application known to modern balneology. *Mineral waters:* Thermal springs. *Season:* Spring and autumn periods greatest activity.

Bath, situated in a valley and at various levels on slopes of surrounding hills, occupies leading position as fashionable inland watering-place, possessing an unrivalled combination of archaeological, historical, social, and scenic attractions, besides the famous waters to which it owes its origin; their healing virtues tried 1903 by 100,000 bathers. It was a bathing establishment time of the Romans; the wonderfully preserved remains of the city's ancient splendour constitute a unique collection of universal interest. It is now a comfortable residential city, with excellent educational, facilities and railway communications. Corporation own hot and cold springs, baths and grand pump-room (a well-organised centre for musical entertainments), and maintain a city band. Theatre Royal, Assembly Rooms (concerts and balls), Art Gallery, Royal Literary and Scientific Institution (Library, reading-room, geological museum), abbey church and various old buildings. Royal Victoria Park (50 acres, 1¼m. carriage drive, promenades, lawns, and plantations), Sidney Gardens (band performances, flower shows), recreation ground (county cricket, football, cycling), golf (18 holes; ladies 9 holes – separate clubs), hunting, archery, tennis, boating, angling.

BEDFORD (1923), County Borough. Pop. 39,183. 50 miles from London. Midland and L. & N.W. Railways. A noted educational centre on the banks of the River Ouse, with charming riverside promenade. Golf Links (18 holes).

BOURNEMOUTH (1905), Hants. County Borough. Pop. 66,000. *Means of access:* L. & S.W. Ry. (107½m. from London) and Midland Ry. *Location:* Extreme S.W. coast of Hants, in sheltered bight between Poole Harbour and Christchurch. *Neighbourhood:* Cliffs, pine-woods, valleys, luxurious growth of trees and shrubs. *Aspect:* South. *Climate:* Mild, equable temperature. *Sunshine:* 1,696 hrs, 1903. *Water Supply:* Constant. *Drainage:* Modern. *Soil:* Sand and gravel. *Front:* High cliffs, covered foliage, intersected rustic paths, broken by deep chines. *Piers:* Bournemouth, 1,238ft., bandstand refreshment kiosk; Boscombe, 600ft. *Beach:* Sandy, no currents, double tides render bathing always practicable. *Bathing:* Mixed. *Baths:* Swimming baths, Turkish and electric at Hydros. *Excursions:* New Forest, 15m.; Corfe Castle, 18m.; Wimborne, 9m; Christchurch Priory, 4m.; Salisbury, 31m.; Stonehenge, 38m. *Season:* Winter. *Annual Fixtures:* Regatta, cricket week, horse show, tennis, golf, and croquet tournament.

Widely-spread town built within recent years on a heath covered with pines, which surround and permeate the locality, contributing to this fashionable town's position as a health resort, aromatic exhalations from pines benefitting pulmonary complaints. East Cliff (oldest residential quarter) separated from West Cliff (newest portion, more elevated) by River Bourne. Town extended more inland through valley than along coast. Valley affords maximum protection from wind, laid out 2 miles as public pleasure gardens, stream running through. Here Invalids' Walk, sheltered quiet, sunny promenade.

Municipal bands, 2 theatres, winter gardens (vocal and instrumental concerts), Shaftesbury Hall (entertainments, lectures, concerts, gymnasium), art gallery, museum, free library, science, art and technical school, drill hall, 3 arcades, coaching, hunting, golf-links (18 holes; ladies 9 holes), 3 large parks, provision for all outdoor pastimes, good educational facilities, excellent London railway service, and direct communication Midlands and North. Electric tramways.

BRIGHTON (1924), Sussex. Pop. 142,427. *Means of access:* Southern Railway. 51 miles from London. *Elevation:* 26 to 462 feet. *Aspect:* South. *Sunshine:* (1922), 1,746 hours. *Water Supply:* Constant. *Drainage:* Modern. *Soil:* Chalk. *Front:* 4½ miles. Marine drive with promenade; lawns, ornamental terrace walks. *Piers:* West Pier, 1,100 feet; Palace Pier, 1,710 feet. *Beach:* Shingle. *Excursions:* Paris, 9 hours via Newhaven; Rottingdean, 4½ miles; Devil's Dyke, 5½ miles; Stanmer Park, 3½ miles; Bramber Castle, 10 miles; Hurst 7½ miles; Ditchling Beacon, 7½ miles.

Society's liveliest seaside rendezvous; favourite resort of Londoners. Great educational facilities. Development of the town due to salubrious location, accessibility to London and resemblance thereto, excellent train service, and its enormous capacity for accommodating and amusing all tastes and all classes all the year round. Racecourse meetings; 6 golf links (18 holes); harriers, foxhounds, county cricket ground, numerous parks and recreation grounds, boating fishing; Royal Pavilion, once a Royal residence, now used for public amusements and concerts; public library, museum, art galleries.

CLACTON-ON-SEA (1928), Essex. Urban District Council. Pop. 7,049. L. & N.E Railway. 70 miles from London. *Aspect:* South. *Climate:* Dry, bracing. *Water Supply:* Constant. *Front:* Sea-wall promenade and cliff walk at different levels, the spaces between the terraces clothed in flowers and tamarisk. *Beach:* Sands. Golf links (18 holes). Popular family summer holiday resort and health resort of convalescents.

DOUGLAS (ISLE OF MAN) (1913), Pop. 22,000. *Means of access:* Steamers from Liverpool, Fleetwood, Heysham, also Ireland and Scotland. *Beach:* Firm sands. *Sea Bathing:* Not mixed. *Excursions:* Numerous by steamboats. *Season:* From Whit week to end of September. Yachting, golf links (18 holes), fishing, coaching, tennis, bowls, mountaineering, two theatres, two large ball-rooms, opera house, two variety halls, hippodrome, bands, public baths, etc. *Sunshine:* (1911) 1,873 hrs.

DROITWICH (1928), Worcestershire. Municipal Borough. Pop. 4,588. L.M. & S. Railway and G.W. Railway. 126 miles from London. 19 miles from Birmingham. *Climate:* Mild. *Neighbourhood:* Undulating woodland. A health resort noted for the curative properties of its brine-laden springs.

EDINBURGH (1929), L. & N.E. Railway and L.M. & S. Railway. Edinburgh possesses a picturesque beauty quite unrivalled. Tourists from all parts of the world are attracted to the metropolis of Scotland by its historical associations with Queen Mary, John Knox, and Sir Walter Scott. Besides the Castle, Holyrood Palace, Scott's Monument and John Knox's House, are many historic buildings, museums, libraries, and a celebrated University.

ENGLISH LAKES (1908), The English Lakes District is one of the most attractive to tourists and holiday-seekers; it is rich in literary and historical associations, affords a unique combination of mountains, lakes, rivers and seas; it is rendered easily accessible by modern railway enterprise, the entire area being covered by a well-arranged system of tours specially designed for the ever-increasing number of pleasure-seekers in search of the gems of the English beauty spots.

Ambleside, Westmoreland. Urban District Council. Pop. 2,536. *Means of access:* Steamer from Lakeside and Windermere, coach and motor from Waterhead Pier and Windermere, 5m. *Elevation:* From 160 to 300 ft. above sea-level. *Immediate Neighbourhood:* Windermere, Grasmere, Langdale, Coniston, Kirkstone, Troutbeck, etc. *Aspect:* Westerly. To all travellers and visitors it offers direct and appreciable charms, the views are of unsurpassed beauty, and the climate bracing. There are excursions through most picturesque scenery to the lakes and mountains. For amusement there is a golf course (9 holes), boating on the lake, and steamer tugs. *Season:* June–Sept.

Kendal, Westmoreland. Pop. 15,000. L. & N.W. Ry., Mid. Ry. The gateway to the Lakes is a beautiful district on the River Kendal. Excellent fishing and coaching.

Keswick, Cumberland. Pop. 4,451. *Means of access:* By rail from Penrith; coach and motor from Waterhead and Ambleside in connection with lake steamer. One of the best of northern centres for the Lake district, and is one of the most romantic places in a region rich in romance. About ½m. from Derwentwater and the Lodore Falls within easy reach. Excursions by coach to the picturesque scenery in the surrounding neighbourhood. Good salmon and trout-fishing in lake and river. Golf course (9 holes).

Windermere, Westmoreland. Urban District Council. Pop. 2,379. *Means of access:* Furness Ry., L. & N.W. Ry. *Elevation:* from 116 ft. to 400 ft. above sea-level. A village to the north of Bowness, commanding splendid views. Situated above the famous lake of the same name. Pleasure steamers run the whole length of the lake, and coaches and motors run to Ambleside, Grasmere, and Ullswater. Splendid fishing and boating.

FALMOUTH (1907), Municipal Borough. Pop. 11,789. *Means of access:* G. W. Ry. and by coasting steamship. *Location:* On south side of Falmouth harbour, 15m. N.N.E. of the Lizard. *Elevation:* Little above sea-level. *Neighbourhood:* Wooded hills. *Aspect:* North-east upon an arm of the sea 10m. in circumference. *Beach:* Shingle, sand as tide recedes. *Climate:* Temperate, equable. *Sunshine:* 1,616 hrs., 1904. *Season:* Summer and winter. Seaport town and watering-place on the S.W. bank of the River Fal, 8m. below Truro, with a magnificent harbour and excellent facilities for yachting and boating. Trees have been planted in many streets. Pier, bathing, park, marine drive. River and sea excursions.

HARROGATE, (1911), Yorkshire, Municpal Borough. Pop. 32,000. N.E. Ry. *Location:* 18m. N. of Leeds, 20m. W. of York. *Elevation:* 321 ft. to 600 ft. *Neighbourhood:* Open moorlands. *Sunshine:* (1909), 1,399 hrs. *Drainage:* Modern. *Soil:* Alluvial, millstone, grit and shale. *Baths:* Numerous large establishments open all the year round, providing complete modern installations, embracing hydropathic, vapour, heat, light, Peat Plombière swimming baths, and other treatments. *Mineral waters:* About 80 varieties of medicinal springs in a small area, one group sulphur, the other iron. Fashionable, select spa and inland resort, celebrated for its mineral springs and bathing palaces; presents many attractions to health-seekers and visitors. Higher Harrogate, open and bracing; Lower Harrogate, milder and sheltered; favourite town for valetudinarians, invalids, and the retired, also a scholastic centre; claims exemption from high summer and low winter temperatures: the Stray, a verdant public common of 200 acres, intersects the town, and is well laid out to retain its

A TIMELINE OF NATIONAL DEBT

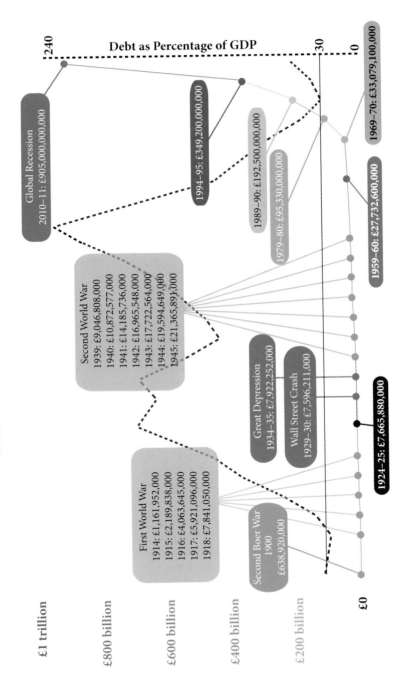

Debt as Percentage of GDP

240

30

0

£1 trillion

£800 billion

£600 billion

£400 billion

£200 billion

£0

Global Recession
2010–11: £905,000,000,000

1994–95: £349,200,000,000

1989–90: £192,500,000,000

1979–80: £95,330,000,000

1969–70: £33,079,100,000

1959–60: £27,732,600,000

Second World War
1939: £9,046,808,000
1940: £10,872,577,000
1941: £14,185,736,000
1942: £16,965,548,000
1943: £17,722,564,000
1944: £19,594,649,000
1945: £21,365,891,000

Great Depression
1934–35: £7,922,252,000

Wall Street Crash
1929–30: £7,596,211,000

1924–25: £7,665,880,000

First World War
1914: £1,161,952,000
1915: £2,189,838,000
1916: £4,063,645,000
1917: £5,921,096,000
1918: £7,841,050,000

Second Boer War
1900
£638,920,000

GREAT WAR CASUALTIES, 1914–1919

The 1940 edition of *Whitaker's* records figures for the number of mobilized, wounded and dead soldiers in the First World War. Although the Armistice between the Allied Powers and Germany occurred on 11 November 1918, fighting continued for several months, until the signing of the Treaty of Versailles on 28 June 1919.

British Empire and Allied and Associated Countries

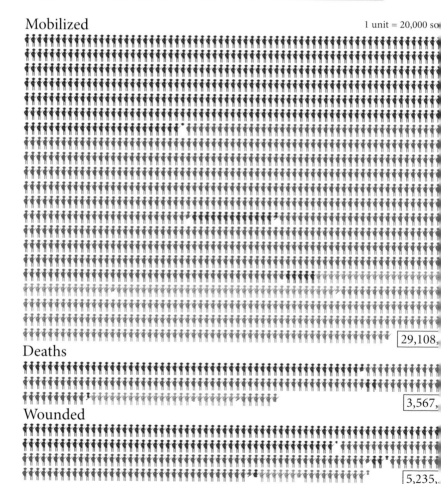

British Empire France Belgium Italy Portugal Romania Serbia USA

Mobilized

1 unit = 20,000 soldiers

29,108,

Deaths

3,567,

Wounded

5,235,

Russian Empire does not appear in the statistics, perhaps on account of its withdrawal
n the war in 1917, which was officially confirmed by the Treaty of Brest-Litovsk on
arch 1918.

ntral Powers

ermany 🛉Austria and Hungary 🛉Bulgaria 🛉Turkey

bilized

1 unit = 20,000 soldiers

22,850,006

aths

3,651,690

ounded

8,544,428

Year	Marriages	Divorces
1913	342,247	827
1932	347,321	4,382
1937	406,117	5,535
1940	531,659	8,495
1943	343,843	11,315
1946	441,100	36,489
1948	446,200	45,755
1953	395,316	32,089
1963	401,137	33,617
1969	451,310	54,278
1983	389,300	160,717
1989	382,023	162,531
1993	341,246	177,805
1999	293,455	156,420
2003	306,214	164,418
2008	275,591	152,960
2013	269,590	129,623

MARRIAGES AND DIVORCES IN GREAT BRITAIN

GREAT BRITAIN AT THE OLYMPICS

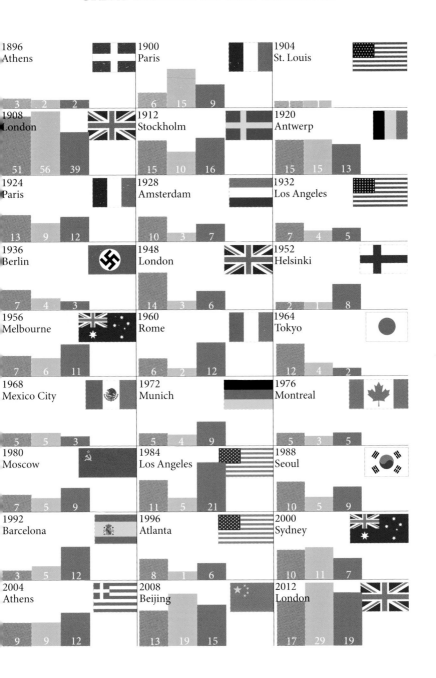

Year	City	Gold	Silver	Bronze
1896	Athens	3	2	2
1900	Paris	6	15	9
1904	St. Louis			
1908	London	51	56	39
1912	Stockholm	15	10	16
1920	Antwerp	15	15	13
1924	Paris	13	9	12
1928	Amsterdam	10	3	7
1932	Los Angeles	7	4	5
1936	Berlin	7	4	3
1948	London	14	3	6
1952	Helsinki	2	1	8
1956	Melbourne	7	6	11
1960	Rome	6	2	12
1964	Tokyo	12	4	2
1968	Mexico City	5	5	3
1972	Munich	5	4	9
1976	Montreal	5	3	5
1980	Moscow	7	5	9
1984	Los Angeles	11	5	21
1988	Seoul	10	5	9
1992	Barcelona	3	5	12
1996	Atlanta	8	1	6
2000	Sydney	10	11	7
2004	Athens	9	9	12
2008	Beijing	13	19	15
2012	London	17	29	19

FLIGHTS BETWEEN THE UK AND ABROAD

Year	Flights by British Aircraft	Year	Flights by Foreign Aircraft
1919		1919	
1920		1920	
1921		1921	
1922		1922	
1923		1923	
1924		1924	
1925		1925	
1926		1926	
1927		1927	
1928		1928	
1929		1929	
1930		1930	
1933		1933	
1936		1936	
1953		1953	
1960		1960	
1963		1963	

1,000   50,000

Total number of flights by British aircraft in 2012: 1,197,871

REGULAR AIR SERVICES IN 1926

ernational air travel began in earnest on 25th August 1919 with the commencement of a
eduled service between Hounslow Heath Aerodrome, Middlesex and Paris-Le Bourget
port. On board were the pilots, one passenger, a consignment of leather, around a dozen
use and several jars of Devonshire cream.

Over the next decade, the range of destinations open to fare-paying passengers
adened significantly. A list of air services first appeared in the 1927 edition of *Whitaker's*,
ailing the range of regular routes during the summer of 1926.

The map below illustrates these flight paths.

lines

erial Airways Ltd
erial Airways Ltd and Sabena Joint Service
erial Airways Ltd and Deutsch-russische
verkehrsgesellschaft
erial Airways Ltd and A. B. Aerotransport
Union
al Dutch Airline (K. L. M.)

Key

❶ Amsterdam
❷ Rotterdam
❸ Essen
❹ Cologne
❺ Dortmund
❻ Cassel
❼ Hamburg
❽ Bremen
❾ Hannover
❿ Magdeburg
⓫ Halle
⓬ Leipzig

RAILWAYS OF THE UNITED KINGDOM

The figures in the graph are taken directly from the selected editions of *Whitaker's Almanack* which would often (but not always) include railway mileage statistics. The trac length figures are based on total route miles (the total extent of routes available for trains operate on).

By 1960, the railways had amassed a deficit of £68m, which increased to £104m in 1962. In order to remedy this and to better serve the needs of the country, the government decided on a radical remodelling of the railway system. In March 1963, the British Railways Board published a report, written by Dr Richard Beeching, on the reshaping of the railways. The main proposals included the closure of many branch lines and about 2,500 of the 7,000 stations to passenger traffic. These proposals were implemen in the mid to late 1960s, and, by 1970, total track length had been reduced significantly, accounting for the noticeable drop in the graph below.

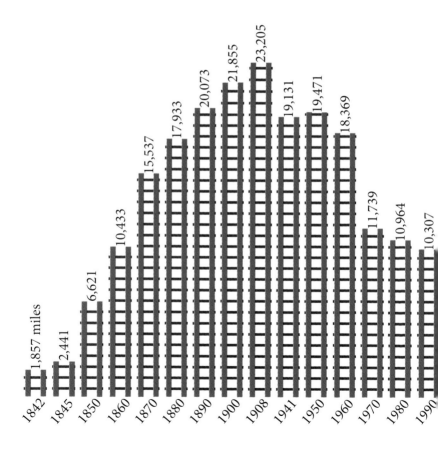

rural charms; the Kursaal, Royal Spa concert-rooms, and gardens are owned by the Corporation, who maintain a military band and an orchestra; covered promenade for water-drinkers; opera house; tennis, lacrosse, golf (18 holes), fox-hunting; coaching.

LLANDRINDOD WELLS, (1925), Central Wales, Urban District Council. L.M. & S. and G.W. Railways. *Elevation:* 750 feet. *Climate:* Bracing. *Mineral Waters:* Sulphur, saline, Lithia, chalybeate, etc. A popular health resort. Its great attractions are its mineral springs, but the beauty of its surroundings and the purity of its air also attract many visitors. Golf links (18 holes)

LOWESTOFT (1927), Suffolk. Pop. 44,326. *Means of Access:* L. & N.E. Railway. *Neighbourhood:* Open, sand dunes and broads. *Climate:* Bracing; absence of fog and mist. *Sunshine:* (1925), 1,746 hours. *Water Supply:* Constant. *Drainage:* Modern. *Soil:* Gravel and sand. A large and important fishing town and high-class summer resort. Good centre for exploring the thousands of acres of lagoons and miles of navigable rivers called the Broads. Excellent fishing, boating. New 18-hole golf links laid out by Braid.

MINEHEAD (1906), Somerset. Urban District Council. Pop. 2,511. G. W. Ry. *Location:* On S. shore of Bristol Channel, 24 m. from Taunton. *Neighbourhood:* Sea and moorland. *Aspect:* East. *Climate:* According to situation on shore or hills. *Water supply:* Constant. *Soil:* Sandstone. *Front:* Asphalted esplanade on sea-wall. *Pier:* With landing stage for excursion steamers. *Beach:* Shingle and sand. *Season:* June to September. *Annual fixture:* Opening meet Devon and Somerset Staghounds (August).

Minehead is a favourite centre, August to December, for members of the Exmoor Hunt; a quiet holiday resort in summer; recommended as a winter residence for invalids.

OBAN (1930), Argyllshire. Pop. 6,344. *Means of Access:* L.M. & S. Railway and steamboat. Oban's natural position, salubrity of climate, and beauty of situation command a high reputation among tourists visiting the Highlands, for whom it is a convenient point of arrival for and departure from the shooting moors. Golf (9 holes). Magnificent drives to numerous places of historic interest.

PERTH (1926), Perthshire. Pop. 33,208. L.M. & S. and L. & N.E. Railways. 22 miles from Dundee, 40 miles from Edinburgh, 450 miles from London. Situated on both sides of the River Tay. It is a great railway centre for tourists and the principal gateway to the Highlands. Golf courses, two (18 holes; ladies 9 holes).

SHORTLANDS (1929), Kent. Southern Railway. 10 miles from London. Situated midway between Beckenham and Bromley. It is a good residential district with many places of interest within the neighbourhood.

STAINES (1910), Market town on River Thames, 6m. S.E. of Windsor. Pleasantly situated and has ample accommodation for the many anglers who make it their headquarters during the season.

TORQUAY (1909), Devon. Market Borough. Pop. 33,625. *Means of access:* G. W Ry., 220m. from London. *Location:* S. E. coast of Devon in the N. recess of Torbay, 25m. S. of Exeter. *Neighbourhood:* Cliffs and hills. *Sunshine:* 1,741 hours, 1907. *Climate:* Mild, soft, equable; luxuriant vegetation. *Water supply:* From Dartmoor; constant, soft. *Drainage:* Modern. *Soil:* Limestone. *Front:* Ornamental promenades and marine drive. *Pier:* 1,500 ft., pavilion, skating rink. *Beach:* Sand and single. *Bathing:* Mixed. *Baths:* Corporation baths (fresh and sea-water, medicated), Turkish. *Excursions:* Rail and river, coaching and marine. *Seasons:* Winter and summer. *Annual Fixtures:* Balls at Easter, Aug., and Christmas; dog show, flower show, regatta, steeple and hurdle races, mobilisation of Fleet. In a curve of Torbay, on a peninsula between the Rivers Dart and Teign, Torquay is built on seven hills, the highest reaching 400 ft., sheltered N. and E.; lower part is built round harbour (enclosed by quay and piers), the houses rising behind in tiers, affording choice of elevation. A fashionable, high-class watering-place, favourite resort for the delicate, and popular winter residence; claims to be warm in winter and cool in summer. Good yachting facilities in the harbour, and safe anchorage in bay. Convenient centre for excursionists over Dartmoor. *Recreations:* Princess Gardens – fêtes, tennis, croquet, bowls, band (plays daily), golf (18 holes and 9 holes), yachting, boating fishing (sea, river and lake), hunting, polo, chess club, public library, theatre; in the Corporation Bath Saloons – balls, concerts, lectures, skating rink; at the recreation ground – football, hockey, tennis, cycle track; model yacht lake in the King's Gardens.

TUNBRIDGE WELLS (1910), Market Borough. Pop. 35,000. *Means of access:* L.B. & S. C. Ry.; S. E. C. Ry. Inland watering-place. A select residential and health resort. The common, 249 acres, is a splendid sloping sweep of verdant heath, furze and bracken, the highest parts, 440 ft. above sea-level; foot of common are its medicinal springs, pump-room, and Pantiles. Open-air and indoor bathing establishments, golf links (18 holes), good hunting centre, coaching.

Tourists in Great Britain
From the 1953 edition

The total number of foreign visitors, arriving in this country rose from 603,000 in 1930 to over 690,000 in 1951, not including tourists from the Republic of Ireland. The large increase in the number of tourists in 1951 is largely accounted for by an increase of 61,000 in the number of foreign visitors from Europe and an increase of over 18,000 in the number of visitors from the Commonwealth.

127,000 United States citizens and 36,000 Canadians visited the United Kingdom in 1951. Tourist earnings from the Dollar Area in the year totalled $69,000,000 (£24,643,000 approximately). The number of visitors from Germany increased by 71 per cent, from 24,000 in 1950 to 41,000 in 1951. Expenditure of all overseas visitors in the United Kingdom in 1951 amounted to £73,000,000 compared with £60,900,000 in 1950.

REVIEWS OF
THE YEAR

The following extracts are taken from the 'Reviews of the Year' or 'Annual Summaries' which constitute articles on specialist fields of interest:

BROADCASTING

Science and Invention of 1927
As recorded in the 1928 edition

TELEVISION PROGRESS – Mr. J. L. Baird [John Logie Baird] has made considerable progress with television during the year, and has considerably increased the distance over which the image of a human face or any other object may be transmitted. On **May 24** he gave a successful demonstration of television between London and Glasgow. Two ordinary Post Office telephone lines were used, one for conversation and the other for television transmission. The telephone lines connecting the two stations were 438 miles long. In some cases the images were unsteady, but in most of the experiments they were steady and clear. At the meeting of the British Association demonstrations were given by Mr. Baird of the television and "noctovision" apparatus, the latter being used over the 200 miles between Leeds and London. It employs infra-red radiation in the place of light, and is regarded by the inventor as likely to be of commercial value at an earlier date than the former, since he hopes to apply it to navigation in fog, the worst enemy the mercantile marine has to face.

Science and Invention of 1929
As recorded in the 1930 edition

TELEVISION IN COLOURS – The addition of colour to previously perfected reproductions in television has been accomplished at the Bell Laboratories in New York where objects in natural colour have been made to appear on a small screen attached to an ordinary telephone. Observers at the demonstration saw a girl in a brightly hued dress eat a ripe red melon, the colour on her cheeks not less apparent than the tints of the fruits, flowers and flags she was handling. Mr. Herbert E. Ives, of the technical staff, explained that "the same light sources for driving the motors and scanning discs of the synchronising system are used as in the monochromatic system. The only new features are the type and arrangement of the neon and argon lamps at the receiving end. The outstanding contributions which made the present achievement possible are the new photo-electric cell, the new gas cells for reproducing the image, and the equipment associated directly with them."

Broadcasting in 1932
As recorded in the 1933 edition

Important developments of 1932 include the transfer of broadcasting headquarters from Savoy Hill to Broadcasting House, the opening of the new Scottish transmitter at Westerglen, the building of a new short-wave station for Empire broadcasts, the establishment of an Empire news service, and the introduction of short television programmes as a regular feature of broadcasting. The developments in the ordinary programmes are less striking, but there has been a welcome increase in the number of relays from foreign stations which is quite in keeping with the B.B.C.'s motto, "Nation shall speak peace unto nation."

The new B.B.C. building in Portland Place had become one of London's architectural points of interest long before the first programme was sent out from it. The transfer from the old premises in Savoy Hill began in the autumn of 1931, but it was not until the early months of 1932 that the main body of the staff moved to the new headquarters. From March onwards, both Broadcasting House and Savoy Hill were used for the transmission of programmes, and on the evening of **May 14** Savoy Hill was closed down, leaving Broadcasting House as the sole headquarters of British broadcasting. Two months later, on **July 7**, Their Majesties the King and Queen [George V. and Queen Mary] paid a visit to Broadcasting House and made a tour of the building.

With its large entrance-hall, its twenty-two studios, including a large concert-hall and a group of ten for dramatic productions, its comprehensive ventilation system and its magnificent technical equipment, Broadcasting House is undoubtedly a worthy home for British broadcasting; but the guiding principle of the building, by which the studios are encased in a central tower and thereby separated from the surrounding offices, has taken away much of the informality which was a pleasant feature of Savoy Hill. Mr. James Agate [theatre critic] has charmingly expressed the difference between the two buildings by putting himself in the position of "an old time sailor who, having learned his job on a four-master, is now confronted with the marvel of funnels and asked where his heart lies. If he is an honest mariner he will speak the truth."

Since 1927 the B.B.C. has transmitted part of its programmes from the experimental short-wave station at Chelmsford, and these transmissions have been enthusiastically received in various parts of the Empire. This service, however, was definitely experimental, and at the end of 1931 the B.B.C. decided to proceed with a comprehensive Empire Broadcasting scheme, which will enable every part of the British Commonwealth of Nations to receive a short-wave programme transmitted from England. The scheme involves the use of a number of different wave-lengths, and the old transmitter at Chelmsford was quite inadequate to the purpose. A new station, equipped with two transmitters, has been built at Daventry, and preliminary transmission tests were begun at the end of 1932. These tests are to be continued until it is possible to determine which are the best wave-lengths for serving the different parts of the Empire, and it is expected that the full Empire service will be inaugurated during 1933.

In anticipation of the opening of the new station, the B.B.C. made an important addition to its short wave transmissions during 1932. A service of Empire news bulletins was established on **January 4**, and the bulletins, which were broadcast each weekday at 12.30 p.m., 6.15 p.m. and midnight, sent the latest news from home and abroad to short-wave listeners overseas.

TELEVISION – Although the day of complete television has not yet arrived, and the majority of broadcasters can still enjoy the privilege of being heard but not seen, each year sees the passing of a further milestone in television's relentless advance. In 1931 transmissions by the Baird process were made from a B.B.C. studio for the first time in the history of broadcasting, and in 1932 television programmes from Broadcasting House became a regular feature of the B.B.C.'s work. These programmes, which are given for half-an-hour on four evenings a week, began on **Monday, August 22**, and the "televised" performances have included singers, musicians, and vaudeville artists, as well as exponents of Yo-Yo and Jiu-Jitsu.

OUTSTANDING BROADCASTS – Of all the material which was broadcast in 1932 there was no item which aroused so much interest and excitement as the verbatim reading of Mr. Neville Chamberlain's War Loan Conversion speech on the evening of **June 30** [Neville Chamberlain was Chancellor of the Exchequer from 1931–7]. This was an important occasion, for it revealed the value of broadcast as a means of conveying important announcements to the general public with the least possible delay. Until the moment when he rose in the House of Commons on **June 30** the secret of Mr. Chamberlain's announcement had been closely guarded, but special arrangements had been made for its immediate communication to the public. A few minutes after he had finished his speech the complete text was broadcast, and to mark the significance of the occasion it was read by Vice-Admiral Sir Charles Carpendale, the controller of the B.B.C., who had recently received his knighthood in the Birthday Honours. In the following month speeches in support and explanation of the scheme were broadcast by Mr. Ramsay MacDonald [Prime Minister from 1929–35], Mr. Stanley Baldwin [Lord President of the Council] and Lord Hailsham and Mr. George Lansbury.

The Prince of Wales [Edward VIII], who is one of the most popular of all broadcasters, was heard in several outstanding items of the year. On January 27 his striking "call to youth," at a meeting organised by the National Council for Social Service, was relayed from the Albert Hall, London; on **Apr. 23** listeners heard his speech on the spirit of Shakespeare and England at the opening of the new Shakespeare Memorial Theatre at Stratford-on-Avon; and on **Aug. 1** the broadcast of the unveiling ceremony of the Somme Memorial at Thiepval included speeches by the Prince of Wales and M. Lebrun, the President of the French Republic.

The chief religious events of the year also figured in the broadcasting programmes. An address by the Archbishop of Canterbury [Cosmo Gordon Lang], in connection with the National Day of Prayer, was relayed from Canterbury Cathedral on Jan. 3.

One of the great benefits of broadcasting is that events which occur overseas can now be brought nearer to the British public than was possible before. Thousands of listeners were able to be present in spirit at the unveiling of the Somme Memorial, and thousands were able to hear the inauguration of two conferences which, though held overseas, vitally concerned the interest of Great Britain. When the World Disarmament Conference opened on Feb. 2, the inaugural speech of Mr. Arthur Henderson, the President of the Conference, was relayed from Geneva, and later in the year the speeches of Mr. Stanley Baldwin, Mr. R. B. Bennett and others were relayed from Ottawa at the opening of the Imperial Economic Conference. The Atlantic was no barrier to the clear reception of the speeches, and part of the ceremony, which had been recorded by the Blattnerphone, was broadcast again for the benefit of those who had not heard the original relay. British listeners were also enabled to sympathise with the French nation in the loss of two distinguished statesmen, for the funeral orations of Mr. Briand, the great Foreign Minister, and M. Doumer, the murdered President, were broadcast by the B.B.C.

In connexion with the transfer of broadcasting headquarters from Savoy Hill to Broadcasting House two items deserve special mention – the first transmission from Broadcasting House and the last from Savoy Hill. The first broadcast from the new headquarters took place on March 15, when Mr. Henry Hall, who had recently succeeded Mr. Jack Payne, introduced the new B.B.C. dance orchestra to the listening public. The last from Savoy Hill was the retrospective programme on May 14, entitled "The End of Savoy Hill." The greater part of the programme, which was devised by Mr. Lance Sieveking, and lasted for more than two and a half hours, was given from Broadcasting House, but the later stages were transmitted from Savoy Hill, where each studio was used for the last time. And the microphones were then cut off. Although the retrospect of the early history of broadcasting was excellently done the programme encountered a good deal of adverse criticism, on the grounds that it was too long, and that after a good beginning it dwindled away into insignificance.

Among other notable broadcasts of the year were Miss Amelia Earhart's account of her flight across the Atlantic, Mr. Neville Chamberlain's speech on his Budget, the appreciations of M. Briand by Lord Cecil of Chelwood and of M. Doumer by Sir John Simon, Mr. Stanley Baldwin's talk on the Ottawa agreements, Sir Samuel Hoare's account of "India since the Round Table Conference," and Mr. Ramsay MacDonald's Empire Day broadcast. In lighter vein, though many listeners will remember it for a long time, was the short message broadcast by the American film comedians, Laurel and Hardy, during their visit to Great Britain.

Television: A Year of Achievement
As recorded in the 1937 edition

The year 1936 will go down in history as television's year of achievement. By the time this article is published regular television programmes, limited, it is true, but representing a definite daily service, will be radiating from the television station which has been established by the British Broadcasting Corporation at Alexandra Palace. In short, television has "arrived."

For some time to come Alexandra Palace will be an experimental television centre, and the future development of the service will depend on many factors. Even the most responsible members of the technical staff at Alexandra Palace are unable to make any pronouncement as to the direction in which the service will be developed to cover the Provinces.

Now that a practical start has been made, it is possible that progress will be fairly rapid. That some of the experts are optimistic is revealed by a recent statement of the chairman of one of the big companies manufacturing television apparatus, that television will be installed in cinemas throughout the country by the end of 1936.

Receivers are now available which are capable of receiving ordinary B.B.C. sound programmes on the short, medium and long waves, as well as television programmes. One such receiver incorporates 23 valves, and will reproduce pictures 9 ins. wide by 7 ins. high. The brilliancy and clearness of the pictures received are controlled by turning a knob in the same way as one operates the volume control of an ordinary broadcast receiver.

Broadcasting in 1937
As recorded in the 1938 edition

It was through broadcasting that the British public learnt, in December 1936, of the Abdication of Edward VIII. Five months later the medium was more happily employed in signalising the Coronation of George VI. Undoubtedly the 1937 Coronation programmes are to be numbered amongst the most impressive which have ever been heard on the air. Anticipating the enormous interest which would attach to the event, the B.B.C. made its arrangements on ambitious lines. The proceedings on **May 12th** occupied some six and a half hours of broadcasting time. The actual ceremony at Westminster Abbey was taken almost in full; and the processions to and from the Abbey were described by commentators at five points of vantage along the route. Extensions to the Empire short-wave transmitting station at Daventry having been completed just in time for the Coronation, the broadcasts were received all over the world. Parts of the day's happenings were televised. In the evening there was a notable feature programme, to which contributions were made by the Dominions and Colonies; and at its conclusion His Majesty, broadcasting for the first time as King Emperor, sent a message to his subjects throughout the Empire.

Once again there was a substantial increase in the number of wireless licence-holders – an increase all the more remarkable, in view of the high figures already achieved. At the end of 1936 the number of licences issued was 7,960,573, which was an increase of 557,464 on the previous year; and by **September 30th, 1937**, the figure had grown to 8,347,800. In the London area alone there were nearly 3,000,000 licence holders. It is interesting to recall that at the end of 1922 – six weeks after the formation of the British Broadcasting Company, Ltd. – there were only 35,774 licences in the whole country; and by 1927 – when the corporation was established – the figure had risen to 2,178,259. Until comparatively recently, 8,000,000 was commonly regarded as saturation point.

British Television Leads the World
As recorded in the 1938 edition

When 1936 drew to its close it was common knowledge that the B.B.C. had spent some months in tentative experiments in television. The British public were waiting expectantly for the curtain to go up on this great new scientific triumph, and there was a sudden quickening of interest when a regular television service was commenced from the new transmitting centre at Alexandra Palace.

When 1937 dawned this service had been running for several weeks. It was creating no little interest amongst the manufacturing section of the wireless industry, and was causing something akin to enthusiasm amongst those of the public who already possessed television receivers and were living inside the 25 miles radius which Alexandra Palace had announced it was able to cover. These pioneer "viewers" reported excellent reception of the B.B.C. transmissions, and it was clear to anyone who made a practical examination of television that it could not be very long before the service was considerably extended.

That optimism has been abundantly justified. At the end of 1937 it can be said that British television has proved its worth. At the same time there remains the obvious reservation that this service can only be enjoyed by only a relatively small proportion of the British public owing to the present restricted range of transmission, and that the extent to which the service is appreciated in the near future depends entirely on the policy of the B.B.C. in providing transmissions for those great areas of Britain in which they are still an untapped well of entertainment and interest.

We hear a lot of what Germany is doing with television, but it is certain that she is providing nothing which can compare with the transmissions from Alexandra

Palace. The same applies to the television achievements of the United States and France. Yet television is in the cradle stage even in Britain itself, but there is little doubt that our own achievements are giving considerable stimulus to its world development.

There has been some successful televising of outdoor events, including the Coronation procession, and it is obvious that here lies one of the most interesting lines of evolution. Some of the difficulties in this pathway of research have been overcome, but it is admitted that many more have yet to be mastered. However, the remarkable Emitron television camera has been frequently used with striking success, and it can be confidently predicted that during the next 12 months outdoor events will take up an even greater part of programme time.

The Coronation of Queen Elizabeth II
As recorded in the 1954 edition

THE QUEEN'S FIRST CHRISTMAS BROADCAST – The Queen followed the practice of her father and grandfather in broadcasting to her people throughout the Commonwealth on Christmas Day. In spite of disturbed atmospheric conditions, Her Majesty was heard clearly in all parts of the world. The Queen, in the first Christmas Day broadcast of her reign, asked for the prayers of all her listeners on her Coronation Day. The Prime Minister of New Zealand, Mr. Holland, announced on Christmas Day that the Queen's Christmas broadcast in 1953 would be made from Government House, Auckland.

THE CORONATION – The sound and television broadcasting of the Coronation ceremony and procession and attendant celebrations was considered on all sides to have been an outstanding success. The original decision to televise only the processions west of the screen in Westminster Abbey was subsequently amended, and viewers saw the whole service except for the Anointing, the Communion prayers and the administration of the Sacrament. Many thousands all over the world were thus enabled to see the actual crowning of Her Majesty. The television transmissions of the procession back to Buckingham Palace were excellent, in spite of the bad weather. Taking into account large-screen presentations in cinemas, church halls, hospitals, etc., it was estimated that not fewer than 20,000,000 people viewed the service in the United Kingdom alone. The television programme lasted for seven hours. Thirty-seven transmitters were used to radiate the sound and television broadcasts in this country. In the evening of Coronation Day, the Queen spoke to her people, and the broadcast was preceded by messages from eight of the Commonwealth Prime Ministers then present in London, from Queen Salote of Tonga and finally from Sir Winston Churchill.

The televised programme of the Coronation was relayed to the Continent, and was seen clearly in France, Belgium, Holland and Western Germany. Telefilms of the service were flown immediately to Canada, reaching Goose Bay, Labrador, at 6.45 p.m., and being seen by audiences in Montreal the same evening. The two chief United States networks (the National Broadcasting Company and the Columbia Broadcasting System) had chartered airliners which flew direct to New York with the films taken by the networks themselves. The films were processed during the journey and were shown during the evening in New York and Boston. During the day 43 languages were used in B.B.C. sound broadcasts, in addition to a continuous English programme on the European and overseas services, and a separate English programme for re-broadcasting in America. Foreign commentators were also given full facilities for independent broadcasts from London.

The televising of the Coronation was a large factor in the increase of television sets in use by the public. On **March 31, 1953**, the latest date for which figures are available, 2,142,452 combined sound and television licences were current, compared with 1,457,000 a year previously.

SPORTS BROADCASTS – Though Football League matches and Rugby Union Internationals continued to be absent from the television programme, many Rugby Union and Rugby League club matches were televised. The Lawn Tennis Championships at Wimbledon and county and Test Match cricket were also still popular. Broadcasting of the Test Matches in particular attracted many viewers and listeners. On the third day of the last Test, the B.B.C. cancelled other programmes to give an almost uninterrupted broadcast of the match from 3 p.m. until the close of play. On the final day, by agreement with the M.C.C., the B.B.C. was allowed to televise the whole of the play, and there was also a ball by ball sound commentary on the Light Programme. An agreement reached between the B.B.C. and Messrs. Topham, the managers of Aintree racecourse, enabled the B.B.C. to broadcast the Grand National.

The State Opening of Parliament
As recorded in the 1960 edition

On **October 28, 1958**, the State Opening of Parliament was televised for the first time. Both the royal procession from Buckingham Palace to the House of Lords and the Queen's reading of her Speech were seen and heard, not only by viewers in this country, but by several millions in Europe. The ceremony was relayed through the Eurovision network to Belgium, Denmark, France, West Germany, the Netherlands, Italy and Switzerland. Reception in most of those countries was good, and it was reported that most of the 2,000,000 sets in West Germany and the 1,000,000 sets in Italy were tuned in to the programme and that 250,000 French people were estimated to have watched it.

Test Match Television
As recorded in the 1960 edition

The M.C.C. announced on **May 5** that a contract had been signed between the M.C.C. and the B.B.C. permitting unlimited television of Test matches by the latter during the ensuing three years.

Viewing Figures
As recorded in the 1960 edition

A report issued by the B.B.C. in January said that in the previous two years the number of people with television sets in their homes had risen from about one-half to two-thirds of the population. There were still 7,500,000 adults who received only B.B.C. television, but 17,000,000 were able to see both B.B.C. and I.T.V. programmes. The average amount of evening viewing in the last quarter of 1958 was 12½ hours a week compared with 11½ hours during the last quarter of 1957. A further statement in July, covering the months of April, May and June, 1959, showed that during those months the average viewer had devoted 9½ hours a week to watching television in the evenings compared with 10½ hours in the corresponding period of 1958, a reduction which was doubtless due to the better weather. The percentage of the adult population viewing during the evening had, however, risen from 18.9 to 20.5, and the television public had increased by 16 per cent.

FILM

Cinematography and Medical Problems

As recorded in the 1915 edition: Science and Invention of 1914

Dr. Gustave Monod, of Vichy, gave a demonstration before the Royal Society of Medicine of the value of cinematography in the analysis of movement and other medical problems, as determined at the Institut-Marey, Boulogne-sur-Seine. The pictures were taken at the rate of 250 a second. The whole process of the act of jumping, walking, and running were shown. Dr. Monod suggested that the method would prove of special value in the training of athletes, and in demonstrating a possible application he showed on the screen two men putting the weight, one of whom put all his strength into the throw, while the other, by a faulty movement at the finish, failed to make full use of his strength. In May an Educational Cinematograph Association was formed in London to encourage the best types of cinematograph production, and to develop a completely educational plan for their use.

Help for British Films

As recorded in the 1928 edition

[The following passage describes the passing of the Cinematograph Act 1927]

An attempt to help British films was made by means of a Government Bill introduced as a sequel to the resolution of the Imperial Conference. Moving the second reading on **March 16**, Sir Philip Cunliffe-Lister [President of the Board of Trade] said that millions of people throughout the Empire were being unconsciously influenced in their ideals and outlooks by films, yet only something like five per cent of the films shown in the British Empire at the present time were of British origin. From the trade point of view the influence of the cinema was no less important. The Empire was flooded with foreign films, he declared. The Bill sought to give some measure of security to the British film industry. It abolished blind-booking [the purchase of unseen pictures] and put a definite time limit on block-booking [the purchase of multiple films as one unit], besides imposing a quota on both renters and exhibitors – on the former in 1928 and on the latter in 1929. The quota was 7½ per cent, rising by 2½ per cent, each year to 25 per cent. The cost of registration would not be more than £400,000 or £500,000, and it was proposed to defray this out of fees. An advisory committee would be set up, consisting of exhibitors, producers and renters, with an independent chairman, as a further measure of efficiency and economy. Mr. Ramsay MacDonald [Leader of the Labour Party] moved the rejection, though he approved of the protection of exhibitors from having foreign films forced upon them, but on **March 22** the second reading was carried by 243 to 135. The Bill was fought line by line in Standing Committee, but this task was completed before the adjournment, the remaining stages being postponed.

British Films Rival Hollywood

As recorded in the 1934 editiion

The British-made film took a big step forward during 1933, and for the first time became a serious competitor of Hollywood productions. Among the leading new pictures shown publicly in London, nearly forty came from British studios, and at least four of them attained international fame. They were *The Good Companions*, founded on Mr. J. B. Priestley's novel, *Rome Express*, *I Was a Spy*, and *The Private Life of Henry VIII.*, in which Mr. Charles Laughton established himself as one of the greatest of film artists. Another very successful film was *Cavalcade*, in which Hollywood closely followed the British production of Mr. Noel Coward's deeply moving play.

A Première in Paris

As recorded in the 1935 edition

Further progress in British film production was made in 1934, and most of the best screen plays seen were the work of British studios, to which many of the leading foreign producers and players were attracted. Among the most important of the year were *Catherine the Great*, which had its world première in Paris, *The Wandering Jew*, *Jew Suss*, *Nell Gwyn*, *The Constant Nymph*, and *Little Friend*. A remarkable film was *Man of Aran*, depicting life on a desolate island off the Irish coast and with no professional artistes. One of the best American productions was *The Barretts of Wimpole Street*, in which Mr. Charles Laughton appeared.

Films of 1935

As recorded in the 1936 edition

The advance in the standard of film production, in respect equally of story, technique and photography, was well maintained in 1935, and the British studios appreciably strengthened their position. Notable among their output were *Sanders of the River* and *The Scarlet Pimpernel*, both founded on popular novels, indeed, many of the most successful screen plays of the year were adaptations, such as *Lorna Doone*, *Bella Donna* and *The Thirty-nine Steps*. Another striking British success was *The Man Who Knew Too Much*, and of the "documentary" films *The Voice of Britain*, illustrating the activities of the B.B.C., struck a new note. Of the American films, *Lives of a Bengal Lancer* was one of the successes of the year; in *Escape Me Never*, Miss Elisabeth Bergner repeated her stage triumph; a step forward in the use of colour was made with *Becky Sharp*, and Max Reinhardt's version of *A Midsummer Night's Dream* showed us a new and restrained Hollywood.

Chaplin's *Modern Times* Banned in Germany

As recorded in the 1937 edition

Despite a number of highly interesting films, both British and American, the event of the year in the cinema world was the presentation of *Modern Times*, the latest production of Charlie Chaplin. Behind a succession of the great comedian's whimsicalities was a background indicting the machinery age which brought the film a ban in Germany and wide popularity in Britain. The States also sent three splendid productions in *Romeo and Juliet*, the last and the best of Irving Thalberg's beautiful screenwork, *Mr. Deeds Goes to Town*, and *Mutiny on the Bounty*, which "starred" our leading actor, Charles Laughton. A home Shakespeare film, *As You Like It*, was a striking addition to British successes, with Elizabeth Bergner and a very good cast. Mr. H. G. Wells saw two of his stories successfully presented – *Things to Come* and *The Man Who Worked Miracles* – and other notable works from studios included *Rhodes of Africa*, *The Ghost Goes West*, *Secret Agent* and *Tudor Rose*.

Disney Comes to Britain

As recorded in the 1939 edition

The outstanding screen success of the year was a production in which no living star appeared – *Snow White and the Seven Dwarfs*, Walt Disney's first full-length film. This fantasy in cartoon, as attractive to the adult as to the children, ran without interruption in the West End for eight months, and even after its general release was still filling its original London house. Although the output of the British studios was slowed down owing to financial considerations, the high standard of their productions was more than maintained, and many American stars were tempted to England to appear in them. The most striking British success was *Sixty Glorious Years*, based upon Queen Victoria's private diaries. Mr. Bernard Shaw took a keen interest in the screen version of his *Pygmalion*, which proved very popular, and the other notable British productions included *St. Martin's Lane*, *A Yank at Oxford*, *The Drum*, *Yellow Sands*, and *Young and Innocent*. Among artists, the greatest triumphs were scored by the young French actress, Danielle Darrieux.

Help for British Films (Part 2)

[The following passage describes the passing of the Cinematograph Films Act 1938]

New proposals to assist the British film industry were made in a Government Bill presented on **Oct. 27**. It provided that renters of films must acquire and exhibitors must show a certain proportion of British films annually for a further ten years. A separate quota for short films was introduced for the first time, and a quality test was instituted in the case of the renters' quota. Any British films on which a minimum of £7,500 had been spent in labour costs and costing at least £1 a foot would qualify for registration automatically. Those below the minimum might be accepted for the quota if the Board of Trade were of opinion that they had special value for the purposes of entertainment.

The Outbreak of the Second World War
As recorded in the 1940 edition

Before the war closed the doors of British studios for a time, they produced several further notable successes, but the most striking of the year's films was *The Lion Has Wings*, made by Alexander Korda in a few weeks. It was a magnificent war picture illustrating Britain before the outbreak of hostilities and in the first month of the campaign, and it showed some of the work of the Royal Air Force, including the raid on German warships at Kiel. The picture was made with Government assistance and was placed on the Secret List during its production, being only released after careful inspection by the censors. Among the best of the pre-war films were *The Citadel* and *Good-bye Mr. Chips*, in each of which Robert Donat added to his reputation; *The Four Feathers*, and *Jamaica Inn*, in which Charles Laughton gave a fine performance. A film version of *The Mikado*, screened in a British Studio, was an interesting feature of the year.

Gable and Leigh Captivate Britain
As recorded in the 1941 edition

More adaptable than the theatre, the cinemas of London suffered less from war conditions than their rivals, being helped by earlier hours of opening and closing. British studios carried on with their arrangements, modified to suit the conditions, and a good proportion of the year's shows were home-products. Among them were several documentary films of the war, the finest being *London Can Take It*, a moving representation of the manner in which the capital of the Empire carried on during the air raids of the autumn. The best of the regular British films was *The Stars Look Down*, adapted from Dr. Cronin's novel, but first place for the year must be given to *Gone with the Wind*, which played simultaneously in the West End at three houses – for nearly three months at one of them. Walt Disney sent another delightful cartoon across the Atlantic – *Pinocchio* – which also ran for many weeks, and a film of the same type, *Gulliver's Travels*, by Max Fleischer, was another success.

War Dominates the Film Industry
As recorded in the 1943 edition

The great majority of films which came from British studios during the year, and quite a number of those flown over from Hollywood, dealt with various phases of the war, several of our own productions being factual instead of fictional – and all the better because of that. Most striking of the home releases – and, in the judgement of many critics, the best picture of the year – was Noel Coward's first essay in film direction, *In Which We Serve*, a stirring and moving story with a warship as its hero, screened and played with restraint and understanding. There were some excellent pictures illustrating the activities of the Royal Air Force, such as *Coastal Command* and *One of Our Aircraft is Missing*, and no admonitions to guard one's conversation were so effective as the Government sponsored *Next of Kin*.

English Film Star Shot Down
As recorded in the 1944 edition

Once again, most of the films produced by British studios had a war atmosphere. One of the most striking was *Life and Death of Colonel Blimp*, not a screen version of Low's creation, but a record of a gallant soldier's life, in which Roger Livesey gave a particularly fine performance. *Desert Victory*, filmed on the battlefields of North Africa under shell-fire and bombing, provided those at home with a wonderful picture of the historic advance of the Eighth Army. A propaganda film for the A.T.S. [*Auxiliary Territorial Service*, the women's branch of the British Army], *The Gentle Sex*, and *The Lamp Still Burns*, a tribute to the nursing profession, were not only excellent entertainment but interesting, because they were the last films directed by Leslie Howard, whose death at the hands of the enemy when a plane in which he was travelling home from Lisbon was shot down, was a real loss to the screen. Among the best of the American films were *Random Harvest*, *The War Against Mrs. Hadley* and *Victory through Air Power*, the latter an experiment by Walt Disney illustrating a plan for winning the war by bombing.

Brief Encounter
As recorded in the 1947 edition

British studios went further ahead during the year, and many of their productions not only held their own against Hollywood in this country, but were acclaimed in the United States. New directors and new writers brought fresh life into the industry, which reached a position that could not have been foreseen by the most sanguine after six years of total war. Most ambitious of the year's home films was *Caesar and Cleopatra*, a technicolour version of Bernard Shaw's play, which ran for some months in the West End and was then generally released to be seen by tens of thousands before crossing the Atlantic. Another fine release, simpler but more appealing, was *Brief Encounter* by Noel Coward, while *Theirs is The Glory* provided a sincere tribute to the airborne men who failed so magnificently at Arnhem.

Great Expectations
As recorded in the 1948 edition

The economic crisis brought a new trouble to the film world. Immediately as the seriousness of the dollar shortage became evident the Government brought into operation a clause inserted in the Finance Act a few months earlier and imposed a tax of 75 per cent of the earnings of imported films. Hollywood at once banned the export to Britain of their productions, but negotiations were soon opened which were expected to result in the lifting of the ban and the showing of more British films in the United States. Before this situation arose home studios had more than held their own with their foreign rivals, and in most lists of the best programmes of the year our own screen plays would be well represented. The adaptation of *Great Expectations* was without doubt one of the most satisfying and successful of English productions, and proved that the drama and humour of Charles Dickens were as effective on the screen as in the novel. An ambitious film, *A Matter of Life and Death*, was another big success, and *Odd Man Out* consolidated James Mason's position as one of our leading actors, and gained one of the awards at the Brussels Festival.

Britain at the Oscars

As recorded in the 1950 edition

The big event of the year in the British film world was the award of the highly-prized "Oscar" of the United States Motion Picture Academy to *Hamlet* as the best film of the year, this being the first time that a film not produced in the States had received the distinction. In addition, Sir Laurence Olivier was given the award of the Academy for the best male acting performance. Another British film, *Red Shoes*, won prizes for the best picture for a colour production and the best musical score of any domestic or foreign picture. The high standard thus set was generally maintained by a large number of British productions during the year, the most noteworthy being *Scott Of The Antarctic*, a screen representation of the great explorer's last endeavour and its tragic outcome, admirably enacted by John Mills in the title role, and his companions, and marked by a careful restraint against over-dramatization.

3-D

As recorded in the 1954 edition

During the greater part of the year, Hollywood – if not the whole film world – was as much concerned with new methods of presentation as with the quality of pictures, and while British producers in no way ignored what was called a technical revolution they were able to show a good proportion of the best films of 1953. The first full-length three dimensional film from the States to be screened in London was *Bwana Devil*, and later examples of the modern system marked a steady improvement. One drawback was that many of the 3-D films necessitated the use of special glasses by the audience. The Coronation provided the most popular of the pictures of the year, both *Elizabeth Is Queen* and *A Queen Is Crowned*, each in colour, being excellent representations of the historic ceremony, which were seen by many millions, not only in England. In the year under review, Charles Chaplin's latest film, *Limelight*, had its world première in London, and pictures made in a dozen countries were on view.

The Dam Busters
As recorded in the 1956 edition

British studios had no reason to be dissatisfied with their work, an unusually large proportion of which consisted of screen adaptations of either novels or stage plays. The most striking presentation was *The Dam Busters*, an extremely effective representation of the planning and organization that were needed to ensure the complete success of the attack by Bomber Command on the German dams, together with some wonderful pictures of the actual onslaught which interfered so greatly with the enemy's production of war materials.

Alec Guinness
As recorded in the 1959 edition

A British Film, *The Bridge On The River Kwai*, had the notable distinction of being selected as the best picture of the year by the British Film Academy and its United States equivalent, and the former chose Alec Guinness as having given the best performance by a British artiste.

Stars of British Film
As recorded in the 1961 edition

While many cinemas throughout the country were obliged to close down, despite the removal of the entertainment tax in the Budget, British films and British players continued to play a large part in the London productions of the year. Among the many artistes who enhanced their reputations were Sir Alec Guinness, Peter Sellers. Kenneth More, Robert Morley, John Mills and Norman Wisdom, and actors of the stage such as Laurence Olivier and Sir Ranulph Richardson again appeared on the screen successfully. A new version of the old classic, *Ben Hur*, proved to be one of the most popular of the American contributions and won a number of "Oscars".

The Eighties
As recorded in the 1984 edition

The film of the year was undoubtedly Sir Richard Attenborough's *Gandhi*, which provoked some controversy, but ultimately won all major awards, and justified Attenborough's 20-year struggle to make it. The subject-matter is a controversial and sensitive one, since it concerned people and events involved in the independence and shaping of the Indian nation.

At the British Academy of Film and Television Awards, *Gandhi* was voted best film, Sir Richard Attenborough best director, Ben Kingsley best actor, and also most outstanding newcomer to films. At the 55th annual Academy Awards in Los Angeles, U.S.A., *Gandhi* was nominated for eleven Oscars and won eight. *Gandhi's* achievement was the more remarkable as it was a British film; the best film award in 1982 had also been awarded to a British film, *Chariots of Fire*, and the American Academy has often been accused of insularity and an inherent desire to protect its own film industry. That *Gandhi* should capture the main awards, and against particularly strong opposition, was a sign that the Academy Awards are now governed by merit more than self-interest.

Monty Python's The Meaning of Life obviously struck a chord with the Cannes Festival Jury, but was generally agreed to be in appalling taste; as with most films by the Monty Python team, those who have acquired the taste find no fault, whilst others should avoid it at all costs.

SCIENCE AND INVENTION

Sailing in the Air
As recorded in the 1869 edition

A meeting of the Aeronautical Society was held at the Crystal Palace, in 1868, at which numerous machines were exhibited that were said to be capable of air-flying, but the practical proof of their value remains to be tested. An ingenious invention is that of M. Kaufman, of Glasgow. It consists of two immense wings, moved by a steam-engine placed between them, and by which they are rapidly moved. The appearance of the machine is that of an enormous bat, but the success attending its use still leaves the ancient Daedalus unshorn of his laurels.

The Channel Tunnel
As recorded in the 1877 edition

The question of forming a railway tunnel beneath the English Channel has long been mooted, especially since Sir John Hawkshaw [civil engineer], in 1865, began his researches into the geological character of the beds and outlying strata, but it was not until 1875 that any practical steps were mutually taken between the English and French Governments. In the summer of 1876 the preliminary works were commenced near Calais. The work had, in October, reached a depth of 122 metres of bored shafts in the chalk, &c. If the first steps be successful, it is possible that the tunnel will be proceeded with, as numerous attempts to improve the sea passage by steamers have failed.

The Telephone
As recorded in the 1878 edition

This instrument for the transmission of sound by electricity has been tried more or less successfully in England and the United States. Several efforts have been made by various persons to utilize electricity in this manner, but to Mr. Graham Bell is due the credit of the first successful demonstration of its practicability. The apparatus consists of ordinary telegraphic coils of insulated wire applied to the poles of a powerful compound permanent magnet. In front is stretched a thin membrane to act as a drum, having a metallic contact-piece cemented to it. A trumpet-shaped mouth collects the waves of sound, which, as they strike the membrane, cause it to vibrate, and transmit similar vibratory motions to the metallic contact-piece. The motion of the latter in front of the poles of the magnet creates an electric disturbance, and a current broken by the intervals of vibration is sent through the wire. To turn the vibrations into sound, a similar instrument is placed at the other end of the wire, where the same process is gone through, but in reversed order. By means of this instrument, spoken words and musical sounds have been made distinctly audible at a distance of several hundred miles.

As recorded in the 1888 edition: The extension of the telephone has greatly advanced during the past year, and long-distance telephony has become quite common, especially in the North and Midlands. A concession has been granted for allowing a telephone cable to be laid from London to Paris. If this step proves successful it is certain to be largely resorted to by business men desiring the most prompt means of communication. The rage for automatic machines has not spared the telephone, at all events on the Continent, where customers place the equivalent of a penny in the slit of the machine, and are forthwith able to talk for three minutes with their friends or customers. The greatest advance in telegraphy is railway-train telegraphy, now proved to be possible by American experiments. Messages were sent from and received on the moving train without difficulty, one even being sent to London and received accurately worded.

Cleopatra's Needle
As recorded in the 1878 edition

In 1820 this obelisk was presented to the British Government by Mehemet Ali [Viceroy of Egypt], but it was not until 1877 that any attempt was made to bring it to this country. Owing to the private munificence of Mr. Erasmus Wilson [surgeon], Mr. Dixon, C.E., was enabled to take the matter in hand. A large iron vessel was built, into which the "needle" was introduced. On the **8th of September** it was safely towed into Alexandria. But on the voyage home in tow of the S.S. *Olga*, in October, a violent storm necessitated the abandonment of this relic. It was discovered next day by the steamer *Fitzmaurice*, and towed into Ferrol, a Spanish port in the Bay of Biscay, where it remained at the time of this Almanack going to press.

As recorded in the 1879 edition: In last year's Almanack the recovery of the obelisk off the coast of Spain was mentioned. It arrived safely in England in March 1878, and was successfully erected on the Thames Embankment in September by the engineering efforts of Mr. Dixon. It was due to the munificence of Mr. Erasmus Wilson, F. R. S., that England became possessed of this monument of antiquity, which possesses an age of 3,500 years.

The Electric Light in Place of Gas

As recorded in the 1879 edition

The application of electricity to general lighting purposes was a very remarkable feature of scientific progress during 1878. Numerous patents were taken out, both here and abroad, for machines to produce the force and also for means of sustaining the light. The electro-dynamitic machines of Wilde, Siemens, and Gramme were chiefly employed, in each of which the electric force is generated by a steam engine, driving a magneto-machine. The difficulty, however, has been to keep up a permanent light, and in this respect Jablochkoff's "candles" have been the most successful [Arc lamps invented by the Russian engineer Pavel Yablochkov, which were used for street lighting in Paris and other European cities]. In October last the Corporation of the City of London and the Metropolitan Board of Works, both resolved to try the practical value of these methods, and in the provinces, and on the Continent the electric light has been adopted for the illumination of large buildings. Inventors are sanguine that the electric light may even be employed in private houses in place of gas.

As recorded in the 1880 edition: Although this source of light will not at present exclude the use of gas, its adoption largely increased during 1879. Numerous large workshops and factories in London and the provincial towns, the embankment of the Thames between Hungerford and Blackfriars Bridges were lighted by it, and eventually it was extended to Waterloo Bridge. The trustees of the British Museum tried it early in the year with but partial success, but in October, under a new system, the results were very satisfactory, the Reading Room being lighted up each evening until 7 o'clock, a great boon to readers. It is also intended to employ the light on foggy days, and thus to confer an additional benefit on literary men using the room.

The Phonograph

As recorded in the 1879 edition

This instrument may be briefly described as one by which sounds may be printed as electricity. It depends on the fact that the vibrations produced by sound, and transmitted by the telephone, can be reproduced by mechanical agency. It is evident that the sounds transmitted by the telephone must act on the drum or receiving instrument, causing it to vibrate to and fro. By substituting a receiving drum of tinfoil for that used, or rather adding one, together with a light steel spring, which carries on its extremity a blunt metallic point, each vibration may be made to form a little dot or dash on the tinfoil. And each of these dots or dashes will depend on the number and length of the vibrations; and consequently, the tinfoil becomes marked just like paper that is printed on. But the paper only shows, as on a book or piece of music, representations of sounds that cannot be reproduced directly from them. On the contrary, the tinfoil can be made to reproduce the exact sounds it has received in the form of vibrations. Consequently, without going into a number of details, these embossed pieces of tinfoil may be sent away to any distance, like an ordinary letter. When the person to whom they are sent receives them, he may place them in another phonograph, and each indentation on the foil, representing a certain number of vibrations per second, is reproduced, affording exactly the same sound that caused it. Thus it is possible to put a person's voice into an envelope, post it, and send it to be reproduced in any part of the world. The voice of the living, and the voices of the dead, may thus be preserved and re-heard as if the persons who originated them were present before us.

Cocaine or Cucaine

As recorded in the 1886 edition

According to Mr. Henry Power, the hydrochlorate of cocaine is a valuable addition to the list of local anaesthetics, and has been used with great success in operations connected with the eye. Since its introduction last year it has been employed in many of the minor cases, and seems to be admirably adapted for cataract operations, which can be performed, after its application for a few moments, without the slightest pain being experienced. Mr. Jessop, of St. Bartholomew's, confirms the opinion of Mr. Power as to the value of this new anaesthetic, by his clinical observations.

Liquid Fuel

As recorded in the 1887 edition

The utilization of petroleum as fuel, in view of the enormous number of recently discovered sources in Russia and other parts of Europe, will do something to allay the fears that exist as to the exhaustion of our coal supplies. Inventors have turned their attention to the liquid fuel, and the latest development has been the building of a steel vessel propelled by a continuous series of explosions of petroleum, similarly to that of a gas-engine. The vessel has no piston or fly-wheel, and the motive power is obtained by a succession of charges of petroleum and heated air, under pressure, and the charges fired by electricity. The explosions occur several times in a minute, the force being expended below the water-level, and the impinging of this force upon the water propels the boat forward.

Photography

As recorded in the 1888 edition

The immense strides which photography has made are mainly due to the introduction of the dry-plate processes, which have in the past year been greatly extended. Instantaneous exposure only being necessary, several ingenious methods of providing detective cameras have followed. One is never certain whether or not his facial expression is being caught and recorded, for the opening of a watch, the pointing of opera-glasses, or even the click of a sham revolver may mean that a portrait has been surreptitiously taken. The watch camera is the invention of Mr. W. J. Lancaster, of Birmingham. The Americans have, however, succeeded in distancing all competitors in this field with their ingenious "pill-box" cameras. Although this is but a toy it will, in moderately skilful hands, take a perfect picture, so that it may be justly regarded as a scientific instrument, although a rough and ready one. An ordinary pill-box with lid is procured; at the back of the box discs of highly-sensitized paper are placed; three or four discs with blanks between each may be carried at one time. In the lid of the box a small hole is made, and at the back of the top of the lid a lens with short focus is placed, or the hole itself will be sufficient to give a fair picture. It is only necessary to hold the box steadily in position, uncovering the hole in the lid for an instant, and return to darkness, so that the plate may be taken out and developed by any of the processes used with the plates of larger and more expensive cameras.

Instantaneous photography has given us a new field in which to exercise the art for the purposes of scientific comparison. The flight of birds, the movements of horses, and other swiftly moving objects are now popular subjects of illustration.

The Manchester Ship Canal
As recorded in the 1890 edition

The Manchester Ship Canal has made most satisfactory progress, and there is every probability that notwithstanding the unfortunate decease on the 25th November, of the able contractor, Mr. T. A. Walker, the task will be completed before the stipulated date, 1st January, 1892. Work was commenced in November, 1887, and up to 26th August last there had been excavated something over 19 millions of cubic yards out of the original estimate of 44 millions, the present monthly output being over one million cubic yards. In addition to about 13,000 human navvies employed there are 96 steam-navvies or excavators, 249 pumping engines, 32 pile-drivers, 5,466 waggons, 163 locomotives, 141 steam-cranes, and 173 horses. The canal will be a little over 35 miles in length from Manchester to the Mersey estuary, and consists essentially of two divisions: a tidal portion from Eastham through the estuary to Runcorn, 12 miles long, and then inland 8 miles further to Warrington, with a bottom width of 120 feet and a depth of 26 feet at low tide; and a canal portion from Warrington to Manchester 15½ miles long, with the same bottom width and depth. The total rise of the canal is 60 feet, the contract price £5,750,000, the engineer, Mr. E. Leader Williams.

Electric Cabs
As recorded in the 1898 edition

During the summer a pioneer band of twelve electric cabs were introduced to the streets of London, and have proved successful. The wheels are driven by an electric motor worked from accumulators in a chamber under the body of the cab, and the controlling gear is at the hand of the driver. As these vehicles are at least as manageable as horse-cabs, and take up much less room, their advent will help to clear the over-crowded metropolitan thoroughfares.

Motor Cars
As recorded in the 1900 edition

There has been a great development of motor cars during the year, especially in France, Belgium and America. They do not compete so successfully with horses in the United Kingdom, but they are gradually coming into fashion. The most favoured are those worked by the Daimler and Denz petroleum motors, and by electricity, but the former are by far the most numerous. An idea that they are unmanageable and dangerous, or break down easily, has been prejudicial to them, but long journeys and races are giving people confidence in them. Motor car races have been a stirring form of sport. It is not unusual for country gentlemen to visit friends 40 or 50 miles distant by motor car and breakfast or dine with them instead of going by train. Farmers are also learning the advantage of sending their produce by motor car instead of by rail. The Parisian fire brigade has adopted the motor car for horse vehicles, and the French military are about to do the same, for transporting baggage and guns. Sportsmen at the moors, tourists and other pleasure seekers are pressing it into their service, and in addition to these light or heavy cars the motor cycle is coming into general use. It is more evident that the motor car is destined to a great future.

Radium
As recorded in the 1902 edition

MM. Curie have discovered that the metal radium and its salts emit mysterious rays which affect the skin, burning and ulcerating it. They should not, therefore, be carried for long on the person.

Mosquitoes and Infection
As recorded in the 1902 edition

Experiments have been carried out in Sierra Leone, by Major Ronald Ross and others, to exterminate the anopheles mosquito, whose bite may infect with malaria. Pools and marshes where they breed are being filled up. Petroleum has also been shed on the water and grass frequented by the pests. American investigators in

Havana have also discovered and proved by experiment that the bite of a mosquito can produce yellow fever of the virulent sort, and even when the patient is treated with an anti-toxic serum.

In 1902 Sir Ronald Ross received the Nobel Prize for Physiology or Medicine, the first Briton to win the award, for his work on malaria.

Iceberg Detection
As recorded in the 1913 edition

As a result of the *Titanic* disaster Sir Hiriam S. Maxim has made a striking suggestion for an apparatus whereby the presence of icebergs might be detected. Bats, he considers, are able to analyse air vibrations by means of leaf-like organs on the head and in much the same way as light-waves are analysed by the eye. The vibrations of their wings are reflected back from any obstacles in their path, and the animal, interpreting the reflected vibrations, avoids the object. The inventor proposes that ocean-going ships should be fitted with a low-frequency siren. The vibrations sent out would be reflected from an iceberg and received again at the ship on a stretched diaphragm of rubbered silk. The movements of the silk would operate to close more or fewer electrical circuits according to the strength of the reflected vibrations, and consequently also according to the size and distance of the object. A recording drum worked in connexion with the diaphragm would enable an exact calculation to be made, and by turning the mouth of the siren in different directions the surroundings of a ship could be accurately mapped out.

Splitting the Atom
As recorded in the 1933 edition

Dr. J. D. Cockroft and Dr. E. T. S. Walton, who had been working for three years on special apparatus in the Cavendish Laboratory, Cambridge, under the direction of Lord Rutherford, have succeeded in "splitting" the atom. Using voltages of between 120,000 and 600,000, they sent several millions of particles per second through a vacuum tube at a speed of 10,000 kilometres per second. It was found that the bombardment of different elements by the particles split light elements, but for every atom split several millions of particles were required. "We concentrated on an atom of hydrogen," Dr. Cockroft said. "We were prepared to work on voltages ranging from 100,000 to 500,000 volts. We found that at 120,000 volts some of the atoms we were bombarding began to break up into helium. These helium atoms came out with energies of the order of 100 to 150 times that of the particles we were firing into them. In one sense it is true that by this means we are turning 120,000 volts into 190,000 volts. But only one particle breaks up for every 10,000,000 we use to bombard it. We are producing from these atoms 100 to 160 times the known energy but only once in 10,000,000 times. Therefore it would only be strictly true to say we were turning 100,000 volts into 160,000 volts if every atom broke up." Dr. Cockroft also said that though the discovery was of immense scientific importance, it was not of immediate practical value.

Loch Ness "Monster"

As recorded in the 1935 edition

During the summer the attention of thousands of people was concentrated on seeing and adding to the description of the world-famed Loch Ness "Monster." The most thorough series of observations was due to Sir Edward Mountain, who for four weeks had twenty watchers posted at points of advantage on the shores of the loch. They reported having seen the creature 21 times, and to have made five photographs. One of these shows the wash of an object, probably bulky and moving at considerable speed, but nothing of the object itself. A second photograph shows a low dark "hump," or perhaps two, but it was noticeable that lines seemed to be continued in both directions. A third photograph shows something short and fairly massive, low in the water, and succeeded by two or three less distinctive "humps," suggesting the head of a large seal, while the "humps" could be water ripples caused by the shoulders and hind quarters.

SPORT

The date in parentheses indicates the edition each of the following extracts was taken from.

THE BOAT RACE
24 Mar. 1877 (1878): The Oxford and Cambridge boat-race ends in a dead-heat; time, 24 minutes 6.5 seconds.

> The Boat Race – the annual rowing competition between Oxford and Cambridge universities on the River Thames – has only finished with one dead heat since the first race in 1829.

THE ASHES
23 July 1884 (1885): Great cricket match at Lord's England, versus Australia, won by the former in a single innings.

> The Ashes is the Test series contested by England and Australia which originates from a match played at the Oval in 1882 which was won by the tourists. Following the win, a newspaper, *The Sporting Times*, wrote of the 'death' of English cricket: "the body will be cremated and the ashes taken to Australia".
>
> The first series in England was held in 1884 and was won by the hosts with a score of 1-0 following victory at Lord's, with A. G. Steel hitting 148.
>
> The first Test was played at Old Trafford with the Oval hosting the third and final Test. The 1884 series was England's first victory in the Ashes.

THE 1908 OLYMPIC GAMES
13 July 1908 (1909): The King [Edward VII.] opened the Olympic Games in the Stadium of the Franco-British Exhibition.

24 July 1908 (1909): The Marathon Race at the Olympic Games was run in great heat. An Italian was the first to break the tape, but a protest as to his having been assisted in the Stadium, after collapsing fifty yards from the finish, was upheld and the trophy awarded to an American. The Queen [Alexandra of Denmark], who was present, afterwards announced her intention of presenting the Italian with a special cup.

The 1908 Summer Olympics, hosted in London for the first time, was the fourth Olympic Games in modern Olympic history. The games lasted a record total of 187 days.

The most extraordinary event occurred at the marathon when the Italian Dorando Pietri became the first to enter the stadium. After collapsing several times and heading off in the wrong direction, he was helped across the finish line by two of the course officials, including Dr Michael Bulger, the chief medical officer.

Following a complaint from the runner-up, Johnny Hayes, Pietri was disqualified. The following day he was awarded a silver cup by Queen Alexandra.

THE 1948 OLYMPIC GAMES
29 July 1948 (1949): Accompanied by Queen [Elizabeth] and Princess Margaret, the King [George VI.] inaugurated at Wembley the XIV Modern Olympiad and saw parade of nations and kindling of Olympic Flame.

Due to the Second World War these were the first Summer Olympics since the 1936 Games held in Berlin. The 1948 Olympics were the first to be broadcast on television.

THE FOUR-MINUTE MILE
6 May 1954 (1955): In a race at Oxford, Roger Bannister became the first man to run a mile in under four minutes, when he returned a time of 3 m. 59.4 sec.

Roger Bannister was a 25-year-old medical student when he became the first person in history to run a mile in under four minutes. The remarkable achievement took place at the Iffley Road track in Oxford and was watched by around 3,000 people. He was knighted in 1975.

16 July 1955 (1956): Stirling Moss became the first Englishman to win the R.A.C. British Grand Prix, crossing the line ahead of his team-mate Juan Fangio, in the race at Aintree before a crowd of more than 100,000.

THE MUNICH AIR DISASTER
6 Feb. 1958 (1959): B.E.A. Elizabethan airliner struck buildings near runway at Munich airport after taking off in snowstorm. Seven members of Manchester

United football team, returning from Belgrade, including English international players Byrne and Taylor, were among the 21 persons killed, who also included several team officials and Mr. Frank Swift, former England goalkeeper. Mr. Matt Busby, manager of Manchester United, and a number of other players were seriously injured. Duncan Edwards, the England wing-half, died in hospital on **Feb. 21**. And the pilot of the aircraft on **March 15**.

The Manchester United team, known as the 'Busby Babes', were returning home from a European Cup match against Red Star Belgrade of Yugoslavia which ended 3-3, enough to send the English team to the semi-finals.

The plane on which the team travelled, along with journalists and supporters, had stopped in Munich to refuel. After two failed attempts to take off due to the bad weather, the captain of the plane attempted a third take off which resulted in the disaster.

Of the 44 people on board the aircraft, twenty died in the crash with three more people later succumbing to their injuries, resulting in a total of 23 deaths. Eight of the 'Busby Babes' died in or as a result of the crash.

---

6 May 1961 (1962): Tottenham Hotspur, by beating Leicester City 2–0 in F.A. Cup Final at Wembley, became first team to win League and Cup in same season since 1897.

THE 1966 WORLD CUP
23 July 1966 (1967): In World Cup quarter-final at Wembley between England and Argentina, Rattin, the Argentinian captain, was sent off field and play was held up for 7 minutes during Argentine protests; later F.I.F.A. suspended 3 Argentine players and said that Argentina would be denied entry to 1970 World Cup unless assurances of good conduct were given.

30 July 1966 (1967): The Queen and the Duke of Edinburgh watched World Cup Final at Wembley, Her Majesty presenting Jules Rimet Trophy to Bobby Moore, captain of the victorious England team.

As hosts of the World Cup, England won the tournament for the first and only time in the nation's history. The final against West Germany is arguably England's most famous match and certainly the most celebrated.

Playing in red in front of 98,000 spectators, England won the game 4–2 which included a hat-trick from striker Geoff Hurst – still the only one ever to be scored in a World Cup final. The England team was managed by Alf Ramsey and captained by Bobby Moore who was carried on his team-mate's shoulders in the celebrations.

The match also featured the famous commentary line of Kenneth Wolstenholme: "They think it's all over. It is now!"

29 May 1968 (1969): Manchester United defeated Benfica 4–1 at Wembley Stadium to become first English club to win European Cup.

The victory marked ten years since the Munich air disaster and featured two survivors from the crash including Bobby Charlton. The game is also remembered for the performance of George Best.

25 Mar. 1977 (1978): The Cambridge boat sank near Barnes Bridge in the University Boat Race with Oxford in the lead, the first sinking for 27 years; Oxford rowed on to complete the course in 18 mins. 58 secs.

RED RUM
2 Apr. 1977 (1978): Red Rum, ridden by Tommy Stack, won the Grand National for a record third time. Charlotte Brew, of Coggeshall, Essex, became the first woman to ride in the Grand National on her gelding Barony Fort, but pulled out of the race four fences from home.

5 July 1980 (1981): Bjorn Borg of Sweden won the Wimbledon men's singles lawn tennis title for a record fifth consecutive time in beating John McEnroe 1–6, 7–5, 6–3, 6–7, 8–6.

COE VS. OVETT
19 Aug. 1981 (1982): Sebastian Coe broke the world mile record by almost three-tenths of a second in a time of 3 min. 48.53 sec. in Zurich; on **Aug. 26.** Steve Ovett regained the record when he recorded 3 min. 48.40 sec. in Koblenz, West Germany; two days later Sebastian Coe regained it with a time of 3 min. 47.33 sec. in Brussels.

Coe and Ovett dominated middle distance running in the 1970s and 80s. Their rivalry was at its fiercest stage at the 1980 Olympic Games in Moscow when Coe won the 1500 metre gold and Ovett won the 800 metre final.

Lord Coe became an MP before becoming chairman of the London Organising Committee for the 2012 Olympics.

Steve Ovett still holds the UK record for the fastest two mile run.

9 Feb. 1983 (1984): The racehorse, Shergar, winner of the 1981 Derby, was stolen by armed and masked men from a stud farm in Co. Kildare in the Irish Republic.

THE HEYSEL STADIUM DISASTER
29 May 1985 (1986): Thirty-eight people died, many of them trampled to death, when a wall and a safety fence collapsed during rioting before the European Cup Final between Liverpool and Juventus in the Heysel Stadium, Brussels; 454 were injured; on **May 31**, the F.A. ordered the withdrawal of all English clubs from European competitions for the coming season; the Belgian Government banned all British football clubs from playing in Belgium; on **June 2**, U.E.F.A. announced that English football clubs had been banned from competing in Europe for an indefinite period; on **June 6**, F.I.F.A. banned English professional soccer clubs from playing anywhere outside England; on **June 8**, British Rail announced it was to stop running football specials for soccer fans and to end cheap excursion fares to fans travelling on scheduled services; on **June 12**, the Prime Minister [Margaret Thatcher] met the F.A. and Football League at Downing Street to discuss soccer hooliganism; on **June 20**, Liverpool were banned by U.E.F.A. from all European club competitions for three seasons.

The Heysel Stadium disaster resulted in the deaths of 39 Juventus fans. The tragedy occurred during a particularly dark era of English football which was often overshadowed by acts of hooliganism.

As a result of the tragedy, English teams were indefinitely banned from European competitions. The ban lasted until the 1990-91 season.

3 Apr. 1993 (1994): The Grand National was declared void after all but nine of the riders failed to realise that a second false start had been indicated; seven horses completed both circuits of the course. After a stewards' inquiry it was said that no recall flag had been shown.

18 Oct. 1995 (1997): The three-times Grand National winner Red Rum died and was buried at Aintree racecourse.

EURO '96
26 June 1996 (1997): In the semi-finals of the European championships Germany beat England 6–5 on penalties at Wembley after sudden-death extra time.

> The European Football Championship of 1996 was hosted by England – the first competition to be held in the country since the 1966 World Cup. After a draw against Switzerland, followed by thrilling wins against Scotland and Holland, England won a rare penalty shoot-out against Spain.
>
> What followed was heartbreak for the host nation as they were defeated by Germany – who went on to lift the trophy – on penalties. Gareth Southgate missed the crucial penalty in a classic moment of recent years.

THE FASTEST BREAK
21 Apr. 1997 (1998): Ronnie O'Sullivan scored the fastest-ever maximum break of 147 at the world snooker championships in Sheffield, when he cleared the table in 5 minutes 20 seconds.

> 16 years after this achievement – which still stands as the record – O'Sullivan won the World Snooker Championship for a fifth time.

28 Sept. 1997 (1999): At Ascot, Frankie Dettori became the first jockey to win all seven races at a meeting.

26 May 1999 (2000): Manchester United became the first English club ever to win the league, FA Cup and European Cup when they beat Bayern Munich 2–1 in the European Cup final in Barcelona. On **27 May** hundreds of thousands of people lined the streets in Manchester to welcome the team back.

THE 2005 ASHES SERIES
12 Sept. 2005 (2006): England won the Ashes series 2–1 after drawing the final Test against Australia at the Oval.

13 Sept. 2005 (2006): Over 25,000 people gathered in Trafalgar Square to celebrate England's Ashes win; thousands more watched the team parade through central London on an open-top bus.

ANDY MURRAY

8 July 2012 (2013): Roger Federer won a record-equalling seventh men's singles Wimbledon title by overcoming Andy Murray in four sets on Centre Court; Murray was attempting to become the first British man since Fred Perry in 1936 to win a major singles title.

Although Andy Murray did not win, his accomplishment in reaching the Wimbledon final was widely regarded as a great success. In a real show of character, Murray won the gold medal at the 2012 Olympic Games by beating Federer on Centre Court four weeks after his Wimbledon loss.

In September 2012, Murray continued an unparalleled year of British sport by ending the 76-year wait for a British male grand slam champion, when he defeated Novak Djokovic in the final of the US Open. On **7 July 2013**, Murray defeated Djokovic on Centre Court to become Wimbledon champion.

THE WEATHER

The date in parentheses indicates the edition each of the following extracts was taken from.

23–30 Mar. 1878 (1879): Heavy Snowstorms throughout the kingdom.

22 Apr. 1884 (1885): At 9.15 a.m. 22nd, an earthquake was felt in the eastern counties, most severely in Colchester. [Measuring 4.6 on the Richter scale, there were reports of as many as five deaths, though this was disputed; more than 1,000 buildings were damaged.]

1927 (1929): A dull and wet summer was the outstanding feature of the weather of 1927. Not since 1879 has a summer compared with it for lack of sunshine and persistent wetness.

7 Jan. 1928 (1929): During the early hours of the 7th an abnormally high tide occurred on the Thames, the tidal reaches attaining their highest level for at least 50 years. Serious flooding occurred at Westminster, Southwark, Putney, and Hammersmith, and fourteen people were drowned through being trapped in basements.

June 1931 (1932): The weather during June was distinguished by a pronounced excess of precipitation everywhere, with the exception of the south-east of England, and by a general deficiency of sunshine. The first three weeks were unsettled, dull and wet, with severe thunderstorms on the 5th, 14th and 19th, followed by generally fine weather during the last week. Notable incidents in the month's weather were the tornado which visited Birmingham on the 14th and the widespread, severe thunderstorms and floods on that day. In most places the 14th was among the warmest days of the month, maximum temperature in London and the south-east exceeding 80° F [27°C]. In the Rickmansworth and Chorley Wood district of Hertfordshire the thunderstorm of the 19th was accompanied by hail of unusual intensity. Mean pressure of the month was slightly above normal in the south, but from 1 millibar to 2 millibars below normal in the north and west. In most districts prevailing winds were south-westerly and generally light or moderate in force. The tornado which occurred in the Birmingham district on the 14th commenced about 14.40 G.M.T. and travelled rapidly from the south to the north-east, causing a very great amount of material damage along its path, which varied in width from 800 to 200 yards [730 to 180 metres]. The storm ceased about 15.15 G.M.T. [. . .] Much flooding occurred during the month as the result of torrential rain accompanied by thunderstorms. At Braunton 59mm. was measured at 9h G.M.T. on the 5th, most of which had fallen since 7h. At Eskdalemuir on the 14th, 31 mm. fell during the hour 18h to 19h; the rainfall was reported to have been of an intensity unparalleled in living memory. Severe floods followed, involving the death of a farmer by drowning and the loss of numerous sheep and cattle. Sunshine aggregates were again below the normal.

Mar. 1947 (1948): Over England and Wales the total precipitation during March exceeded that of any previous March in the series back to 1869. There was three times the average in parts of Somerset, the Upper Thames and Lower Severn Valleys. In the case of the Thames Valley above Teddington the general rainfall (including snow) for the 7 days March 4 to 10 was 2.12 inches [54 mm] and for the 12 days March 4 to 15 as much as 3.59 inches [91 mm], compared with the average for the whole of March of 2.08 inches [53 mm]. When the partial thaw occurred on March 11 the river had therefore to cope with the melting snow as well as the rainfall, the renewed flow of some of the smaller streams which had ceased owing to frost earlier in the cold spell, and in addition there was initially little percolation into the saturated and frozen ground. A gust of 98 m.p.h. was recorded at Mildenhall (Suffolk) on March 16.

Taking into account the temperature, duration of frost, snowfall and prevalence of easterly winds the winter of 1946–47 was probably the most severe for a century.

2 June 1952 (1953): The Coronation was completed and shortly afterwards the Queen, the central figure of a colourful procession, left the Abbey to meet again her people, waiting patiently in showers of rain to show their affection.

On the Coronation day of Queen Elizabeth II the maximum temperature was 11.7 °C; the minimum temperature was 6.7 °C; there was 1.5 mm of rainfall and just 2.2 hours of sunshine.

15 Aug. 1952 (1953): Rainfall of 9 inches [229 mm] on Exmoor caused rivers to overflow and become raging torrents, which carried huge boulders and trees along and caused widespread damage in North Devon and Somerset; West Lyn river left its bed and tore through High Street at Lynmouth, destroying or damaging beyond repair 60 houses and hotels and smashing all public services and 17 bridges. Lynmouth had to be completely evacuated. Death toll in areas affected was over 30 and damage to public services about £2,000,000.

1 Feb. 1953 (1954): Lashed by winds of gale force, exceptionally high tides during night and early morning smashed defences on both sides of North Sea, causing heavy loss of life and great damage by flooding from the Humber to North England, heavier death roll and vast inundations in the Netherlands and considerable destruction to some Belgian coast resorts. In England, worst-hit localities were Sutton and Mablethorpe, King's Lynn, where River Ouse burst its banks, Hunanston, Cromer, Great Yarmouth, Felixstowe, Harwich, Clacton, Canvey Island (where practically all inhabitants were evacuated), Sheerness and Whitstable. Number of dead was officially placed at 307, including 12 Americans. Over 32,000 persons were evacuated from their homes and about 25,000 houses and more than 150,000 acres of agricultural land were flooded.

1962 (1964): The year began and ended with bitterly cold weather and widespread snow cover. Mean temperature was below the 1921–50 average in each month after February, apart from October. Over England and Wales it was the coldest year since 1919, over Scotland 1952 was colder. With easterly winds predominating during March it was the coldest March this century over much of the country. The spring over England and Wales was the coldest this century, although over Scotland the spring of 1951 was colder.

Jan. 1963 (1964): The very cold weather, with winds from the east, which set in on December 23 continued during most of the month. Mean temperature was below 32° F [0°C] nearly everywhere, apart from the extreme south-west and north-west, giving for England and Wales the coldest January since 1814 and the coldest month this century, being rather colder than February 1947. [...] Fog, dense at night, with spectacular rime deposits, persisted over parts of the Midlands and London area from the 23rd to the 25th. The sea froze at several places, including near Herne Bay, and the Thames was frozen over in places and there were ice-floes near Tower Bridge.

Feb. 1963 (1964): Bitterly cold weather predominated, with almost continuous frost, often severe at night. Although over England and Wales February 1963 was not as cold as that of 1947, the winter as a whole ranked as one of the coldest since 1740.

14 Jan. 1968 (1969): A deepening depression moving eastwards on the 14th brought strong winds to northern districts, a gust of 134 m.p.h. being recorded on Great Dun Fell (Westmoreland) while more than 2 inches [51 mm] of rain fell in parts of western Scotland. Extensive gale damage, with some loss of life, occurred in central Scotland, especially in Glasgow. Further disturbances brought a renewal of gale force winds and heavy rains on the 16th and 18th. On the 19th an anticyclone developed over the English Channel and covered the British Isles on the 22nd.

Sept. 1968 (1970): Cool, showery weather, with local thunderstorms, persisted during the first three days, but the 4th to 9th became drier and milder. Rain spread across the country on the 5th. On the 6th an anticyclone developed off south-west England and moved to the north-east. Rain occurred in the north-west on the 8th, but in south-east England the 9th and 10th were the warmest days of the month with afternoon temperatures reaching 25·6° C (78°F.) on the 10th at Camden Square (London) and Gillingham (Kent). In the south thunderstorms developed on the 10th. The 11th and 12th were cooler with heavy rains, more than 2 inches [51 mm] being recorded in parts of Northumberland during the night of 12–13th. The 13th was mainly dry, as a depression formed to the south-west of England to bring nearly

2 inches [51 mm] of rain on the 14th to the Isles of Scilly. During the three days, 14th to 16th, parts of Surrey, Kent and Essex recorded 6–8 inches [152–203 mm] in persistent rains, followed by widespread and disastrous floods in south-east England, especially in the east Molesey area. At Purleigh, Essex, 2.2 inches [56 mm] fell in 42 mins. on the 14th.

June 1976 (1977): It was the driest June in England and Wales since 1925 and following the previous dry months 17 counties had a serious shortage of water. The month started unsettled but by the 3rd it had become dry over much of the country and many central and eastern districts stayed dry until the middle of the month. [...] The hot spell from the 23rd onwards caused traffic congestion, industrial troubles, heat exhaustion, etc., and fires. Towards the end of the month large fires were reported in Norfolk, Suffolk, Surrey, Essex, Hampshire and North Yorkshire. The army were called in to control the moor fires near Whitby (North Yorkshire). Sunshine was above normal in most areas but in much of central and western Scotland and west coast regions of England and Wales it was less than normal. It was the dullest June on record at Benbecula (Western Isles).

June 1977 (1978): The 7th and 8th were generally showery. [The Queen's Silver Jubilee was on the 7th.]

Oct. 1987 (1989): Rainfall totals were well above normal generally but near normal in north-west Scotland. It was the fourth wettest October in England and Wales since 1727. On the 8th hailstones of 10–20 mm. (0.4–0.8 inches) fell at Slaidburn (Lancs.) On the 9th torrential rain caused flooding and road accidents in south-eastern areas as gales swept the south coast. Floods brought commuter traffic in London to a halt. Snow fell at Alwen (Clwyd) on the 9th. Further heavy rain brought more severe flooding to many parts of the south east on the 10th. In Essex some villages were almost cut off when the river Stour burst its banks, and flooding to a depth of 4 m. (13.1 ft) occurred near Colchester. On the 16th a violent storm with heavy rain brought chaos to southern England. The winds were probably the strongest for 250 years. Millions of trees were uprooted or broken, many crashed into power lines and houses, or fell across roads and railway lines. The damage and disruption was enormous and the cost almost incalculable: the insured loss from the storm, about £1.5 billion, was the greatest on record for a natural disaster anywhere in the world (including earthquakes and tropical hurricanes). Some large areas were without electricity for up to a fortnight. The violent winds produced several gusts of over 90 knots (104 mph) and at Shoreham-by-Sea (W. Sussex) a mean hourly wind of 72 knots (83 mph) was recorded just before a power failure stopped the recorder. This is the highest mean wind ever recorded below 200 m. (656 ft.) in the United Kingdom. A gust of 100 knots (115 mph) was estimated from the recorder just after the power failure. On the 17th and 18th there were strong winds and heavy rain in western and northern Wales. Trecastle (Powys) had 22.2 cm. (8.7 inches) of rain from the 14th to the 18th, 77mm. (3.0 inches) more than the normal amount for the month. There was widespread flooding, worst around Carmarthen and in the areas of the rivers Teifi and Tywi. At Glanrhyd near Llandeilo a Swansea to Shrewsbury train plunged into the river when the bridge gave way, killing four people. On the 20th torrential rain brought flooding to large areas of Northern Ireland, with floodwater up to 3m. (9.8 ft.) deep in Strabane (Co. Londonderry).

Jan. 1990 (1991): The 25th brought severe gales to England and Wales with gusts of up to 93 knots (107 mph) at Aberporth (Dyfed) and Gwennap Head (Cornwall). Gusts above 80 knots (92 mph) were widespread on southern and western coasts, and gusts of more than 70 knots (81 mph) occurred in many areas of central and southern England and Wales. Very extensive structural damage occurred and large numbers of trees were blown down over a much greater area than that affected by the storm of October 1987. Many people were injured and several were killed. Road and rail traffic was severely disrupted and large areas were left without electricity.

> Known as the Burns' Day Storm because it began on the 25 January, it claimed 97 lives and cost UK insurers £3.37 billion.

7 Dec. 2006 (2008): A tornado struck Kensal Rise in West London injuring six people and leaving many people homeless; a number of residential houses were seriously damaged.